MANCHESTER UNITED OFFICIAL YEARBOOK 1999

Compiled and Edited by Cliff Butler
Assisted by Ivan Ponting

Contributors
MARTIN EDWARDS
ALEX FERGUSON
BARRY MOORHOUSE
CLIFF BUTLER
IVAN PONTING

Thanks to
ARTHUR ALBISTON, NEIL BAILEY, DR PHILIP BATTY, RUTH BAYLEY, DAVE BUSHELL, DIANE CLIFFORD, JOHN COOKE, TONY COTON, MIKE COX, JIMMY CURRAN, MARK EDWARDS, SHARON FAULKNER, JULIAN FLANDERS, ALASTAIR GOURLAY, TREVOR LEA, EDDIE LEACH, HANS LOKOY, PAUL McGUINNESS, TOMMY MARTIN, STUART MATHIESON, DAVID MEEK, ALBERT MORGAN, DEBBIE NEWALL, CLARE NICHOLAS, NICKY PARIS, OLE PEDERSEN, MATT PROCTOR, NIGEL REECE, ARTHUR ROBERTS, DAVID RYAN, JIMMY RYAN, JIM SANDFORD, PETER SMITH, TOM STATHAM, CRAIG STEVENS, TIM TAYLOR, TONY WHELAN, DAVID WILLIAMS, TRACEY WOODWARD, STUART WORTHINGTON, ALEC WYLIE, ANNE WYLIE AND EVERYONE WHO SUPPLIED INFORMATION THROUGHOUT THE 1998-99 SEASON

THANKS ALSO TO ALL THE CLUBS WHO KINDLY GRANTED PERMISSION IN ALLOWING THEIR OFFICIAL CLUB CRESTS TO BE REPRODUCED IN THIS PUBLICATION

Photographs
ACTION IMAGES AND JOHN PETERS

Design and editorial
DESIGN/SECTION FROME

First published in 1999 by
MANCHESTER UNITED BOOKS
an imprint of ANDRE DEUTSCH
76 Dean Street, London W1V 5HA

in association with
MANCHESTER UNITED FOOTBALL CLUB PLC
OLD TRAFFORD MANCHESTER M16 0RA

CIP data for this title is available from the British Library

ISBN
0-233-99741-5 (HARDBACK)
0-233-99453-X (PAPERBACK)

Printed and bound in the UK by
BUTLER & TANNER LTD. FROME AND LONDON

CONTENTS

MANCHESTER UNITED FOOTBALL CLUB PLC

Directors

C.M. EDWARDS (Chairman)

J.M. EDELSON

SIR BOBBY CHARLTON CBE

E.M. WATKINS LL.M.

R.L. OLIVE

P.F. KENYON

D.A. GILL

Chief Executive

C. MARTIN EDWARDS

Manager

ALEX FERGUSON CBE

Secretary

KENNETH R. MERRETT

Honours

EUROPEAN CHAMPION CLUBS' CUP – Winners: 1968 • 1999

EUROPEAN CUP WINNERS' CUP – Winners: 1991

FA PREMIER LEAGUE – Champions: 1993 • 1994 • 1996 • 1997 • 1999
Runners-up: 1995 • 1998

FOOTBALL LEAGUE DIVISION ONE – Champions: 1908 • 1911 • 1952 • 1956 • 1957 • 1965 • 1967
Runners-up: 1947 • 1948 • 1949 • 1951 • 1959 • 1964 • 1968 • 1980 • 1988 • 1992

FA CHALLENGE CUP – Winners: 1909 • 1948 • 1963 • 1977 • 1983 • 1985 • 1990 • 1994 • 1996 • 1999
Finalists: 1957 • 1958 • 1976 • 1979 • 1995

FOOTBALL LEAGUE CUP – Winners: 1992
Finalists: 1983 • 1991 • 1994

EUROPEAN SUPER CUP – Winners: 1991

FA CHARITY SHIELD – Winners: 1908 • 1911 • 1952 • 1956 • 1957 • 1983 • 1993 • 1994 • 1996 • 1997
Joint Holders: 1965 • 1967 • 1977 • 1990

CLUB TELEPHONE NUMBERS

Main Switchboard (General Enquiries)	872 1661
	930 1968
Ticket and Match Information	872 0199
Commercial Department	872 3488
Merchandising Switchboard	877 6077
Megastore	848 8181
Mail Order Hotline	877 9777
United Review Subscriptions	877 9777
Magazine Subscriptions	0990 442442
Development Association	872 4676
Membership and Supporters' Club	872 5208
Conference and Catering	872 3331
Museum and Tour Centre	877 4002
United in the Community	708 9451
Manchester United Radio (Matchdays only)	872 1413
Red Cafe	930 2930
Club Call	0891 121161*
Web Site	WWW.MANUTD.COM
MUTV	0870 8486888

* *Calls cost 50p per minute at all times*

Chairman's Message

I have always looked upon my annual responsibility of welcoming you all to the pages of the *Manchester United Official Yearbook* as one of the most pleasing duties of the season. And that is all the more true on this occasion following the incredible events, which we witnessed, as the club became the first ever to collect the classic treble of FA Carling Premiership, FA Cup and UEFA Champions League.

The yearbook has become recognised as the definitive record of the club's playing activities and this year it will document the most successful season any English club has ever enjoyed. To win one trophy at the end of a hard season is cause for celebration, and rightly so, but to scoop the game's three most prestigious honours is, as so many people have said, close to 'Roy of the Rovers' stuff. The last ten days of the 1998-99 season will remain forever in the memory of everyone connected with Manchester United.

The drama, excitement, passion and emotion became almost too intense to bear, but in the end it was worth all the anxiety to see our club claim an unparalleled chapter in football history. I know I shall never forget the scenes at Old Trafford, Wembley and Nou Camp as one of the game's great stories was being written and I'm sure my sentiments are shared with the millions of people to whom Manchester United is a way of life.

I recall Sir Matt Busby saying in 1968, after United had won the European Cup for the first time, that the triumph was the start, and not the end, of a glorious era. And that is exactly how I look upon these latest remarkable achievements. We have all long believed United to be the greatest football club in the World. We can now make that claim happy in the knowledge that once again we are proud and honoured to be the 'Champions of Europe'.

Alex Ferguson, his players and staff, are to be congratulated on bringing so much glory to Old Trafford, and you the fans should also feel mighty proud of yourselves for the incomparable support you have given to the team and club.

Enjoy reading and recalling the moments of a great season in this new enlarged and improved edition of the club yearbook. I know I will!

C. Martin Edwards

Manager's Message

I can well remember as a youngster being taken along to Hampden Park in Glasgow to watch Manchester United play Rangers in a Coronation Cup match. I cannot recall exactly what it was, but there was something about United which really impressed me. Matt Busby was in his early days as boss at Old Trafford but he had already stamped his mark on the club after his post-war team had collected the FA Cup and League Championship.

Even then there seemed to be something almost magical about United and never in my wildest dreams did I ever think that I would myself be manager at Manchester United when the club became the first in English football to achieve 'The Treble'.

Football can be so incredibly emotional, and that day at Hampden was just one of my many thoughts as I watched the lads taking on Bayern Munich. I was of course aware of the fact that it was the 90th anniversary of Sir Matt Busby's birth.

As the season entered its last two weeks I could feel the pressure mounting as our place in the game's record books loomed larger. I once said that in my opinion it was virtually impossible for the treble to be won in modern football, and particularly by an English club. I suppose I now have to take those words back, although I would be very surprised if we ever see it achieved again. European football is set to expand over the next few years and it will become increasingly difficult to spread the load of so many games across a squad of players.

Having said that, we have a group of players who never cease to surprise me and I'm convinced they are capable of virtually anything. To say they never know when they are beaten would be stating the painfully obvious. But I have to admit that as the seconds ticked away in Barcelona I was already composing myself to take defeat with dignity. Then came 60 seconds which will be etched on all our memories for eternity. In football terms it was without a doubt the greatest moment in my life. The final weeks of last season will remain with me until the day I die and those moments at the end of the game at Nou Camp when Teddy Sheringham and Ole Gunnar Solskjaer scored will never be far from my thoughts.

Little Alex Ferguson, from Govan, is so proud to be manager of Manchester United and immensely honoured to be compared with the late, great Sir Matt Busby.

Truly great moments like that are there to be cherished.

Alex Ferguson

AUGUST

WEDNESDAY 12	v LKS LODZ	H
SATURDAY 15	v LEICESTER CITY	H
SATURDAY 22	v WEST HAM UNITED	A
WEDNESDAY 26	v LKS LODZ	A

BECKHAM 7

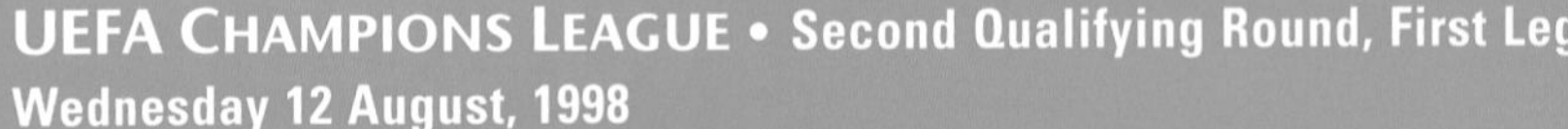

MANCHESTER UNITED 2

GIGGS 16
COLE 81

1. Peter SCHMEICHEL
2. Gary NEVILLE
3. Denis IRWIN
16. Roy KEANE
5. Ronny JOHNSEN
6. Jaap STAM
7. David BECKHAM
8. Nicky BUTT
9. Andy COLE
18. Paul SCHOLES
11. Ryan GIGGS

SUBSTITUTES

4. David MAY
10. Teddy SHERINGHAM
12. Phil NEVILLE
14. Jordi CRUYFF
20. Ole Gunnar SOLSKJAER (18) 82
21. Henning BERG
31. Nick CULKIN

MATCH REPORT

After their Charity Shield debacle against Arsenal, United needed a stabilising performance to kick-start their season, which is exactly what they produced against the Polish champions. It wasn't spectacular, certainly not a contest worth consigning to the memory bank, but it was passably efficient and laid a solid foundation for progress to the UEFA Champions League proper.

In all honesty, it helped that the visitors appeared to be devoid of attacking ambition, opting for a packed defence, which invited the Reds to pummel them almost at will. Accordingly,

Ryan Giggs shoots past Wyparlo to give United the lead

Old Trafford • 8.00pm • Attendance 50,906
Referee Atanus Ouzounov, Bulgaria

0 LKS LODZ

1. Boguslaw WYPARLO
16. Darlington OMODIAGBE
3. Tomasz KOS
4. Witold BENDKOWSKI
25. Tomasz CEBULA
6. Grzegorz KRYSIAK
7. Rafal PAWLAK
8. Dzidoslaw ZUBEREK
9. Rafal NIZNIK
33. Tomasz WIESZCZYCKI
19. Zbigniew WYCISKIEWICZ

SUBSTITUTES

2. Jacek PASZULEWICZ (8) 72
12. Michal SLAWUTA
15. Rodrigo CARBONE (9) 57
17. Ariel JAKUBOWSKI (16) 85
20. Jacek PLUCIENNIK
21. Pietr MATYS
23. Artur BUGAJ

Andy Cole rises to head United's second goal

Ferguson's men poured forward from the off and but for indifferent finishing, inconsistent crossing and a plucky display by Lodz keeper Wyparlo, they must have put the outcome of the tie beyond doubt. As it was, a sweet sidestep and neat shot from Giggs after 16 minutes and a late header from Cole plumped up an acceptable cushion for the second leg.

Jaap Stam, the world's most expensive defender, was not taxed on his senior debut and Roy Keane showed encouraging mobility after his lengthy injury lay-off. Clearly, though, rather tougher tests would lie ahead.

Ryan Giggs takes on the Lodz defence

MANCHESTER UNITED 2

SHERINGHAM 79
BECKHAM 90

1. Peter SCHMEICHEL
2. Gary NEVILLE
3. Denis IRWIN
16. Roy KEANE
5. Ronny JOHNSEN
6. Jaap STAM
7. David BECKHAM
8. Nicky BUTT
9. Andy COLE
18. Paul SCHOLES
11. Ryan GIGGS

SUBSTITUTES

4. David MAY
10. Teddy SHERINGHAM (2) 77
12. Phil NEVILLE
21. Henning BERG (6) h-t
31. Nick CULKIN

Leicester keeper Kasey Keller claims the ball under pressure from Andy Cole

MATCH REPORT

United needed a change of pace after their virtual stroll against the Poles and it was provided by Martin O'Neill's feisty Foxes. Indeed, for much of the game it seemed possible that the Reds would plunge to a morale-sapping home defeat. They were saved by a trademark Beckham free-kick three minutes into stoppage time, an inspired intervention which nevertheless put a flattering gloss on a distinctly below-par team performance.

The script began to go seriously awry from the beginning, with the new central-defensive partnership of Stam and Johnsen clearly needing more time to gel. First the home rearguard was

Old Trafford • 3.00pm • Attendance 55,052
Referee Neale Barry, Scunthorpe

2 LEICESTER CITY

7 HESKEY
76 COTTEE

1. Kasey KELLER
14. Robbie SAVAGE
3. Frank SINCLAIR
18. Matt ELLIOTT
5. Steve WALSH
6. Mustafa IZZET
7. Neil LENNON
37. Theo ZAGORAKIS
9. Emile HESKEY
27. Tony COTTEE
11. Steve GUPPY

SUBSTITUTES

4. Gerry TAGGART (18) 89
10. Garry PARKER
15. Pontus KAAMARK
22. Pegguy ARPHEXAD (1) 61
25. Stuart WILSON (27) 83

David Beckham celebrates United's equalising goal in the dying moments of the game with Roy Keane, Nicky Butt and Ryan Giggs

pierced by Heskey, who poked home from an Izzet cross, then Cottee spurned two fine chances to put the visitors out of sight.

After the interval United continued to splutter ineffectively, offering only intermittent threat to the visitors' goal, and when Cottee's header doubled Leicester's lead with only a quarter of an hour remaining, the Mancunians' outlook was bleak. However, three minutes later Sheringham nudged a Beckham shot wide of substitute keeper Arphexad, then the England midfielder struck at the death.

Later Alex Ferguson admitted that it was debatable whether United deserved a point. They must have been poor!

FA Carling Premiership
Saturday 22 August, 1998

West Ham United 0

12. Shaka HISLOP
20. Andrew IMPEY
17. Stan LAZARIDIS
19. Ian PEARCE
15. Rio FERDINAND
6. Neil RUDDOCK
18. Frank LAMPARD
8. Trevor SINCLAIR
29. Eyal BERKOVIC
10. John HARTSON
11. Steve LOMAS

SUBSTITUTES

7. Marc KELLER
16. John MONCUR
22. Craig FORREST
24. Samassi ABOU (29) 72
30. Javier MARGAS

MATCH REPORT

In normal circumstances, the debut display of a £12.6 million marksman would have come in for intense and not necessarily complimentary scrutiny from the massed ranks of the media.

Andy Cole tries to show debutant Dwight Yorke the way by getting in a shot despite the close attentions of West Ham defender Andy Impey

Boleyn Ground • 3.00pm • Attendance 26,039
Referee Peter Jones, Loughborough

0 MANCHESTER UNITED

1. Peter SCHMEICHEL
2. Gary NEVILLE
3. Denis IRWIN
16. Roy KEANE
5. Ronny JOHNSEN
21. Henning BERG
7. David BECKHAM
8. Nicky BUTT
9. Andy COLE
19. Dwight YORKE
11. Ryan GIGGS

SUBSTITUTES

4. David MAY
10. Teddy SHERINGHAM (9) 70
12. Phil NEVILLE (2) 52
18. Paul SCHOLES
31. Nick CULKIN

But happily for Dwight Yorke, who seemed understandably at something of a loss for much of the afternoon in a team which he had joined only 48 hours earlier, the spotlight's unforgiving glare was directed firmly elsewhere.

The recipient of all the unwanted attention was, of course, David Beckham, who had been promised unremitting persecution by an hysterical section of the Hammers' support as a result of his World Cup sending-off. As it turned out his ordeal was less torrid than expected and he passed his test of character with flying colours, refusing to be provoked by the chorus of catcalls which greeted his every touch and concentrating on the game.

The football? Though West Ham pressed forward enterprisingly in the first half they carried little threat. Meanwhile United should have been awarded a penalty when the referee was unsighted as Ruddock handled Giggs' cross, and Hislop was forced to make fine saves from Cole. In the second period, the visitors, with Keane increasingly dominant, seized the midfield initiative without making a telling strike. No goals, then, but a briskly competent away display by the white-shirted Reds.

David Beckham salutes United's travelling fans

LKS LODZ 0

1. Boguslaw WYPARLO
17. Ariel JAKUBOWSKI
3. Tomasz KOS
4. Witold BENDKOWSKI
5. Tomasz LENART
6. Grzegorz KRYSIAK
7. Rafal PAWLAK
8. Dzidoslaw ZUBEREK
9. Rafal NIZNIK
33. Tomasz WIESZCZYCKI
19. Zbigniew WYCISZKIEWICZ

SUBSTITUTES

2. Jacek PASZULEWICZ
12. Michal SLAWUTA
20. Jacek PLUCIENNIK (5) 82
21. Piotr MATYS (8) 52
23. Artur BUGAJ (17) 85

MATCH REPORT

United exercised the utmost care in stifling the life out of a Lodz side transformed from their passive mode of two weeks earlier. Now, with a two-goal deficit to make up, they sprang into instant attack, the nimble Niznik signalling Polish intentions by nipping beyond a startled Irwin and shooting uncomfortably close to Schmeichel's post after a mere 20 seconds of action.

The Reds reacted calmly, containing their eager but relatively unsophisticated opponents by lengthy bouts of simple, safe passing and by defending firmly when possession was lost. By such unspectacular means, gradually the sting was extracted

United's team line-up to face LKS Lodz

LKS Stadium • 9.05pm • Attendance 8,000
Referee Graziano Cesari, Italy

0 MANCHESTER UNITED

1. Peter SCHMEICHEL
12. Phil NEVILLE
3. Denis IRWIN
16. Roy KEANE
5. Ronny JOHNSEN
6. Jaap STAM
7. David BECKHAM
8. Nicky BUTT
18. Paul SCHOLES
10. Teddy SHERINGHAM
11. Ryan GIGGS

SUBSTITUTES

4. David MAY
9. Andy COLE
14. Jordi CRUYFF
17. Raimond VAN DER GOUW
20. Ole Gunnar SOLSKJAER (11) 65
21. Henning BERG
30. Wesley BROWN

Paul Scholes tussles for the ball with Lodz's Rafal Pawlak

from Lodz and the visitors began to create occasional chances, the best of which fell to Sheringham, who headed wide from a Giggs corner when well placed.

Later Beckham, Keane and Butt all had chances to register while United's only instant of true alarm came when Johnsen deflected a Kos free-kick perilously close to his own net. By the end the Reds were ambling, their mission accomplished with ease. Pretty it was not, but it had been supremely professional.

August in Review

WEDNESDAY 12	v LKS LODZ	H	2-0
SATURDAY 15	v LEICESTER CITY	H	2-2
SATURDAY 22	v WEST HAM UNITED	A	0-0
WEDNESDAY 26	v LKS LODZ	A	0-0

PLAYER IN THE FRAME

David Beckham

Following his World Cup trauma, David was placed under a merciless media spotlight and became the subject of moronic abuse up and down the country. He could have wilted under the pressure, but he didn't. Instead he answered his critics by concentrating on his work, his late equaliser against Leicester on the opening day of the Premiership season providing a telling early retort.

FA Carling Premiership

UP TO AND INCLUDING
SUNDAY 30 AUGUST 1998

	P	W	D	L	F	A	Pts
Liverpool	3	2	1	0	6	2	7
Aston Villa	3	2	1	0	4	1	7
Nottingham Forest	3	2	0	1	4	3	6
Charlton Athletic	3	1	2	0	5	0	5
Wimbledon	3	1	2	0	4	2	5
Arsenal	3	1	2	0	2	1	5
Leeds United	3	1	2	0	2	1	5
West Ham United	3	1	2	0	1	0	5
Leicester City	3	1	1	1	4	3	4
Coventry City	3	1	1	1	2	2	4
Blackburn Rovers	3	1	1	1	1	1	4
Sheffield Wednesday	3	1	0	2	3	2	3
Derby County	3	0	3	0	1	1	3
Tottenham Hotspur	3	1	0	2	2	6	3
MANCHESTER UNITED	2	0	2	0	2	2	2
Middlesbrough	3	0	2	1	2	4	2
Newcastle United	3	0	2	1	2	5	2
Chelsea	2	0	1	1	2	3	1
Everton	3	0	1	2	0	3	1
Southampton	3	0	0	3	2	9	0

SEPTEMBER

WEDNESDAY 9	v CHARLTON ATHLETIC	H
SATURDAY 12	v COVENTRY CITY	H
WEDNESDAY 16	v FC BARCELONA	H
SUNDAY 20	v ARSENAL	A
THURSDAY 24	v LIVERPOOL	H
WEDNESDAY 30	v BAYERN MUNICH	A

FA CARLING PREMIERSHIP
Wednesday 9 September, 1998

MANCHESTER UNITED 4

SOLSKJAER 39, 63
YORKE 45, 48

1. Peter SCHMEICHEL
12. Phil NEVILLE
3. Denis IRWIN
16. Roy KEANE
5. Ronny JOHNSEN
6. Jaap STAM
7. David BECKHAM
18. Paul SCHOLES
20. Ole Gunnar SOLSKJAER
19. Dwight YORKE
15. Jesper BLOMQVIST

SUBSTITUTES

9. Andy COLE (20) 68
10. Teddy SHERINGHAM (19) 68
17. Raimond VAN DER GOUW
21. Henning BERG (3) 57
33. Mark WILSON

MATCH REPORT

What with ongoing turbulence over the proposed takeover by BSkyB and an indifferent start to their Premiership campaign, United were in pressing need of a lift when they entertained sparky top-flight newcomers Charlton Athletic. They got it, thanks to a brace of goals each from the ebullient Yorke, who was making his home debut, and the popular Solskjaer.

However, there was no instant gratification for their frustrated fans, even though Yorke's integration into the Reds' fluent passing game was immediately apparent. During the first half-hour the home side made and missed chances with equal

Ole Gunnar Solskjaer scores United's equaliser

Old Trafford • 8.00pm • Attendance 55,147
Referee Paul Durkin, Portland

1 CHARLTON ATHLETIC

32 KINSELLA

1. Sasa ILIC
2. Danny MILLS
3. Chris POWELL
4. Neil REDFEARN
12. Steve BROWN
6. Eddie YOUDS
7. Shaun NEWTON
8. Mark KINSELLA
9. Andy HUNT
10. Clive MENDONCA
11. John ROBINSON

SUBSTITUTES

13. Andy PETTERSON
15. Keith JONES (8) 76
16. Paul MORTIMER (7) 56
19. Steve JONES (10) 71
23. Stuart BALMER

Dwight Yorke takes on Eddie Youds and Neil Redfearn on his home debut

alacrity, but when the inevitable goal arrived it came from Charlton's Kinsella, who beat Schmeichel with a deflected drive. Dismay in the Old Trafford stands was only temporary. Within seven minutes Solskjaer had levelled after a rather fortuitous passing interchange with Yorke, then the Tobagan provoked the night's most ecstatic celebration by heading home from a Beckham free-kick shortly before the break. Three minutes after the resumption another Beckham delivery was converted by Yorke following a touch by Solskjaer and the Norwegian completed the scoring with a diving header from a centre by Berg. As United coasted towards the final whistle, with debutant Blomqvist bedding himself in unflashily on the left flank, the stadium was engulfed by a heady mixture of rapture and relief.

MANCHESTER UNITED 2

YORKE 20
JOHNSEN 48

1. Peter SCHMEICHEL
2. Gary NEVILLE
12. Phil NEVILLE
16. Roy KEANE
5. Ronny JOHNSEN
6. Jaap STAM
7. David BECKHAM
18. Paul SCHOLES
20. Ole Gunnar SOLSKJAER
19. Dwight YORKE
11. Ryan GIGGS

SUBSTITUTES

8. Nicky BUTT (7) 78
9. Andy COLE
15. Jesper BLOMQVIST (11) 78
17. Raimond VAN DER GOUW
21. Henning BERG

MATCH REPORT

The momentum of United's season moved up a notch as they comfortably outclassed a woefully lacklustre Coventry side, then eased back on the throttle with the forthcoming Barcelona clash in mind. The Reds settled for a goal in either half, the first a slightly mishit tap-in by Yorke following incisive work by the splendid Scholes – Dwight's third goal in three appearances – and the second a firm dispatch by Johnsen after efforts by Yorke and Scholes had been blocked.

Those were the bare bones of the victory, but there was far more to admire from a home viewpoint. For instance, Stam was in gratifyingly commanding form at the back, linking smoothly with Johnsen, and suggesting that hysterical press condemnation of earlier performances could be discounted. Paul Scholes and David Beckham both played well, and nothing could dampen the spirits of the 55,193 fans in attendance, not even media speculation about the proposed takeover of the club.

But the man who riveted the attention most vividly was Yorke. Effervescent and inventive, he offered an imaginative link between midfield and attack, he continued to show a good understanding with Solskjaer, and always looked capable of breaching the Sky Blue wall erected to frustrate him. Like a certain Frenchman before him, the Tobagan entertained no doubts that he was born to grace the Old Trafford stage.

That said, the visitors were so poor that their manager, Gordon Strachan, compared their approach to that of a dentist's patient who knew that pain was coming soon!

Old Trafford • 3.00pm • Attendance 55,193
Referee Uriah Rennie, Sheffield

0 COVENTRY CITY

1. Magnus HEDMAN
13. Jean-Guy WALLEMME
3. David BURROWS
30. Barry QUINN
5. Richard SHAW
6. Gary BREEN
7. Darren HUCKERBY
27. Marc EDWORTHY
9. Dion DUBLIN
12. Paul TELFER
11. George BOATENG

SUBSTITUTES

4. Paul WILLIAMS
14. Trond SOLTVEDT
15. Paul HALL (7) 73
16. Steve OGRIZOVIC
29. Sam SHILTON

Jean-Guy Wallemme keeps Dwight Yorke away from the Coventry goal

UEFA CHAMPIONS LEAGUE • Group D
Wednesday 16 September, 1998

MANCHESTER UNITED 3

1. Peter SCHMEICHEL
2. Gary NEVILLE
3. Denis IRWIN
16. Roy KEANE
21. Henning BERG
6. Jaap STAM
7. David BECKHAM
18. Paul SCHOLES
20. Ole Gunnar SOLSKJAER
19. Dwight YORKE
11. Ryan GIGGS

SUBSTITUTES

4. David MAY
8. Nicky BUTT (20) 55
9. Andy COLE
10. Teddy SHERINGHAM
12. Phil NEVILLE (3) 79
15. Jesper BLOMQVIST (11) 84
17. Raimond VAN DER GOUW

GIGGS 17
SCHOLES 25
BECKHAM 64

MATCH REPORT

This was football the way it used to be played, at least in the rosy-hued imagination of soccer romantics. It was a night of rapturous entertainment and end-to-end thrills, with United veering from passages of play as enchanting as any they have compiled during the Ferguson era to dire moments of demoralisation and disarray.

Appropriately the game began with a flourish as the Reds penetrated Barcelona's fragile rearguard only for Beckham to shoot wildly and inaccurately instead of seeking out the better-placed Yorke. Thereafter, however, the bounteously gifted midfielder made ravishing amends, going on to deliver one of his most compelling performances.

First he supplied the centre which led to Solskjaer rapping the Spaniards' bar, then climaxed a flowing move by launching a deep cross from the right which Giggs rose to head home with all the power and certainty of a latter-day Tommy Taylor. Beckham's next telling contribution was to find Yorke whose spellbinding overhead kick rebounded from keeper Hesp and Luis Enrique for Scholes to crash home. The by now rampant Reds nearly scored a third goal when Yorke robbed Abelardo and fed Solskjaer, but he was just offside.

Now Barcelona adjusted their hitherto impractically attacking formation and surged back into contention. First a Rivaldo 'goal' was wrongly disallowed for offside, then Anderson took

Paul Scholes celebrates United's second goal

Old Trafford • 7.45pm • Attendance 53,601
Referee Stefano Braschi, Italy

3 FC BARCELONA

47 ANDERSON
60 GIOVANNI (penalty)
71 LUIS ENRIQUE (penalty)

13. Ruud HESP
2. Michael REIZIGER
12. SERGI
21. LUIS ENRIQUE
5. ABELARDO
15. COCU
7. Luis FIGO
23. ZENDEN
9. ANDERSON
10. GIOVANNI
11. RIVALDO

SUBSTITUTES

1. VITOR BAIA
6. OSCAR
16. Dragan CIRIC
22. OKUNOWO
24. ROGER
26. XAVI (10) 68

Dwight Yorke attempts a spectacular overhead kick that rattled the bar and rebounded for Scholes to score

advantage of confusion in United's defence to score just after the interval. Next Giovanni netted from the spot after Rivaldo tumbled contentiously when under challenge from Stam, and the Reds were reeling.

Cue Beckham and a curling 25-yard free-kick of utter perfection which restored the lead, but only briefly. As Barca exerted more frenetic pressure, Butt handled during a goalmouth mêlée – an offence for which he was sent off – and Luis Enrique converted the penalty. In the end it was a fair result to a breathtaking contest which neither side deserved to lose.

Ryan Giggs celebrates his 17th-minute strike

FA CARLING PREMIERSHIP
Sunday 20 September, 1998

ADAMS 14
ANELKA 44
LJUNGBERG 80

1. David SEAMAN
2. Lee DIXON
3. Nigel WINTERBURN
4. Patrick VIEIRA
14. Martin KEOWN
6. Tony ADAMS
15. Ray PARLOUR
16. Stephen HUGHES
9. Nicolas ANELKA
10. Dennis BERGKAMP
11. Marc OVERMARS

SUBSTITUTES

5. Steve BOULD
8. Fredrik LJUNGBERG (9) 80
12. Christopher WREH
13. Alex MANNINGER
19. Remi GARDE

MATCH REPORT

For a club with serious aspirations to regaining their Premiership crown, the home of the new Champions was hardly the place to endure the footballing equivalent of a calamitous day at the office. But that's how it was for the black-shirted Reds at Highbury. Distressingly for the visiting fans, their team succumbed rather limply to a vastly more determined Gunners side which recorded its fourth successive triumph over United, giving rise to inescapable fears that they had established a telling psychological edge.

With Giggs partnering Yorke up front and Blomqvist occupying the left flank, the Mancunians' attack might have been expected to exhibit dazzling movement, but it never happened. Instead Arsenal, for whom Vieira, Overmars and the entire defence were outstanding, assumed comprehensive domination, taking the lead when Adams outjumped Stam to head in from Hughes' free-kick.

True, United enjoyed no vestige of luck, as evidenced by Beckham's 25-yard shot which beat Seaman, struck one post and narrowly eluded the other,

Roy Keane battles with Arsenal's Stephen Hughes for dominance of the midfield

Arsenal Stadium • 4.00pm • Attendance 38,142
Referee Graham Barber, Pyrford

0 MANCHESTER UNITED

1. Peter SCHMEICHEL
2. Gary NEVILLE
3. Denis IRWIN
16. Roy KEANE
21. Henning BERG
6. Jaap STAM
7. David BECKHAM
8. Nicky BUTT
15. Jesper BLOMQVIST
19. Dwight YORKE
11. Ryan GIGGS

SUBSTITUTES

12. Phil NEVILLE
14. Jordi CRUYFF
17. Raimond VAN DER GOUW
18. Paul SCHOLES
20. Ole Gunnar SOLSKJAER

Jaap Stam holds off Arsenal's Patrick Vieira

but after that isolated scare the Gunners resumed the ascendancy. This was underlined a minute before the break when Anelka eluded Stam to net at the second attempt after Schmeichel had saved his first effort.

In the second half Arsenal were able to cruise in the broiling sunshine, particularly after Butt was sent off – his second dismissal in four days – for tripping Vieira when the Frenchman was bearing down on goal. A miserable afternoon for United was completed when a loose ball reached home debutant Ljungberg, just on as a substitute for Anelka, who chipped a third goal with casual ease.

MANCHESTER UNITED 2

IRWIN (penalty) 19
SCHOLES 80

1. Peter SCHMEICHEL
2. Gary NEVILLE
3. Denis IRWIN
16. Roy KEANE
12. Phil NEVILLE
6. Jaap STAM
7. David BECKHAM
18. Paul SCHOLES
20. Ole Gunnar SOLSKJAER
19. Dwight YORKE
11. Ryan GIGGS

SUBSTITUTES

8. Nicky BUTT (18) 88
9. Andy COLE (20) 70
15. Jesper BLOMQVIST
17. Raimond VAN DER GOUW
21. Henning BERG

MATCH REPORT

It all came right in the end, but behind that satisfying 2-0 scoreline lies the tale of a distinctly curious encounter with the old enemy.

For the opening 19 minutes, United's superiority was absolute with the Anfield men virtually supine, having adopted a policy of passive containment. Such an approach, when faced with a bevy of attackers as talented as those at Alex Ferguson's disposal, is one which requires a well-nigh watertight defence. As recent events had demonstrated, that was an asset Liverpool did not possess. Thus a home goal seemed inevitable, and duly it arrived, albeit controversially, when McAteer was harshly adjudged guilty of handball and Irwin netted from the spot.

Now the tenor of the game was transformed. The visitors emerged from their shell, taking control of midfield although failing dismally to achieve penetration, thanks hugely to the giant contribution of new central defensive partners Stam and Gary Neville, who allowed Owen and company barely a kick. However, in its turn, United's apparent switch to unadventurous mode

Paul Scholes is congratulated after scoring United's second goal

Old Trafford • 8.00pm • Attendance 55,181
Referee Steve Lodge, Barnsley

0 LIVERPOOL

19. Brad FRIEDEL
15. Patrik BERGER
20. Stig Inge BJORNEBYE
4. Jason McATEER
23. Jamie CARRAGHER
6. Phil BABB
7. Steve McMANAMAN
17. Paul INCE
13. Karlheinz RIEDLE
10. Michael OWEN
11. Jamie REDKNAPP

SUBSTITUTES

1. David JAMES
8. Oyvind LEONHARDSEN
9. Robbie FOWLER (13) 75
14. Vegard HEGGEM
21. Dominic MATTEO

Andy Cole fires in a shot at goal

worried the home support and they were mightily relieved when Riedle's 63rd-minute strike was correctly disallowed for offside.

Only late in the contest, with Liverpool flagging visibly, did the Red Devils resume the offensive and it was from a typically incisive counter-attack that the points were clinched. Yorke nudged a Cole cross behind Scholes, who altered direction adroitly and dispatched the sweetest of left-foot curlers into the far top corner of Friedel's net from some 16 yards. Thereafter United might have doubled their tally but that would have been unduly savage punishment for the deflated Merseysiders. As it was, they were left to ponder the wisdom of their bizarrely negative start.

UEFA CHAMPIONS LEAGUE • Group D
Wednesday 30 September, 1998

BAYERN MUNICH 2

ELBER 11, 90

1. Oliver KAHN
2. Markus BABBEL
3. Bixente LIZARAZU
16. Jens JEREMIES
25. Thomas LINKE
20. Hasan SALIHAMIDZIC
19. Carsten JANCKER
8. Thomas STRUNZ
9. Giovan de Souza ELBER
10. Lothar MATTHAUS
11. Stefan EFFENBURG

SUBSTITUTES

4. Samuel Osei KUFFOUR
12. Sven SCHEUER
17. Thorsten FINK (16) 82
18. Michael TARNAT
24. Daei DAEI (19) 63
28. Berkant GOKTAN (20) 63

MATCH REPORT

An uncharacteristic but undeniably colossal late blunder by Peter Schmeichel, for once impetuous where he is usually so imperturbable, cost United a famous away victory. They led 2-1 with only seconds remaining when he rushed to claim a long throw which should have been left to Stam. He failed to reach it and Elber turned in the equaliser in the ensuing confusion.

The Brazilian, a thorn in the visitors' side all evening, had steered Bayern into an early lead, possibly from an offside position, after which United consolidated calmly before building pressure of their own. This paid off when Beckham shrugged off a challenge from Lizarazu to deliver an exquisite cross from which Yorke scored with a full-length diving header.

Now, with Sheringham excelling in a deep-lying role, the Red Devils began to control proceedings, which was reflected by another goal four minutes after the interval when Scholes beat keeper Kahn courageously in a 50-50 challenge before walking the ball into the net.

Thus stung, Bayern poured forward through the curtains of rain which enveloped the Olympic Stadium, and

United Manager Alex Ferguson and Ex-Player/Director Sir Bobby Charlton admire Munich's Olympic Stadium before the game

Olympic Stadium, Munich • 7.45pm • Attendance 55,000
Referee Marc Batta, France

2 MANCHESTER UNITED

30 YORKE
49 SCHOLES

1. Peter SCHMEICHEL
2. Gary NEVILLE
3. Denis IRWIN
16. Roy KEANE
12. Phil NEVILLE
6. Jaap STAM
7. David BECKHAM
18. Paul SCHOLES
19. Dwight YORKE
10. Teddy SHERINGHAM
15. Jesper BLOMQVIST

SUBSTITUTES

4. David MAY
9. Andy COLE
4. Jordi CRUYFF (15) 69
17. Raimond VAN DER GOUW
20. Ole Gunnar SOLSKJAER
21. Henning BERG
30. Wesley BROWN

David Beckham and Lothar Matthaus clash in midfield

they created a succession of chances, all missed or dealt with by the splendid Schmeichel.

The aberration which followed will remain long in the memory, but should not obscure the excellence of his earlier work. Alex Ferguson referred to the equaliser as a kick in the teeth but doubtless would have settled for a draw beforehand. Perhaps more worrying for the United boss was a needless booking for Beckham, which would keep him out of the next UEFA Champions League encounter.

SEPTEMBER IN REVIEW

WEDNESDAY 9	v CHARLTON ATHLETIC	H	4-1
SATURDAY 12	v COVENTRY CITY	H	2-0
WEDNESDAY 16	v FC BARCELONA	H	3-3
SUNDAY 20	v ARSENAL	A	0-3
THURSDAY 24	v LIVERPOOL	H	2-0
WEDNESDAY 30	v BAYERN MUNICH	A	2-2

PLAYER IN THE FRAME

Paul Scholes

Three delightful but contrasting goals epitomised Paul's inestimable value. First there was the opportunism of his close-range strike at home to Barcelona, then the exquisite technique showcased by the late curler which tied up the Old Trafford triumph over Liverpool, and finally the raw courage with which he contested a 50-50 ball with the Bayern keeper before putting United ahead in Munich.

FA CARLING PREMIERSHIP

UP TO AND INCLUDING MONDAY 28 SEPTEMBER 1998

	P	W	D	L	F	A	Pts
Aston Villa	7	5	2	0	8	1	17
Derby County	7	3	3	1	6	3	12
Wimbledon	7	3	3	1	11	9	12
West Ham United	7	3	3	1	7	5	12
Newcastle United	7	3	2	2	13	7	11
MANCHESTER UNITED	**6**	**3**	**2**	**1**	**10**	**6**	**11**
Leeds United	7	2	5	0	8	4	11
Liverpool	7	3	2	2	12	9	11
Chelsea	6	3	2	1	10	7	11
Arsenal	7	2	4	1	6	3	10
Sheffield Wednesday	7	3	0	4	8	5	9
Middlesbrough	7	2	3	2	8	8	9
Tottenham Hotspur	7	2	2	3	8	14	8
Charlton Athletic	7	1	4	2	11	10	7
Everton	7	1	4	2	4	5	7
Nottingham Forest	7	2	1	4	5	9	7
Leicester City	7	1	3	3	6	8	6
Blackburn Rovers	7	1	2	4	5	10	5
Coventry City	7	1	2	4	4	12	5
Southampton	7	0	1	6	3	18	1

October

SATURDAY 3	v SOUTHAMPTON	A
SATURDAY 17	v WIMBLEDON	H
WEDNESDAY 21	v BRONDBY IF	A
SATURDAY 24	v DERBY COUNTY	A
WEDNESDAY 28	v BURY	H
SATURDAY 31	v EVERTON	A

FA CARLING PREMIERSHIP
Saturday 3 October, 1998

SOUTHAMPTON 0

1. Paul JONES
29. Phil WARNER
15. Francis BENALI
4. Carlton PALMER
5. Claus LUNDEKVAM
6. Ken MONKOU
7. Matthew LE TISSIER
14. Stuart RIPLEY
18. Wayne BRIDGE
10. Egil OSTENSTAD
11. David HOWELLS

SUBSTITUTES

13. Neil MOSS
16. James BEATTIE (14) 64
23. Scott HILEY
24. Steve BASHAM
28. Kevin GIBBENS (5) 56

Andy Cole turns in celebration after scoring United's second goal

MATCH REPORT

For once, United enjoyed a good day at The Dell, where they had lost on their three previous visits. Arriving this time without the injured Schmeichel, Giggs and Scholes, they demonstrated forcibly the depth of their squad, winning comfortably and leaving their hosts marooned at the foot of the table.

But it was Southampton who fashioned the first chance, Howells squandering a free header on two minutes, an act of profligacy for which his side was to be punished swiftly. Cole broke free on the left and crossed to Yorke whose scuffed shot from close range trickled into the net.

The Dell • 3.00pm • Attendance 15,251
Referee David Elleray, Harrow-on-the-Hill

3 MANCHESTER UNITED

12 YORKE
60 COLE
75 CRUYFF

17. Raimond VAN DER GOUW
2. Gary NEVILLE
3. Denis IRWIN
16. Roy KEANE
12. Phil NEVILLE
6. Jaap STAM
7. David BECKHAM
8. Nicky BUTT
9. Andy COLE
19. Dwight YORKE
15. Jesper BLOMQVIST

SUBSTITUTES

10. Teddy SHERINGHAM (19) 73
14. Jordi CRUYFF (15) 73
20. Ole Gunnar SOLSKJAER
21. Henning BERG
24. Wesley BROWN (3) 79

Jaap Stam and Southampton's Ken Monkou challenge for the ball in a scramble following a Southampton corner

The Saints reacted with spirit and mounted their most impressive spell but United, with Keane showing signs of returning to his best, soaked up their attacks without due alarm.

On the hour, with Southampton growing increasingly desperate, they were put to the sword by Blomqvist, sparkling on the left flank in the absence of Giggs, whose delightful pass sent in Cole to neatly sidefoot the Red Devils further ahead. It only remained for the substitute Cruyff to dispatch an immaculate 14-yard volley for the third. It was United's first away victory and lifted them to second place in the Premiership.

FA CARLING PREMIERSHIP
Saturday 17 October, 1998

MANCHESTER UNITED 5

17. Raimond VAN DER GOUW
2. Gary NEVILLE
12. Phil NEVILLE
16. Roy KEANE
24. Wesley BROWN
6. Jaap STAM
7. David BECKHAM
15. Jesper BLOMQVIST
9. Andy COLE
19. Dwight YORKE
11. Ryan GIGGS

SUBSTITUTES

13. John CURTIS (12) 74
14. Jordi CRUYFF (7) 57
18. Paul SCHOLES (11) 66
20. Ole Gunnar SOLSKJAER
21. Henning BERG

COLE 19, 88
GIGGS 45
BECKHAM 47
YORKE 52

MATCH REPORT

This was Manchester United in all their power and glory, very close to their opulent best. They scored five times, struck the woodwork twice, saw several efforts cleared off the line and were prevented from reaching double figures by a succession of scintillating saves by Sullivan. This was, without doubt, the best league performance of the season to date played out in front of the biggest crowd, and a perfect warm-up for next Wednesday's Champions League match against Brondby.

The Reds exhibited no hint of a weakness, and even when Euell nullified Cole's earlier strike with a goal ludicrously

Andy Cole slots the ball past Scotland's new number one goalkeeper, Neil Sullivan, to make it 1-0 to United after 19 minutes

Old Trafford • 3.00pm • Attendance 55,265
Referee Gary Willard, Worthing

1 WIMBLEDON

39 EUELL

1. Neil SULLIVAN
2. Kenny CUNNINGHAM
3. Alan KIMBLE
4. Chris PERRY
5. Dean BLACKWELL
6. Ben THATCHER
20. Jason EUELL
8. Robbie EARLE
15. Carl LEABURN
10. Andy ROBERTS
16. Michael HUGHES

SUBSTITUTES

11. Marcus GAYLE (15) h-t
12. Neal ARDLEY (3) h-t
13. Paul HEALD
18. Mark KENNEDY
23. Carl CORT

against the run of play, they merely resumed their domination and regained the lead through a Giggs header from a Blomqvist cross on the stroke of half-time.

The home side's superiority was rubbed in ruthlessly through strikes from Beckham, who beat Sullivan with a low shot from 25 yards, and Yorke shortly after the interval and a late effort from Cole completed the rout. It could have been much worse if Neil Sullivan in the Dons' goal had not celebrated his Scotland call-up with a brilliant performance by saving late efforts from both Cole and Blomqvist.

Alex Ferguson's satisfaction could hardly have been more comprehensive. The partnership between Yorke and Cole showed signs of growing into something really special; Keane's rehabilitation appeared complete; and with young Brown, a natural central defender deployed at right-back making his league debut, another gem has been unearthed.

As defeated Dons' manager Joe Kinnear summed up philosophically after the match: 'There is no shame in being beaten by a great team'.

Andy Cole dances the Lambada after his second goal

UEFA Champions League • Group D
Wednesday 21 October, 1998

Brondby IF 2

DAUGAARD 35
SAND 90

1. Mogens KROGH
2. Ole BJUR
16. Bo JENSEN
4. Per NIELSEN
19. Kenneth RASMUSSEN
6. Alan Jensen RAVN
14. Soren COLDING
8. Kim DAUGAARD
12. Ebbe SAND
13. Bo HANSEN
24. Thomas LINDRUP

SUBSTITUTES

5. Da Silva VRAGEL (16) 27
9. Jesper THYGESEN
15. Ruben BAGGER (13) 67
17. Soren KROGH
21. Mikkel JENSEN (4) 31
22. Emeka ANDERSON
23. Mads OLSEN

MATCH REPORT

Two-goal Ryan Giggs runs at the heart of the Brondby defence

After two draws against top-quality opposition, United were desperate for their first victory of the European campaign when they faced Brondby, perceived as Group D's weakest side. It was delivered in exhilarating style as the Danes were buried beneath an avalanche of goals, finishing on the business end of the most comprehensive away triumph in Champions League history.

The Reds got off to a perfect start after two minutes when Brown, playing with a maturity beyond his tender years, rampaged down the right and delivered a routine cross which Krogh, the Danish keeper, spilled to the feet of Giggs. The Welshman, who was to cause constant problems for the home defence in his free-roving role, accepted the gift with relish.

Parken Stadium, Copenhagen • 7.45pm • Attendance 40,315
Referee Vitor Manuel Melo Pereira, Portugal

6 MANCHESTER UNITED

2, 21 GIGGS
28 COLE
55 KEANE
60 YORKE
62 SOLSKJAER

1. Peter SCHMEICHEL
2. Gary NEVILLE
12. Phil NEVILLE
16. Roy KEANE
30. Wesley BROWN
6. Jaap STAM
15. Jesper BLOMQVIST
18. Paul SCHOLES
9. Andy COLE
19. Dwight YORKE
11. Ryan GIGGS

SUBSTITUTES

14. Jordi CRUYFF (11) 61
17. Raimond VAN DER GOUW
20. Ole Gunnar SOLSKJAER (9) 61
21. Henning BERG
23. Michael CLEGG
29. John CURTIS
33. Mark WILSON (19) 66

Spurred on by the reverse Brondby went for gung-ho adventure, piling forward with apparent abandon which left huge gaps for the visitors to exploit on the counter.

Duly they did so. Giggs headed his second from a Blomqvist centre, then Cole made it three after dazzling interplay with Yorke, and the twice-taken free-kick converted by Daugaard after 35 minutes already smacked of consolation.

So it proved, with Keane, Yorke and Solskjaer – with his first touch after coming on as a substitute – adding second-half nails to the Brondby coffin. Sand's injury-time reply offered merely a semblance of respectability to a result which, thanks to Bayern's defeat of Barcelona, left the Reds at the summit of Group D.

Ole Gunnar Solskjaer makes it six with his first touch

FA CARLING PREMIERSHIP
Saturday 24 October, 1998

DERBY COUNTY 1

BURTON 75

1. Russell HOULT
16. Jacob LAURSEN
3. Stefan SCHNOOR
4. Darryl POWELL
17. Spencer PRIOR
6. Igor STIMAC
18. Lee CARSLEY
8. Dean STURRIDGE
9. Paulo WANCHOPE
10. Rory DELAP
24. Deon BURTON

SUBSTITUTES

2. Horacio CARBONARI
5. Tony DORIGO (16) h-t
19. Steve ELLIOTT
21. Mart POOM
27. Francesco BAIANO

MATCH REPORT

After their cakewalk in Copenhagen, the Reds were in curiously sluggish mode for their attempt to earn their first win of the decade at the home of Derby County. Indeed, for most of the afternoon their normal zest and aggression were notable for their absence and it took a late triple substitution by Alex Ferguson to salvage a point. The manager was not amused, admitting that, in the end, a draw was probably more than his side deserved.

Jim Smith's Rams, who faced United on the back of three straight defeats, reacted boldly to their crisis of form by selecting three front-runners – Wanchope, Sturridge and Burton – and resorting largely to route-one methods to ensure their gainful employment. Chances were few and far between and much of the action was arid, but the Reds found themselves pinned back for lengthy periods and when slack marking allowed Burton to knock Powell's low cross into Schmeichel's net some quarter of an hour from the end, Derby could claim reasonably to deserve the lead.

Ferguson had seen enough. With eight minutes remaining he hauled off Giggs, Butt and Gary Neville and sent on Blomqvist, Scholes and Cruyff to try and salvage something from the game. Within four minutes the Dutchman had saved the day, poaching an equaliser with another four minutes still left on the clock. Thereafter Yorke almost pinched all three points with a header from a Blomqvist cross but, on the balance of play, a win for United would have been a travesty.

Pride Park • 3.00pm • Attendance 30,867
Referee Paul Durkin, Portland

1 MANCHESTER UNITED

86 CRUYFF

1. Peter SCHMEICHEL
2. Gary NEVILLE
12. Phil NEVILLE
16. Roy KEANE
24. Wesley BROWN
6. Jaap STAM
7. David BECKHAM
8. Nicky BUTT
9. Andy COLE
19. Dwight YORKE
11. Ryan GIGGS

SUBSTITUTES

14. Jordi CRUYFF (8) 82
15. Jesper BLOMQVIST (11) 82
17. Raimond VAN DER GOUW
18. Paul SCHOLES (2) 82
21. Henning BERG

Andy Cole receives close attention from the Derby defence

WORTHINGTON CUP • Third Round
Wednesday 28 October, 1998

MANCHESTER UNITED 2

SOLSKJAER 106
NEVLAND 115

1. Peter SCHMEICHEL
23. Michael CLEGG
13. John CURTIS
4. David MAY
12. Phil NEVILLE
21. Henning BERG
33. Mark WILSON
28. Philip MULRYNE
20. Ole Gunnar SOLSKJAER
14. Jordi CRUYFF
34. Jonathan GREENING

SUBSTITUTES

2. Gary NEVILLE
18. Paul SCHOLES (33) 70
22. Erik NEVLAND (28) h-t
24. Wesley BROWN (23) 70
27. Terry COOKE

MATCH REPORT

Valuable experience for some United youngsters, much-needed revenue for Bury and always the chance of an upset . . . there didn't seem too much wrong with the widely maligned Worthington Cup when these two friendly neighbours met at a rain-lashed Old Trafford.

Brave, determined and well organised, the Shakers stretched the Reds fully before succumbing to two goals in the second period of extra time.

Despite publicity to the contrary, a home starting line-up which included Berg, May, Phil Neville, Cruyff and Solskjaer hardly came into the untried category. However, it was rookies such as midfielder Wilson and marksman Greening who took the eye and who went closest to scoring in a first half during which Bury's best chance fell to Lucketti, who headed wide of van der Gouw's goal from a Patterson free kick.

After the break, with the rain easing slightly, but the wind picking up, Nevland for United and Preece for Bury almost broke the deadlock, and Woodward might have settled proceedings in the visitors' favour near the end of normal time.

The crowd of over 52,000, including an estimated 10,000 travelling supporters, continued to cheer on the teams. Eventually the Reds prevailed through a Solskjaer left-footer which went in off a post right at the start of the second period of extra time, and a close-range effort from Nevland nine minutes later that followed fine work from Brown. The Shakers, though, had done themselves proud.

Old Trafford • 8.00pm • Attendance 52,495
Referee Keith Burge, Tonypandy

0 BURY

after extra time

1. Dean KIELY
2. Andy WOODWARD
3. Dean BARRICK
4. Nick DAWS
5. Chris LUCKETTI
6. Steve REDMOND
7. Chris SWAILES
8. Mark PATTERSON
9. Laurent D'JAFFO
10. Lennie JOHNROSE
11. Tony ELLIS

SUBSTITUTES

12. Andy PREECE (9) 58
13. Patrick KENNY
14. John FOSTER
15. Rob MATTHEWS
16. Lutel JAMES (11) 63

Jonathan Greening impresses in his first game of the season, catching the eye with some clever runs and several shots on target

Erik Nevland celebrates his goal five minutes from the end of extra time

FA CARLING PREMIERSHIP
Saturday 31 October, 1998

EVERTON 1

FERGUSON 31

1. Thomas MYHRE
12. Craig SHORT
3. Michael BALL
4. Olivier DACOURT
5. Dave WATSON
6. David UNSWORTH
7. John COLLINS
15. Marco MATERAZZI
9. Duncan FERGUSON
26. Ibrahima BAKAYOKO
29. Danny CADAMARTERI

SUBSTITUTES

2. Alex CLELAND
13. Paul GERRARD
14. Tony GRANT
27. Richard DUNNE (12) 67
36. Jamie MULLIGAN

MATCH REPORT

United could derive massive satisfaction from this comprehensive demolition of a rumbustiously competitive Everton side, which hitherto had been undefeated in ten matches. It wasn't just the emphatic, perhaps faintly flattering margin of victory but the manner in which it was achieved, the Reds matching the Merseysiders for strength and determination while eclipsing them in terms of quality. In addition the understanding between Yorke and Cole continued to burgeon, the youthful Brown looked ever more at home in the top flight and the rapidly blossoming Blomqvist offered further compelling evidence that, at last, United had found a credible deputy for Giggs.

The hosts made a bright start, with the combative Ferguson stretching Stam and company, but their impetus was jolted when Cole and Scholes set up Yorke for his eighth goal in 12 outings. United doubled their tally when the unchallenged Short nodded a Beckham cross into his own net, but Everton hopes were revived when Ferguson soared above his markers to head past Schmeichel from Ball's free-kick. Amazingly, it was the Blues' first Premiership goal of the season at Goodison.

After the interval Walter Smith's men enjoyed a period of territorial ascendancy but no luck, as Stam nudged the ball against his own woodwork, then Collins hit a post and Bakayoko and Short missed inviting chances. But United

David Beckham helps Jesper Blomqvist celebrate his first ever goal for Manchester United

Goodison Park • 3.00pm • Attendance 40,079
Referee Peter Jones, Loughborough

4 MANCHESTER UNITED

14 YORKE
23 SHORT (o.g.)
59 COLE
64 BLOMQVIST

1. Peter SCHMEICHEL
2. Gary NEVILLE
12. Phil NEVILLE
16. Roy KEANE
24. Wesley BROWN
6. Jaap STAM
7. David BECKHAM
18. Paul SCHOLES
9. Andy COLE
19. Dwight YORKE
15. Jesper BLOMQVIST

SUBSTITUTES

3. Denis IRWIN (12) 67
14. Jordi CRUYFF
17. Raimond VAN DER GOUW
20. Ole Gunnar SOLSKJAER
21. Henning BERG

weathered the storm and broke away to settle matters with two goals in six minutes. The brilliant Blomqvist was centrally involved on both occasions, first setting up Cole for a clinical finish, then nodding his own first goal for United after Myhre had saved his initial shot.

Jesper Blomqvist and Everton's Danny Cadamarteri challenge for the ball

October in Review

SATURDAY 3	v SOUTHAMPTON	A	3-0
SATURDAY 17	v WIMBLEDON	H	5-1
WEDNESDAY 21	v BRONDBY IF	A	6-2
SATURDAY 24	v DERBY COUNTY	A	1-1
WEDNESDAY 28	v BURY	H	2-0
SATURDAY 31	v EVERTON	A	4-1

PLAYER IN THE FRAME

Roy Keane

After taking some six weeks to regain full effectiveness following his lengthy lay-off of the previous campaign, Roy was back to his dynamic best. This was demonstrated with vivid clarity at The Dell, where his dynamic thrusts from deep laid the foundations for United's first away win of the season, and he contributed a lovely goal to the drubbing of Brondby in Sweden.

FA Carling Premiership

UP TO AND INCLUDING
MONDAY 2 NOVEMBER 1998

	P	W	D	L	F	A	Pts
Aston Villa	10	6	4	0	11	3	22
Manchester United	**10**	**6**	**3**	**1**	**23**	**9**	**21**
Arsenal	11	5	5	1	13	5	20
Middlesbrough	11	4	5	2	17	12	17
Liverpool	11	4	4	3	18	12	16
Chelsea	9	4	4	1	13	9	16
Leicester City	11	4	4	3	11	10	16
West Ham United	11	4	4	3	12	12	16
Tottenham Hotspur	11	4	3	4	14	18	15
Charlton Athletic	11	3	5	3	19	16	14
Leeds United	11	2	8	1	11	8	14
Derby County	11	3	5	3	10	9	14
Newcastle United	11	4	2	5	15	16	14
Wimbledon	11	3	5	3	16	19	14
Everton	11	2	6	3	7	10	12
Sheffield Wednesday	11	3	2	6	8	10	11
Blackburn Rovers	11	2	3	6	11	15	9
Nottingham Forest	11	2	3	6	8	17	9
Coventry City	11	2	2	7	7	17	8
Southampton	11	1	3	7	6	23	6

NOVEMBER

WEDNESDAY 4	v BRONDBY IF	H
SUNDAY 8	v NEWCASTLE UNITED	H
WEDNESDAY 11	v NOTTINGHAM FOREST	H
SATURDAY 14	v BLACKBURN ROVERS	H
SATURDAY 21	v SHEFFIELD WEDNESDAY	A
WEDNESDAY 25	v FC BARCELONA	A
SUNDAY 29	v LEEDS UNITED	H

MANCHESTER UNITED 5

BECKHAM 7
COLE 13
P. NEVILLE 16
YORKE 28
SCHOLES 62

1. Peter SCHMEICHEL
2. Gary NEVILLE
3. Denis IRWIN
16. Roy KEANE
12. Phil NEVILLE
6. Jaap STAM
7. David BECKHAM
18. Paul SCHOLES
9. Andy COLE
19. Dwight YORKE
15. Jesper BLOMQVIST

SUBSTITUTES

8. Nicky BUTT
14. Jordi CRUYFF (15) h-t
17. Raimond VAN DER GOUW
20. Ole Gunnar SOLSKJAER (9) 53
21. Henning BERG
29. John CURTIS
30. Wesley BROWN (12) 32

MATCH REPORT

David Beckham is congratulated on the first goal of the match by team mates Jesper Blomqvist, Andy Cole, Dwight Yorke and Gary Neville

With the victory in Copenhagen fresh in their minds, complacency might have been the Reds' most dangerous foe when Brondby paid their return visit. In the event, the very idea seemed preposterous, with United scoring three times in the opening 16 minutes annihilating the Danes at a canter.

Old Trafford • 7.45pm • Attendance 53,250
Referee Lubos Michel, Slovakia

0 BRONDBY IF

22. Emeka ANDERSEN
2. Ole BJUR
18. Aurelijus SKARBALIUS
4. Per NIELSEN
19. Kenneth RAMUSSEN
6. Allan JENSEN RAVN
7. John JENSEN FAXE
8. Kim DAUGAARD
12. Ebbe SAND
14. Soren COLDING
15. Ruben BAGGER

SUBSTITUTES

3. Anders BJERREGAARD
5. Da Silva VRAGEL
9. Jesper THYGESEN (15) 68
13. Bo HANSEN (12) 77
17. Soren KROGH (2) 74
21. Mikkel JENSEN
30. Kim DREJS

Beckham began the destruction with a 30-yard free-kick which sneaked low past the right hand of stand-in keeper Andersen, who would have been disappointed not to repel it. Next came the goal of the night, a delectable chip from Cole after some telepathic sorcery with Yorke, and then Phil Neville contributed a rare strike for the third. Andersen allowed a Yorke header from Beckham's cross to squirm underneath him for the fourth, and the first-half scoring was complete.

To their credit, Brondby never abandoned their own attacking inclinations but Schmeichel was equal to dealing with their rare incursions and it was left to Scholes to wrap up proceedings just after the hour mark with a lovely individual effort, netting from a narrow angle after leaving several helpless opponents in his wake.

Counting a pre-season drubbing in a friendly, United had now scored 17 times in three meetings with the Danes. But it is not the case that they should not be dismissed as cannon fodder. After all, they had beaten Bayern Munich earlier in the competition and, three years earlier, had claimed a glorious victory against Liverpool at Anfield. Placed in such a context, the Reds' achievement assumed considerable proportions.

Phil Neville scores a rare goal after 16 minutes

FA Carling Premiership
Sunday 8 November, 1998

Manchester United 0

1. Peter SCHMEICHEL
2. Gary NEVILLE
3. Denis IRWIN
16. Roy KEANE
24. Wesley BROWN
6. Jaap STAM
7. David BECKHAM
18. Paul SCHOLES
9. Andy COLE
19. Dwight YORKE
15. Jesper BLOMQVIST

SUBSTITUTES

5. Ronny JOHNSEN (24) 58
8. Nicky BUTT (5) 83
14. Jordi CRUYFF
17. Raimond VAN DER GOUW
20. Ole Gunnar SOLSKJAER (15) 89

MATCH REPORT

After the prolific derring-do of recent weeks, the Reds' encounter with Ruud Gullit's transitional Newcastle side proved to be a pronounced anti-climax. The Magpies crowded the midfield and succeeded in stifling an attack which had accumulated 26 goals in its last seven outings.

It was a shrewd tactical ploy by the Dutchman, who might have been celebrating the capture of all three points – and his club's second Old Trafford victory in 34 attempts – had the referee not interpreted Irwin's 39th-minute flattening of Dalglish inside the box as a legitimate shoulder charge.

Yet the Mancunians had begun in extravagant mode, successive backheels by Cole and Yorke fashioning an opening for the normally reliable Scholes, who missed the target. It was a wondrous move, but as a sample of the afternoon's entertainment it proved sorely misleading.

Apart from their penalty claim, the closest Newcastle went to scoring was a Shearer free-kick, which had Schmeichel scrabbling across his line with undignified haste. Meanwhile the jaded hosts'

Newcastle's Stephen Glass is challenged by Wes Brown

Old Trafford • 3.00pm • Attendance 55,174
Referee Stephen Dunn, Bristol

0 NEWCASTLE UNITED

1. Shay GIVEN
16. Laurent CHARVET
38. Andrew GRIFFIN
4. David BATTY
28. Aaron HUGHES
34. Nikolaos DABIZAS
15. George GEORGIADIS
12. Dietmar HAMANN
9. Alan SHEARER
25. Paul DALGLISH
17. Stephen GLASS

SUBSTITUTES

2. Warren BARTON
3. Stuart PEARCE
11. Gary SPEED (12) 67
13. Steven HARPER
24. Nolberto SOLANO

David Batty crowds Paul Scholes out of the midfield

best chance fell to Beckham, who was sent through exquisitely by Gary Neville only to clip the ball wide of the advancing Given.

Thus the Tynesiders departed with a deserved share of the spoils, leaving Alex Ferguson to bemoan a flat performance.

MANCHESTER UNITED 2

SOLSKJAER 57, 60

17. Raimond VAN DER GOUW
23. Michael CLEGG
13. John CURTIS
4. David MAY
21. Henning BERG
33. Mark WILSON
34. Jonathan GREENING
8. Nicky BUTT
20. Ole Gunnar SOLSKJAER
14. Jordi CRUYFF
28. Philip MULRYNE

SUBSTITUTES

22. Erik NEVLAND
29. Alex NOTMAN
30. Ronnie WALLWORK (4) h-t
35. Paul TEATHER
36. Ryan FORD

MATCH REPORT

Nicky Butt battles with Steve Stone and Scot Gemmill of Forest

The vast and growing gulf between the superpowers of English soccer and the rest was demonstrated vividly as Manchester United fielded a virtual reserve side, yet still defeated their Premiership colleagues, Nottingham Forest.

Old Trafford • 8.00pm • Attendance 37,237
Referee Rob Harris, Oxford

1 Nottingham Forest

68 STONE

1. Dave BEASANT
2. Matthieu LOUIS-JEAN
3. Alan ROGERS
15. Craig ARMSTRONG
5. Steve CHETTLE
27. Andy GRAY
7. Steve STONE
8. Scot GEMMILL
29. Marlon HAREWOOD
14. Dougie FREEDMAN
11. Chris BART-WILLIAMS

SUBSTITUTES

4. Nigel QUASHIE
13. Mark CROSSLEY
19. Jean-Claude DARCHEVILLE
22. Des LYTTLE
40. Pierre VAN HOOIJDONK (29) 63

Of course, the Reds' reserves are pretty special, as evidenced by the identity of their two-goal match-winner, the Norwegian international Solskjaer. And just to emphasise the point more forcibly, both his strikes were engineered by Cruyff, the owner of a considerable collection of Holland caps.

For all that, Forest had the better of a first half in which van der Gouw was in frequent action, saving splendidly from Harewood, Bart-Williams and Gemmill, while Forest keeper Beasant had to wait until the 27th minute to get a proper feel of the ball. Although possession was shared equally between the teams, Forest had the better chances and skipper-for-the-night Berg had to make several timely interventions to prevent a Nottingham breakthrough.

However, following a goalless first period, United reappeared for the second half in livelier form, and Cruyff had twice threatened Beasant's goal before his two link-ups inside three minutes with Solskjaer proved decisive. The first came when Greening fed the Dutchman, who slipped a pass to the running Norwegian, and the second was a carbon copy. Forest hit back with a 25-yard scorcher from Stone but could make no further impression, which meant the Reds were through to the last eight of the Worthington Cup.

Ole Gunnar Solskjaer celebrates his two-goal haul

FA CARLING PREMIERSHIP
Saturday 14 November, 1998

MANCHESTER UNITED 3

1. Peter SCHMEICHEL
2. Gary NEVILLE
13. John CURTIS
18. Paul SCHOLES
12. Phil NEVILLE
6. Jaap STAM
7. David BECKHAM
8. Nicky BUTT
9. Andy COLE
19. Dwight YORKE
15. Jesper BLOMQVIST

SUBSTITUTES

3. Denis IRWIN
14. Jordi CRUYFF (18) 63
16. Roy KEANE (14) 81
20. Ole Gunnar SOLSKJAER (15) 67
21. Henning BERG

SCHOLES 31, 59
YORKE 43

MATCH REPORT

After surging smoothly into a seemingly impregnable three-goal lead, United were pegged back by ten-man Blackburn, whose two strikes midway through the second half set up an unexpectedly tense finale.

In fact, Rovers had been the brighter starters and Davies had spurned an early chance to snatch the lead when his hurried chip cleared not only the stranded Schmeichel, but also the crossbar. Thereafter, though, the Reds slipped into their familiar sweet-passing rhythm and should have registered when Filan dropped the ball at Cole's feet only for the striker to shoot against an upright instead of into the gaping net.

Paul Scholes scores United's first from a pass by Dwight Yorke

Old Trafford • 3.00pm • Attendance 55,198
Referee Mike Reed, Birmingham

2 Blackburn Rovers

66 MARCOLIN
74 BLAKE

13. John FILAN
2. Jeff KENNA
3. Callum DAVIDSON
4. Tim SHERWOOD
5. Darren PEACOCK
6. Stephane HENCHOZ
19. Damien JOHNSON
23. Christian DAILLY
14. Nathan BLAKE
10. Kevin DAVIES
12. Damien DUFF

SUBSTITUTES

8. Kevin GALLACHER (10) 78
18. Dario MARCOLIN (12) 52
20. Gary CROFT (3) 56
22. Alan FETTIS
27. David DUNN

Dwight Yorke celebrates United's second

However, the home side's growing ascendancy paid off twice before the interval. First Yorke fed Scholes, who cut in from the left to score with a crisp, low cross-shot, then Butt flicked on a Beckham drive and Yorke netted from ten yards.

When Sherwood was dismissed after 48 minutes following a petty clash with Beckham and then Scholes increased United's advantage from an acute angle after a clever dribble, there would have been few in the ground to forecast what would follow. But Blackburn unceremoniously evicted their hosts from the comfort zone through Marcolin's left-footer and a header from Blake and the result was in doubt until the final whistle.

SHEFFIELD WEDNESDAY 3

ALEXANDERSSON 15, 73
JONK 55

33. Pavel SRNICEK
2. Peter ATHERTON
20. Andy HINCHCLIFFE
4. Wim JONK
22. Emerson THOME
6. Des WALKER
26. Niclas ALEXANDERSSON
8. Benito CARBONE
25. Petter RUDI
10. Andy BOOTH
32. Danny SONNER

SUBSTITUTES

13. Matt CLARKE
14. Francesco SANETTI
16. Ritchie HUMPHREYS
18. Dejan STEFANOVIC
24. Jim MAGILTON

MATCH REPORT

A paltry record of one win in their previous eight visits to Sheffield Wednesday might have been expected to ensure that United were on their mettle. It didn't. For most of the afternoon they looked sloppy, seemingly complacent, perhaps with minds turning towards their forthcoming joust at the Nou Camp. Whatever, they got what they deserved at Hillsborough – precisely nothing.

After a misleadingly bright opening by the Reds, in which a clever chip from Blomqvist narrowly cleared Srnicek's bar, a Carbone-inspired Wednesday assumed the upper hand and took the lead after Schmeichel reached an undemanding 20-yard shot from Alexandersson with routine ease, only to fumble the ball inexplicably over his own line.

True Yorke and Cole combined beautifully for the former Newcastle marksman to restore parity with the deftest of finishes, and United might have had a penalty when Irwin was felled by Alexandersson, but the referee wanted nothing to do with it. Still, things were looking up for the Red Devils at the end of the first half.

But after surviving a brief flurry of Mancunian initiatives shortly before the break, it was Wednesday who wrested control of proceedings. First Jonk tucked in a rebound after Schmeichel had blocked a Booth effort, then Carbone set up Alexandersson, who scored his second of the afternoon and put the match beyond the Reds' reach. Once again, Hillsborough, not one of United's favourite venues, proved an unhappy hunting ground.

Hillsborough • 3.00pm • Attendance 39,475
Referee David Elleray, Harrow-on-the-Hill

1 MANCHESTER UNITED

29 COLE

1. Peter SCHMEICHEL
2. Gary NEVILLE
3. Denis IRWIN
16. Roy KEANE
12. Phil NEVILLE
6. Jaap STAM
7. David BECKHAM
18. Paul SCHOLES
9. Andy COLE
19. Dwight YORKE
15. Jesper BLOMQVIST

SUBSTITUTES

8. Nicky BUTT (15) 57
17. Raimond VAN DER GOUW
20. Ole Gunnar SOLSKJAER (16) 83
21. Henning BERG
24. Wesley BROWN (3) 65

Not even the towering Jaap Stam could do anything to prevent Wednesday's three goals

UEFA CHAMPIONS LEAGUE • Group D
Wednesday 25 November, 1998

FC BARCELONA 3

ANDERSON 1
RIVALDO 57, 73

13. Ruud HESP
2. Michael REIZIGER
12. SERGI
23. ZENDEN
22. OKUNOWO
26. XAVI
7. Luis FIGO
8. Albert CELADES
9. ANDERSON
10. GIOVANNI
11. RIVALDO

SUBSTITUTES

16. Dragan CIRIC
24. ROGER
25. ARNAU
27. MARIO
33. CUADRADO

MATCH REPORT

This was a night of pure, intoxicating fantasy, outstripping even the glittering contest between these two breathtakingly attack-minded adversaries at Old Trafford back in September. The result was the same though, six goals being shared, which massaged United's quarter-final aspirations while extinguishing those of the gallant, expansive Catalans.

The drama began after only 49 seconds when Giovanni crossed from the left, Irwin failed to clear and Anderson gulled Gary Neville before clubbing an unstoppable shot into United's net. Suddenly there were visions of a humiliating repetition of the Reds' Nou Camp nightmare of 1994, a scenario given added weight by Barcelona's non-stop wave of assaults, orchestrated with such ravishing flair by Rivaldo.

However, United stood firm, with Schmeichel outstanding, and they transformed the complexion of the game when inspired footwork by Blomqvist set up Yorke to equalise with a pulverising, low drive from the edge of the box.

Thereafter, though Luis Figo buzzed menacingly, the visitors grew ever more composed and were worthy of the lovely goal which yielded the lead, a perfect finish from Cole after a mesmerising interchange with Yorke. That ascendancy was short-lived, though, with Rivaldo's briskly executed curling free-kick leaving Schmeichel confused and leaden-footed.

Still the action ebbed and flowed relentlessly and the Reds

Dwight Yorke celebrates his equaliser...

Nou Camp Stadium • 7.45pm • Attendance 54,213
Referee Gunter Benko, Austria

3 MANCHESTER UNITED

25, 68 YORKE
53 COLE

1. Peter SCHMEICHEL
2. Gary NEVILLE
3. Denis IRWIN
16. Roy KEANE
30. Wesley BROWN
6. Jaap STAM
7. David BECKHAM
18. Paul SCHOLES
9. Andy COLE
19. Dwight YORKE
15. Jesper BLOMQVIST

SUBSTITUTES

8. Nicky BUTT (7) 82
12. Phil NEVILLE
17. Raimond VAN DER GOUW
20. Ole Gunnar SOLSKJAER
21. Henning BERG
29. John CURTIS
33. Mark WILSON

...then heads his second to make the score 3-2

regained the upper hand with a classic strike of stunning simplicity, Beckham crossing unerringly for Yorke to head powerfully past Hesp. Undismayed, Rivaldo and company, who had to win to remain in the competition, redoubled their efforts and the Brazilian netted the game's final goal with a clever overhead kick. Still he was not done, rapping Schmeichel's bar with a glorious 30-yarder, but Ferguson's men held on to celebrate one of the finest hours in United's rich European history.

Andy Cole celebrates United's colossal performance

MANCHESTER UNITED 3

1. Peter SCHMEICHEL
2. Gary NEVILLE
12. Phil NEVILLE
16. Roy KEANE
24. Wesley BROWN
6. Jaap STAM
18. Paul SCHOLES
8. Nicky BUTT
9. Andy COLE
19. Dwight YORKE
20. Ole Gunnar SOLSKJAER

SUBSTITUTES

10. Teddy SHERINGHAM (18) 72
11. Ryan GIGGS (9) 65
13. John CURTIS
17. Raimond VAN DER GOUW
21. Henning BERG (6) 77

SOLSKJAER 45
KEANE 46
BUTT 78

MATCH REPORT

Ole Gunnar Solskjaer scores the first goal

Nicky Butt has many laudable attributes but he is not renowned as a spectacular match-winner. However, with the end of this compellingly entertaining encounter in sight and the scores level, the grittily resilient midfielder came up with a strike of which any specialist marksman would have been proud. Accepting a pass from Phil Neville on the edge of the area, Butt swivelled adroitly and dispatched a savagely rising drive beyond the despairing dive of substitute keeper Paul Robinson.

Old Trafford • 4.00pm • Attendance 55,172
Referee Graham Poll, Tring

2 LEEDS UNITED

30 HASSELBAINK
52 KEWELL

1. Nigel MARTYN
18. Gunnar HALLE
20. Ian HARTE
4. Alf-Inge HAALAND
21. Martin HIDEN
25. Jonathan WOODGATE
12. David HOPKIN
37. Stephen McPHAIL
9. Jimmy Floyd HASSELBAINK
10. Bruno RIBEIRO
19. Harry KEWELL

SUBSTITUTES

6. David WETHERALL (21) 26
8. Clyde WIJNHARD
16. Danny GRANVILLE
36. Paul ROBINSON (1) h-t
39. Alan SMITH (10) 85

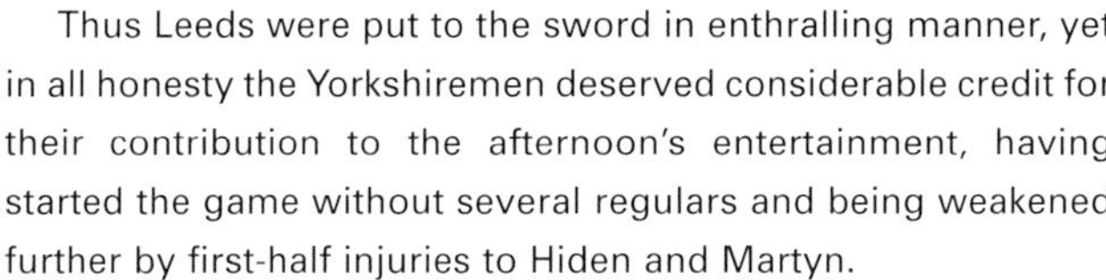

Thus Leeds were put to the sword in enthralling manner, yet in all honesty the Yorkshiremen deserved considerable credit for their contribution to the afternoon's entertainment, having started the game without several regulars and being weakened further by first-half injuries to Hiden and Martyn.

That said, it had been against the run of play when Hasselbaink, given undue time and space by the Reds' rearguard, shot the visitors ahead via the foot of a post. Leeds retained the advantage for some quarter of an hour, but then were undone by lightning United raids either side of the interval. First Solskjaer was freed by Yorke to beat the ailing Martyn from a narrow angle, then Butt and Scholes combined beautifully to send in Keane for a ten-yard howitzer which gave the newly-arrived Robinson no vestige of a chance.

That might have been the signal for a Manchester romp, but David O'Leary's Leeds are made of stern stuff and soon they were level, courtesy of a slip by Brown and a precision chip from the excellent Kewell. More end-to-end exchanges ensued, and then came Butt's decisive intervention.

Gary Neville congratulates Roy Keane on scoring the second goal just after half time

November in Review

WEDNESDAY 4	v BRONDBY IF	H	5-0
SUNDAY 8	v NEWCASTLE UNITED	H	0-0
WEDNESDAY 11	v NOTTINGHAM FOREST	H	2-1
SATURDAY 14	v BLACKBURN ROVERS	H	3-2
SATURDAY 21	v SHEFFIELD WEDNESDAY	A	1-3
WEDNESDAY 25	v FC BARCELONA	A	3-3
SUNDAY 29	v LEEDS UNITED	H	3-2

PLAYER IN THE FRAME

Andy Cole

Andy has received plenty of brickbats in his time, but now bouquets were in order. His swashbuckling and prolific partnership with Dwight Yorke continued to develop, the pair proving particularly irresistible in Barcelona, where the Englishman collected one of the most brilliant goals of his career to take his tally to the season thus far to nine.

FA Carling Premiership

UP TO AND INCLUDING
MONDAY 30 NOVEMBER 1998

	P	W	D	L	F	A	Pts
Aston Villa	14	8	5	1	22	12	29
Manchester United	**14**	**8**	**4**	**2**	**30**	**16**	**28**
West Ham United	15	7	5	3	20	16	26
Arsenal	15	6	7	2	15	7	25
Chelsea	13	6	6	1	22	13	24
Leeds United	15	5	8	2	22	14	23
Middlesbrough	15	5	8	2	22	17	23
Liverpool	15	6	4	5	26	19	22
Derby County	15	5	6	4	15	14	21
Wimbledon	15	5	5	5	19	25	20
Newcastle United	15	5	4	6	19	19	19
Tottenham Hotspur	15	5	4	6	19	23	19
Leicester City	15	4	6	5	16	18	18
Everton	15	4	6	5	10	15	18
Charlton Athletic	15	3	7	5	25	23	16
Sheffield Wednesday	15	4	4	7	14	15	16
Coventry City	15	4	3	8	13	21	15
Nottingham Forest	15	2	5	8	12	24	11
Southampton	15	2	5	8	12	24	11
Blackburn Rovers	15	2	3	10	14	24	9

WEDNESDAY 2	v TOTTENHAM HOTSPUR	A
SATURDAY 5	v ASTON VILLA	A
WEDNESDAY 9	v BAYERN MUNICH	H
SATURDAY 12	v TOTTENHAM HOTSPUR	A
WEDNESDAY 16	v CHELSEA	H
SATURDAY 19	v MIDDLESBROUGH	H
SATURDAY 26	v NOTTINGHAM FOREST	H
TUESDAY 29	v CHELSEA	A

TOTTENHAM HOTSPUR 3

ARMSTRONG 48, 55
GINOLA 85

1. Ian WALKER
2. Stephen CARR
22. Andy SINTON
23. Sol CAMPBELL
5. Colin CALDERWOOD
6. Allan NIELSEN
32. Luke YOUNG
18. Steffen IVERSEN
9. Darren ANDERTON
14. David GINOLA
11. Chris ARMSTRONG

SUBSTITUTES

7. Ruel FOX (5) h-t
10. Les FERDINAND
13. Espen BAARDSEN
16. Clive WILSON
25. Stephen CLEMENCE

MATCH REPORT

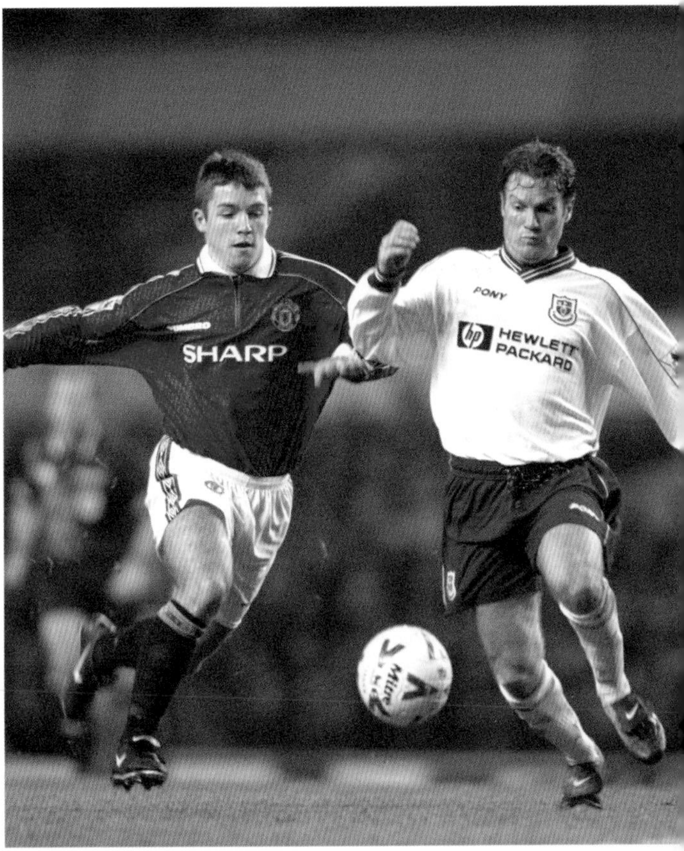

White Hart Lane • 7.45pm • Attendance 35,702
Referee Peter Jones, Loughborough

1 MANCHESTER UNITED

70 SHERINGHAM

17. Raimond VAN DER GOUW
23. Michael CLEGG
13. John CURTIS
12. Phil NEVILLE
5. Ronny JOHNSEN
21. Henning BERG
34. Jonathan GREENING
8. Nicky BUTT
20. Ole Gunnar SOLSKJAER
10. Teddy SHERINGHAM
11. Ryan GIGGS

SUBSTITUTES

7. David BECKHAM (13) 86
15. Jesper BLOMQVIST (34) 86
29. Alex NOTMAN (8) 72
30. Ronnie WALLWORK
31. Nick CULKIN

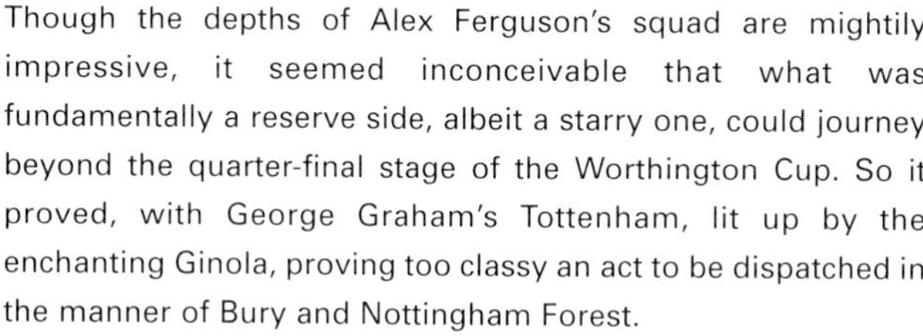

Though the depths of Alex Ferguson's squad are mightily impressive, it seemed inconceivable that what was fundamentally a reserve side, albeit a starry one, could journey beyond the quarter-final stage of the Worthington Cup. So it proved, with George Graham's Tottenham, lit up by the enchanting Ginola, proving too classy an act to be dispatched in the manner of Bury and Nottingham Forest.

The first half was a dour, rather lifeless affair in which the two teams effectively cancelled each other out, but the game sprang to life straight after the interval when Nielsen centred, the newly-introduced Fox nodded on and Armstrong beat van der Gouw with a looping header. Soon United were two down, this time Ginola dancing down the left touchline before crossing for Armstrong to net again with his head, this time at the near post.

Now the Reds pushed forward, with Greening prominent, and Butt missed a good chance before Sheringham, a former White Hart Lane favourite who had been subjected to constant barracking, reduced the arrears with an expert flick of his forehead from a Phil Neville pass.

It was a spirited response by the visitors, who now went in search of an equaliser, only for Ginola to settle matters with a trademark 25-yarder near the end.

Alex Notman, making his senior debut, fights for the ball with Tottenham's Andy Sinton

ASTON VILLA 1

JOACHIM 55

1. Michael OAKES
15. Gareth BARRY
3. Alan WRIGHT
4. Gareth SOUTHGATE
5. Ugo EHIOGU
6. Steve WATSON
7. Ian TAYLOR
17. Lee HENDRIE
14. Dion DUBLIN
12. Julian JOACHIM
11. Alan THOMPSON

SUBSTITUTES

16. Simon GRAYSON
18. Fabio FERRARESI
22. Darius VASSELL
30. Adam RACHEL
32. Aaron LESCOTT

MATCH REPORT

With only one point separating United from table-topping Villa, perhaps it was not surprising that their meeting should be a tense, scrappy affair, far removed from the free-flowing encounter predicted by optimistic purists.

The afternoon began, predictably enough, with a fusillade of jeers for Yorke from his former fans, and an error-strewn first half did little to lift the general mood. Villa made most of the early running, but though they enjoyed the major share of possession they created few clear-cut chances and United

Dwight Yorke hurdles Ugo Ehiogu en route to the Villa goal

Villa Park • 3.00pm • Attendance 39,241
Referee Mike Riley, Leeds

1 MANCHESTER UNITED

47 SCHOLES

1. Peter SCHMEICHEL
2. Gary NEVILLE
3. Denis IRWIN
16. Roy KEANE
24. Wesley BROWN
6. Jaap STAM
7. David BECKHAM
18. Paul SCHOLES
9. Andy COLE
19. Dwight YORKE
15. Jesper BLOMQVIST

SUBSTITUTES

5. Ronny JOHNSEN
8. Nicky BUTT (9) 70
10. Teddy SHERINGHAM
11. Ryan GIGGS (15) h-t
17. Raimond VAN DER GOUW

contained their assaults with relative comfort. The lively Hendrie came closest to a breakthrough after rounding Schmeichel, only for the opportunity to evaporate when he became entangled with his team-mate Taylor.

Still, the home side could feel aggrieved on the run of play when the Red Devils snatched the lead shortly after the interval, Cole's clever cross from the right being repelled by Oakes but only to the feet of Scholes, who netted emphatically.

Villa's equaliser some eight minutes later was deserved, but owed plenty to fortune, a speculative long-range effort from Joachim catching Irwin's shin and coming wide of the stranded Schmeichel.

Not long after that Thompson rattled United's post with a scorching 25-yard free-kick and Villa exerted more pressure, but without creating undue alarm in the Reds' rearguard. Still, come the final whistle, Alex Ferguson would have been more satisfied with his point than John Gregory.

Paul Scholes celebrates after putting United in the lead just after half-time

UEFA CHAMPIONS LEAGUE • Group D
Wednesday 9 December, 1998

MANCHESTER UNITED 1

KEANE 43

1. Peter SCHMEICHEL
2. Gary NEVILLE
3. Denis IRWIN
16. Roy KEANE
30. Wesley BROWN
6. Jaap STAM
7. David BECKHAM
18. Paul SCHOLES
9. Andy COLE
19. Dwight YORKE
11. Ryan GIGGS

SUBSTITUTES

5. Ronny JOHNSEN (3) h-t
8. Nicky BUTT (19) 64
10. Teddy SHERINGHAM
12. Phil NEVILLE
15. Jesper BLOMQVIST
17. Raimond VAN DER GOUW
21. Henning BERG

MATCH REPORT

It was a night of palpitations and feverish mathematical calculations as United advanced into the UEFA Champions League quarter-finals. Thanks to a draw with the Germans and favourable results elsewhere, the Reds went through as one of the two best group runners-up, and as the competition's top

Roy Keane shoots United into the lead from the edge of the box

Old Trafford • 7.45pm • Attendance 54,434
Referee Dick Jol, Holland

1 BAYERN MUNICH

56 SALIHAMIDZIC

- 1. Oliver KAHN
- 2. Markus BABBEL
- 3. Bixente LIZARAZU
- 4. Samuel Osei KUFFOUR
- 20. Hasan SALIHAMIDZIC
- 16. Jens JEREMIES
- 21. Alexander ZICKLER
- 8. Thomas STRUNZ
- 9. Giovane de Souza ELBER
- 10. Lothar MATTHAUS
- 11. Stefan EFFENBERG

SUBSTITUTES

- 5. Thomas HELMER
- 12. Sven SCHEUER
- 14. Mario BASLER (21) 81
- 18. Michael TARNAT
- 19. Carsten JANCKER (9) 81
- 25. Thomas LINKE (10) 61

scorers to date their progress was richly deserved.

Though 21 full internationals started the match, the first performer to take the eye was the odd man out, young Wesley Brown, who executed a characteristically smooth challenge on the menacing Salihamidzic which set the tone for an outstandingly composed personal performance.

However, if the rookie was not nervous, the majority of the home support was as a surprisingly open match developed. Both Yorke and Cole went close for United, but Elber was a whisker away from giving Bayern the lead and Effenberg was worryingly influential in midfield.

The breakthrough craved by the Reds and by their supporters came shortly before the break when Beckham found Giggs on the left, where the Welshman initially miscontrolled the ball before recovering to beat Strunz and slip an inviting delivery into the path of the marauding Keane. From the edge of the box the skipper's low shot fizzed into the net and Old Trafford erupted with joy and relief.

Straight after the interval Johnsen, on for the injured Irwin, spurned a double chance, first miscuing from close range, then thrashing the ball over the bar. Now Bayern raised their tempo and after Schmeichel had saved magnificently from Kuffour they equalised when Salihamidzic scuffed home following a corner.

Thereafter United responded positively, and Scholes and Cole both went close, but there was no denying that, to United fans, that final half an hour seemed like an eternity.

FA Carling Premiership
Saturday 12 December, 1998

TOTTENHAM HOTSPUR 2

CAMPBELL 71, 90

1. Ian WALKER
2. Stephen CARR
22. Andy SINTON
23. Sol CAMPBELL
32. Luke YOUNG
6. Allan NIELSEN
7. Ruel FOX
14. David GINOLA
9. Darren ANDERTON
10. Les FERDINAND
11. Chris ARMSTRONG

SUBSTITUTES

5. Colin CALDERWOOD
13. Espen BAARDSEN
20. Jose DOMINGUEZ
21. Rory ALLEN (7) 83
25. Stephen CLEMENCE

MATCH REPORT

After two characteristic examples of Solskjaer opportunism had eased United into a seemingly decisive lead, a combination of Gary Neville's dismissal and a spirited Spurs fightback cost the Reds two precious points at the end of a tempestuous clash.

It all began swimmingly for the visitors with Sheringham fired up for his return to Tottenham and Beckham making destructive incursions into the left flank of the Spurs' defence. First he slipped his marker to cross for Giggs, whose diving header was parried by Walker but only to the feet of the voracious Solskjaer, who half-volleyed home from close range. Then came another precision delivery from the Beckham boot and the Norwegian pounced again, this time dispatching a slick first-time shot at the near post despite being under heavy challenge from a defender.

However, the balance of power shifted dramatically after 39 minutes when Gary Neville was sent off for his second bookable offence, the felling of Ginola. Tottenham began the second half with renewed fervour and the referee brandished cards so regularly that United finished with seven bookings (including Neville's pair) and Spurs with two.

Ole Gunnar Solskjaer is congratulated by David Beckham, Roy Keane and Teddy Sheringham

White Hart Lane • 3.00pm • Attendance 36,079
Referee Uriah Rennie, Sheffield

2 MANCHESTER UNITED

11, 18 SOLSKJAER

1. Peter SCHMEICHEL
2. Gary NEVILLE
12. Phil NEVILLE
16. Roy KEANE
5. Ronny JOHNSEN
6. Jaap STAM
7. David BECKHAM
8. Nicky BUTT
20. Ole Gunnar SOLSKJAER
10. Teddy SHERINGHAM
11. Ryan GIGGS

SUBSTITUTES

9. Andy COLE (10) 75
14. Jordi CRUYFF
15. Jesper BLOMQVIST (11) 87
17. Raimond VAN DER GOUW
21. Henning BERG (20) h-t

Andy Cole, Jaap Stam and Roy Keane combine to stop Tottenham's Les Ferdinand getting in a header on goal

Despite the inevitable pressure, though, the ten men held out until some 20 minutes from the end, when Campbell headed in powerfully from an Anderton free-kick. Soon after that Nielsen squandered a fine chance to equalise, but an away victory seemed the most likely outcome until Anderton and Campbell combined again at the death.

United had had a player sent off and thrown away a two-goal lead, but the point gained was enough to send them to the top of the Premiership table for the first time this season.

FA CARLING PREMIERSHIP
Wednesday 16 December, 1998

MANCHESTER UNITED 1

COLE 45

1. Peter SCHMEICHEL
2. Gary NEVILLE
3. Denis IRWIN
16. Roy KEANE
24. Wesley BROWN
6. Jaap STAM
18. Paul SCHOLES
8. Nicky BUTT
9. Andy COLE
19. Dwight YORKE
15. Jesper BLOMQVIST

SUBSTITUTES

5. Ronny JOHNSEN
7. David BECKHAM (19) 61
10. Teddy SHERINGHAM (18) 85
11. Ryan GIGGS (15) 77
12. Phil NEVILLE

MATCH REPORT

For the second successive match, United succumbed to a late equaliser, though in fairness it should be emphasised that Chelsea were worth their point. Indeed, the visitors' undeniable class was underpinned with a gritty resilience which signalled their emergence as genuine title contenders.

The Reds, with Giggs and Beckham confined to the bench, began enterprisingly enough and Cole might have registered after six minutes when set up by Yorke following a Blomqvist cross. As a distinctly tetchy first half wore on, United held territorial sway without finding their most effective rhythm while it took the Blues 39 minutes to fashion a clear opening. However, the deadlock was broken shortly before the interval when a low Butt drive was blocked and Cole netted with a beautifully precise 15-yard shot.

In the second period, which saw two United bookings added to Chelsea's five of the first half, the Reds created most chances – Cole, Scholes and Blomqvist all went close – while the visitors played impressively neat and controlled football under pressure. Indeed, their poise

Andy Cole and Chelsea's Michael Duberry wait for the ball to come down

Old Trafford • 8.00pm • Attendance 55,159
Referee Graham Barber, Pyrford

1 CHELSEA

83 ZOLA

- 1. Ed DE GOEY
- 2. Dan PETRESCU
- 3. Celestine BABYARO
- 12. Michael DUBERRY
- 21. Bernard LAMBOURDE
- 14. Graeme LE SAUX
- 17. Albert FERRER
- 16. Roberto DI MATTEO
- 19. Tore Andre FLO
- 25. Gianfranco ZOLA
- 11. Dennis WISE

SUBSTITUTES

- 7. Bjarne GOLDBAEK
- 8. Gustavo POYET (14) 45
- 13. Kevin HITCHCOCK
- 22. Mark NICHOLLS
- 28. Jody MORRIS

increased in the final quarter and it came as no surprise when Poyet freed Zola to chip deftly over Schmeichel to level the scores with seven minutes remaining.

Andy Cole scores to give United the lead

FA CARLING PREMIERSHIP
Saturday 19 December, 1998

MANCHESTER UNITED 2

BUTT 62
SCHOLES 70

1. Peter SCHMEICHEL
2. Gary NEVILLE
3. Denis IRWIN
16. Roy KEANE
5. Ronny JOHNSEN
12. Phil NEVILLE
7. David BECKHAM
8. Nicky BUTT
9. Andy COLE
10. Teddy SHERINGHAM
11. Ryan GIGGS

SUBSTITUTES

15. Jesper BLOMQVIST
17. Raimond VAN DER GOUW
18. Paul SCHOLES (7) 64
20. Ole Gunnar SOLSKJAER (12) 79
24. Wesley BROWN

MATCH REPORT

It seemed scarcely credible: United were three down at home with less than an hour played and there could be no complaints about the scoreline. Quite simply, the subdued Reds, who had gone five games without victory even before this swingeing reverse, had been comprehensively outplayed by Bryan Robson's team, in which a certain Gary Pallister was utterly outstanding.

In fact, it had been United who had launched the game's first wave of attacks but Middlesbrough had looked well-organised at the back, tidy in midfield and menacing up front, so when Ricard opened the scoring from a Deane cutback it was hardly a shock.

Nicky Butt heads United back into the match

Old Trafford • 3.00pm • Attendance 55,152
Referee Gary Willard, Worthing

3 MIDDLESBROUGH

24 RICARD
31 GORDON
59 DEANE

1. Mark SCHWARZER
29. Colin COOPER
3. Dean GORDON
4. Steve VICKERS
5. Gianluca FESTA
6. Gary PALLISTER
7. Robbie MUSTOE
16. Andy TOWNSEND
19. Hamilton RICARD
10. Brian DEANE
15. Neil MADDISON

SUBSTITUTES

11. Alan MOORE (7) 72
12. Mikkel BECK (15) 83
23. Clayton BLACKMORE
25. Ben ROBERTS
28. Robbie STOCKDALE

Paul Scholes doubles the score...

However, when Gordon hammered in a volley from outside the box and Deane made it three some 14 minutes into the second period, Old Trafford was dumbfounded. The home defence, badly missing the injured Stam, was in tatters. Only a Giggs header shortly before the break had threatened the visitors' equilibrium.

That all changed after Butt hit back with a header from a Beckham cross. Now United put 'Boro under virtual siege and soon Scholes squeezed a shot just inside a post for the second. Thereafter it was one-way traffic but the north-easterners held out with only one serious alarm, when Cole's shot was partially blocked by Schwarzer and Vickers cleared off the line.

Clearly Alex Ferguson, who missed the match due to a family bereavement, had work to do ahead of the busy holiday schedule.

...and Ryan Giggs can't believe the result

FA Carling Premiership
Saturday 26 December, 1998

MANCHESTER UNITED 3

JOHNSEN 28, 60
GIGGS 62

1. Peter SCHMEICHEL
12. Phil NEVILLE
3. Denis IRWIN
16. Roy KEANE
5. Ronny JOHNSEN
21. Henning BERG
7. David BECKHAM
8. Nicky BUTT
18. Paul SCHOLES
10. Teddy SHERINGHAM
11. Ryan GIGGS

SUBSTITUTES

15. Jesper BLOMQVIST (11) 75
17. Raimond VAN DER GOUW
20. Ole Gunnar SOLSKJAER (18) 63
24. Wesley BROWN
34. Jonathan GREENING (16) 66

MATCH REPORT

United returned to winning ways after a six-match hiatus during which defensive frailties had threatened to undermine their season. Thus the clean sheet, their first since early November, was practically as welcome as the trio of goals scored.

Clearly United were desperate for a win and, with that purpose in mind, could hardly have faced more suitable opponents than under-strength Forest, who were looking for their first triumph in 16 Premiership outings.

Still, the Reds began in lacklustre fashion with attacking inspiration apparently lacking, but that all changed after 28 minutes. Beckham crossed, Giggs' header was saved, but from

Ryan Giggs takes on Forest's Matthieu Louis-Jean

Old Trafford • 3.00pm • Attendance 55,216
Referee Jeff Winter, Stockton

0 NOTTINGHAM FOREST

1. Dave BEASANT
2. Matthieu LOUIS-JEAN
3. Alan ROGERS
4. Nigel QUASHIE
5. Steve CHETTLE
15. Craig ARMSTRONG
7. Steve STONE
14. Dougie FREEDMAN
9. Neil SHIPPERLEY
10. Andy JOHNSON
11. Chris BART-WILLIAMS

SUBSTITUTES

12. Chris DOIG (5) 68
13. Mark CROSSLEY
17. Thierry BONALAIR (11) 54
19. Jean-Claude DARCHEVILLE
20. Glyn HODGES (7) 77

the ensuing corner Johnsen netted with a precise downwards nod.

Now, at last, self-belief began to flow through the United ranks and it was surprising that the beleaguered Nottingham rearguard held out for so long before conceding a second goal, plundered powerfully by Johnsen following a Berg header.

The best was yet to come. Two minutes later Sheringham slipped the ball to Beckham, who delivered a first-time dispatch to Giggs. The ball bounced invitingly, and the multi-gifted Welshman chipped the ball with delicate precision over the advancing Beasant. A rather mundane match had been illuminated by a moment of pure footballing beauty.

Ronny Johnsen (far right) heads United's first from a corner

FA CARLING PREMIERSHIP
Tuesday 29 December, 1998

CHELSEA 0

1. Ed DE GOEY
2. Dan PETRESCU
3. Celestine BABAYARO
12. Michael DUBERRY
5. Frank LEBOEUF
14. Graeme LE SAUX
17. Albert FERRER
28. Jody MORRIS
19. Tore Andre FLO
25. Gianfranco ZOLA
16. Roberto DI MATTEO

SUBSTITUTES

6. Marcel DESAILLY (28) 73
7. Bjarne GOLDBAEK (14) 88
13. Kevin HITCHCOCK
22. Mark NICHOLLS
32. Mikael FORSSELL

MATCH REPORT

Widespread allegations of Peter Schmeichel's declining standards in the autumn of his career, fuelled by his own decision to leave Old Trafford at season's end, were made to appear nonsensical by the giant Dane's commanding performance at the home of Championship-challenging Chelsea.

True, he was aided by the profligacy of the Blues' forwards, especially the normally reliable Flo and the captivating Zola, but during a first period in which Gianluca Vialli's men launched wave after wave of attacks, it was Schmeichel who stood between the Reds and a rout. Some of his saves were world-class and as the half wore on he grew in dominance, several times emerging victorious from one-on-one duels with the diminutive Italian.

The nearest United came to registering during a hectic first 45 minutes came when Cole danced past De Goey, only for his shot to be blocked on the line by Duberry.

The second half began along the same lines as the first, but slowly Sheringham's replacement of Scholes altered the Reds' attacking emphasis, and soon they began

Andy Cole gets past Chelsea's Ed De Goey, only to have his shot blocked on the line

Stamford Bridge • 8.00pm • Attendance 34,741
Referee Mike Riley, Leeds

0 MANCHESTER UNITED

1. Peter SCHMEICHEL
2. Gary NEVILLE
3. Denis IRWIN
16. Roy KEANE
5. Ronny JOHNSEN
6. Jaap STAM
7. David BECKHAM
8. Nicky BUTT
9. Andy COLE
18. Paul SCHOLES
11. Ryan GIGGS

SUBSTITUTES

10. Teddy SHERINGHAM (18) 60
12. Phil NEVILLE
15. Jesper BLOMQVIST
17. Raimond VAN DER GOUW
21. Henning BERG

Roy Keane and Chelsea's Roberto Di Matteo tussle for the ball

to enjoy a period of marked superiority over the home team.

As the game entered its final quarter the action swayed from end to end, and the visitors were outraged on 80 minutes when Leboeuf, who had already been cautioned, floored Beckham, who was making for goal. There was no retribution from referee Mike Riley, though, and a minute later United themselves enjoyed an escape as Schmeichel made yet another outstanding save from Zola.

In the end, the Reds could be satisfied with a mightily hard-earned point, while the Blues were left to rue their early inaccuracy in front of goal.

DECEMBER IN REVIEW

WEDNESDAY 2	v TOTTENHAM HOTSPUR	A	1-3
SATURDAY 5	v ASTON VILLA	A	1-1
WEDNESDAY 9	v BAYERN MUNICH	H	1-1
SATURDAY 12	v TOTTENHAM HOTSPUR	A	2-2
WEDNESDAY 16	v CHELSEA	H	1-1
SATURDAY 19	v MIDDLESBROUGH	H	2-3
SATURDAY 26	v NOTTINGHAM FOREST	H	3-0
TUESDAY 29	v CHELSEA	A	0-0

PLAYER IN THE FRAME

Ronny Johnsen

In the wake of the home defeat by Middlesbrough, United's season was in need of an instant tonic and it was provided by Ronny Johnsen. The Norwegian weighed in with two goals in the Boxing Day victory over Nottingham Forest which launched the Red Devils on a marathon unbeaten run, putting them in with a realistic chance of the treble.

FA CARLING PREMIERSHIP

UP TO AND INCLUDING MONDAY 28 DECEMBER 1998

	P	W	D	L	F	A	Pts
Aston Villa	20	11	6	3	31	20	39
Chelsea	19	9	9	1	31	17	36
Arsenal	20	9	8	3	22	11	35
Manchester United	**19**	**9**	**7**	**3**	**39**	**23**	**34**
Leeds United	19	8	8	3	32	17	32
West Ham United	20	9	5	6	24	23	32
Liverpool	20	9	4	7	36	25	31
Middlesbrough	20	7	9	4	32	26	30
Wimbledon	19	8	5	6	25	30	29
Leicester City	20	7	7	6	23	21	28
Derby County	20	6	10	4	20	18	28
Tottenham Hotspur	20	7	6	7	28	30	27
Newcastle United	20	6	6	8	24	28	24
Everton	20	5	8	7	13	21	23
Sheffield Wednesday	20	6	4	10	21	22	22
Blackburn Rovers	20	4	6	10	20	28	18
Coventry City	20	4	5	11	16	29	17
Charlton Athletic	20	3	7	10	23	31	16
Southampton	20	3	5	12	16	38	14
Nottingham Forest	20	2	7	11	18	36	13

JANUARY

SUNDAY 3	v MIDDLESBROUGH	H
SUNDAY 10	v WEST HAM UNITED	H
SATURDAY 16	v LEICESTER CITY	A
SUNDAY 24	v LIVERPOOL	H
SUNDAY 31	v CHARLTON ATHLETIC	A

FA CUP (Sponsored by AXA) • Third Round
Sunday 3 January, 1999

MANCHESTER UNITED 3

COLE 68
IRWIN (penalty) 82
GIGGS 90

1. Peter SCHMEICHEL
24. Wesley BROWN
3. Denis IRWIN
16. Roy KEANE
21. Henning BERG
6. Jaap STAM
15. Jesper BLOMQVIST
8. Nicky BUTT
9. Andy COLE
19. Dwight YORKE
11. Ryan GIGGS

SUBSTITUTES

10. Teddy SHERINGHAM (9) 84
12. Phil NEVILLE (24) 75
14. Jordi CRUYFF
17. Raimond VAN DER GOUW
20. Ole Gunnar SOLSKJAER (15) 73

MATCH REPORT

Denis Irwin scores from the penalty spot

The fire and the passion with which the Red Devils reacted to going a goal behind to Middlesbrough answered the week's most preposterous question in suitably emphatic fashion. Were

Old Trafford • 4.00pm • Attendance 52,232
Referee Graham Barber, Pyrford

1 MIDDLESBROUGH

53 TOWNSEND

1. Mark SCHWARZER
2. Curtis FLEMING
3. Dean GORDON
29. Colin COOPER
15. Neil MADDISON
6. Gary PALLISTER
7. Robbie MUSTOE
8. Paul GASCOIGNE
19. Hamilton RICARD
10. Brian DEANE
16. Andy TOWNSEND

SUBSTITUTES

12. Mikkel BECK (8) 75
13. Marlon BERESFORD
14. Philip STAMP (7) 62
23. Clayton BLACKMORE
28. Robbie STOCKDALE

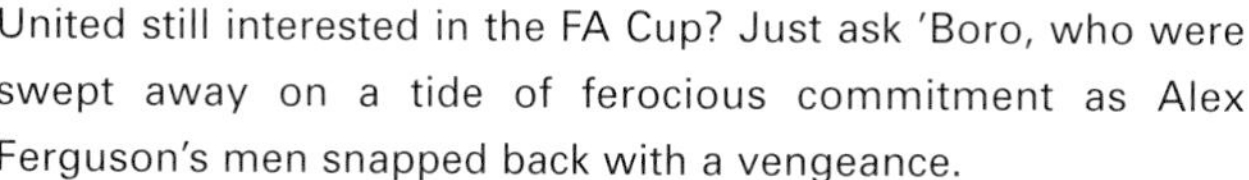

United still interested in the FA Cup? Just ask 'Boro, who were swept away on a tide of ferocious commitment as Alex Ferguson's men snapped back with a vengeance.

In truth the first half had been something of a disappointment for the Old Trafford multitude when, after a bright start in which Giggs, Cole and the ever-improving Brown had been prominent, United had failed to make telling inroads into a stout and resolute rearguard. Though pinned back most of the time, the visitors did not seem unduly stretched and when they struck on the break – Townsend netting with a precise cross-shot after Deane had headed on a long ball from Cooper – fears of a repeat of their successful pre-Christmas raid began to loom.

But this time the Reds' responded to adversity with deadly effect. First Giggs fed Cole, who shrugged off a challenge from Pallister before lashing home a shot at the near post. Then, with the home side increasingly ascendant, they nosed in front when Maddison was adjudged to have fouled Butt in the area and Irwin scored from the spot. True, it was a softish penalty, as even the United manager admitted, but his team merited the lead on the balance of play. Thereafter it was left to Giggs to garnish the occasion with a narrow-angled drive after a sweet one-two interchange with Solskjaer. A point was well and truly made.

Ryan Giggs and Phil Neville celebrate after United's third and last goal

FA CARLING PREMIERSHIP
Sunday 10 January, 1999

MANCHESTER UNITED 4

YORKE 10
COLE 40, 68
SOLSKJAER 81

17. Raimond VAN DER GOUW
24. Wesley BROWN
3. Denis IRWIN
16. Roy KEANE
21. Henning BERG
6. Jaap STAM
15. Jesper BLOMQVIST
8. Nicky BUTT
9. Andy COLE
19. Dwight YORKE
11. Ryan GIGGS

SUBSTITUTES

5. Ronny JOHNSEN (24) 78
7. David BECKHAM
14. Jordi CRUYFF (16) 84
20. Ole Gunnar SOLSKJAER (8) 78
31. Nick CULKIN

MATCH REPORT

Dwight Yorke slams the ball past Neil Ruddock to give United the lead...

With all due respect to a demoralised West Ham, the biggest threat to the Red Devils' dominance of an utterly one-sided contest was that the match might be abandoned through a repetition of the power failure which had delayed kick-off by 45 minutes. For the first time in weeks, United approached the fluency expected of champions as they put the Hammers to the sword with ruthless and joyful efficiency.

Old Trafford • 4.00pm • Attendance 55,180
Referee Mike Reed, Birmingham

1 WEST HAM UNITED

89 LAMPARD

12. Shaka HISLOP
19. Ian PEARCE
17. Stan LAZARIDIS
4. Steve POTTS
15. Rio FERDINAND
6. Neil RUDDOCK
18. Frank LAMPARD
8. Trevor SINCLAIR
29. Eyal BERKOVIC
10. John HARTSON
11. Steve LOMAS

SUBSTITUTES

2. Tim BREACKER
22. Craig FORREST
24. Samassi ABOU
26. Joe COLE (8) h-t
39. Ezy IRIEKPEN

With the visitors looking ill at ease from the start, Hislop barely had time to adjust his gloves before shots were raining in and it seemed only a matter of time before the home side made their domination pay. So it proved, the inevitable occurring after ten minutes when Keane located Cole, who spun like a scarlet top before finding Yorke on the right margin of West Ham's box. The Tobagan met the ball with pulverising force, drilling a savage drive into the net's far corner.

Thereafter chances proliferated for the Mancunians, for whom Blomqvist was a constant threat, but it was not until five minutes before the break, when Butt's miskicked shot rebounded from a post for Cole to complete the formalities, that the lead was doubled.

After the break it was more of the same, with West Ham's only chink of light being provided by the form of teenage prodigy Joe Cole, on as a substitute for Sinclair, who brightened up their ideas. But the Reds' romp continued with goals for Andy Cole and Solskjaer, while Lampard's late strike offered scant consolation to the travelling Londoners.

...and celebrates yet another important strike

FA CARLING PREMIERSHIP
Saturday 16 January, 1999

LEICESTER CITY 2

ZAGORAKIS 35
WALSH 75

1. Kasey KELLER
15. Pontus KAAMARK
19. Rob ULLATHORNE
4. Gerry TAGGART
5. Steve WALSH
6. Mustafa IZZET
7. Neil LENNON
25. Stuart WILSON
27. Tony COTTEE
37. Theo ZAGORAKIS
11. Steve GUPPY

SUBSTITUTES

10. Garry PARKER (25) 74
16. Stuart CAMPBELL (15) 74
21. Graham FENTON (27) 89
22. Pegguy ARPHEXAD
29. Stefan OAKES

MATCH REPORT

Goal-hungry United carried on where they had left off against West Ham, this time at the expense of Leicester. The Foxes, deprived of four key players through illness, injury and suspension, were simply butchered by the Reds, who could easily have finished with double figures.

The massacre commenced with a swagger, Cole dummying an Irwin centre to leave Yorke with a relatively routine tap-in. Pluckily, though, Leicester refused to capitulate and regained parity before the interval when Zagorakis thundered a fulminating drive past Schmeichel from 25 yards.

Dwight Yorke makes it 4-1 with a shot from a narrow angle

Filbert Street • 3.00pm • Attendance 22,091
Referee Steve Dunn, Bristol

6 MANCHESTER UNITED

10, 64, 86 YORKE
50, 62 COLE
90 STAM

1. Peter SCHMEICHEL
24. Wesley BROWN
3. Denis IRWIN
16. Roy KEANE
21. Henning BERG
6. Jaap STAM
7. David BECKHAM
15. Jesper BLOMQVIST
9. Andy COLE
19. Dwight YORKE
11. Ryan GIGGS

SUBSTITUTES

5. Ronny JOHNSEN
12. Phil NEVILLE (24) h-t
17. Raimond VAN DER GOUW
18. Paul SCHOLES
20. Ole Gunnar SOLSKJAER

Jaap Stam scores his first goal for United

But United emerged for the second period with renewed purpose, and soon Giggs freed Cole through the middle to slip the ball under Keller. Then the ubiquitous Yorke, whose arrival at Old Trafford had added immensely to the team's creativity, eluded Walsh and sent in Cole for the third.

Next it was Yorke's turn to register, rolling the ball home from the narrowest of angles, before Leicester hit back when a Guppy shot was deflected in by Walsh. That proved the merest of blips in the Reds' progress, Yorke completing his hat-trick by popping home the rebound after Cole had rapped the bar, then Stam stabbing in the sixth following a glorious pass from Beckham.

Suddenly United's indifferent form of November and December was but a distant memory.

FA CUP (Sponsored by AXA) • Fourth Round
Sunday 24 January, 1999

MANCHESTER UNITED 2

YORKE 88
SOLSKJAER 90

1. Peter SCHMEICHEL
2. Gary NEVILLE
3. Denis IRWIN
16. Roy KEANE
21. Henning BERG
6. Jaap STAM
7. David BECKHAM
8. Nicky BUTT
9. Andy COLE
19. Dwight YORKE
11. Ryan GIGGS

SUBSTITUTES

5. Ronny JOHNSEN (21) 81
12. Phil NEVILLE
17. Raimond VAN DER GOUW
18. Paul SCHOLES (8) 68
20. Ole Gunnar SOLSKJAER (3) 81

MATCH REPORT

Rarely can the climax of a game, any game, have been greeted with such riotous euphoria as that which boiled over at Old Trafford as Liverpool were ejected from the FA Cup in truly stunning manner. As the match had worn on, United fans had become increasingly conditioned to impending defeat, courtesy of an early header by Owen. Despite the Red Devils' almost total domination of the second half, the final minutes were approaching and the Anfielders continued to resist courageously, if at times fortunately.

But a deadly double sting in the tail of this pulsatingly dramatic confrontation was in store. After 88 minutes Redknapp fouled Johnsen and Beckham delivered a sumptuously flighted free-kick which eluded Carragher and found Cole, whose unselfishly cushioned header gifted the predatory Yorke with the simplest of tap-ins.

The ground was engulfed in a tidal wave of relief yet that was as nothing to the pure rapture which was to follow. Deep in stoppage time, Scholes seized possession in the Liverpool box only for the ball to squirt away to Solskjaer, who wrong-footed the Merseysiders' defence before dispatching a clinical drive through the legs of a defender, beating James at his near post.

Ole Gunnar Solskjaer celebrates his last-minute winner which sent everyone into a frenzy of excitement...

Old Trafford • 12.00pm • Attendance 54,591
Referee Graham Poll, Tring

1 LIVERPOOL

3 OWEN

1. David JAMES
14. Vegard HEGGEM
12. Steve HARKNESS
23. Jamie CARRAGHER
21. Dominic MATTEO
20. Stig Inge BJORNEBYE
17. Paul INCE
15.Patrik BERGER
9. Robbie FOWLER
10. Michael OWEN
11. Jamie REDKNAPP

SUBSTITUTES

3. Bjorn Tore KVARME
4. Jason McATEER (11) 71
7. Steve McMANAMAN
8. Oyvind LEONHARDSEN
19. Brad FRIEDEL

Now ecstasy cascaded from the stands, in stark contrast to the creeping despair which prevailed as United's earlier pressure, during which Keane had hit the woodwork twice, had come to nothing.

However, Liverpool deserved a measure of sympathy. They had taken an early lead in a difficult FA Cup tie away from home and their three central defenders, Carragher, Matteo and Harkness, had performed nobly and for their afternoon's endeavours to end in such a disappointing manner amounted, in sporting terms, to cruelty beyond belief.

...after slamming the ball into the net through Jamie Carragher's legs

FA Carling Premiership
Sunday 31 January, 1999

Charlton Athletic 0

28. Simon ROYCE
2. Steve BROWN
3. Chris POWELL
4. Neil REDFEARN
5. Richard RUFUS
23. Carl TILER
15. Keith JONES
8. Mark KINSELLA
9. Andy HUNT
39. Martin PRINGLE
11. John ROBINSON

SUBSTITUTES

1. Sasa ILIC
7. Shaun NEWTON
17. Mark BRIGHT (9) 78
26. Paul KONCHESKY
27. Scott PARKER (39) 83

MATCH REPORT

Dwight Yorke rises majestically to head home Paul Scholes' cross...

The Valley • 4.00pm • Attendance 20,043
Referee Gary Willard, Worthing

1 MANCHESTER UNITED

89 YORKE

1. Peter SCHMEICHEL
2. Gary NEVILLE
3. Denis IRWIN
16. Roy KEANE
21. Henning BERG
6. Jaap STAM
7. David BECKHAM
8. Nicky BUTT
9. Andy COLE
19. Dwight YORKE
11. Ryan GIGGS

SUBSTITUTES

5. Ronny JOHNSEN
12. Phil NEVILLE
17. Raimond VAN DER GOUW
18. Paul SCHOLES (8) 82
20. Ole Gunnar SOLSKJAER (7) 71

United ascended to the Premiership summit thanks to a last-minute winner from Yorke, whose consistent excellence continued to confound critics who believed his £12.6 million transfer fee to be exorbitant.

Overall, it wasn't one of the Reds' more scintillating performances and the hard-working Addicks could consider themselves a trifle unlucky to finish empty-handed, but Alex Ferguson's men never give up any cause and they reaped the benefit for their persistence.

It took the visitors some 35 minutes to make any impression on a resolute Charlton defence, but then three chances materialised in quick succession, only to be spurned by Butt, Giggs and Berg. Then, just before the interval, the hosts engineered their most clear-cut opening when Schmeichel pushed a Kinsella corner to Redfearn, who blazed over the bar from just inside the penalty area.

The second period followed a similar pattern and a stalemate looked increasingly inevitable until towards the end when Butt, more attack-minded than in previous campaigns, failed with a trio of goal attempts.

And so to the 89th-minute dénouement, when the busy Scholes, on as a substitute for Butt, twisted cleverly to dink a diagonal cross from the right and Yorke rose to head into Royce's net via the foot of a post.

...and shares his joy with Roy Keane

January in Review

SUNDAY 3	v MIDDLESBROUGH	H	3-1
SUNDAY 10	v WEST HAM UNITED	H	4-1
SATURDAY 16	v LEICESTER CITY	A	6-2
SUNDAY 24	v LIVERPOOL	H	2-1
SUNDAY 31	v CHARLTON ATHLETIC	A	1-0

PLAYER IN THE FRAME

Henning Berg

After a lengthy interlude out of the side, Henning stormed back into the reckoning with a series of outstanding performances as United won all of their five games during January. Alongside Jaap Stam, the Norwegian looked calm and decisive, and he impressed particularly in the FA Cup meetings with Middlesbrough and Liverpool.

FA Carling Premiership

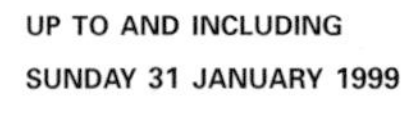
UP TO AND INCLUDING
SUNDAY 31 JANUARY 1999

	P	W	D	L	F	A	Pts
Manchester United	23	12	8	3	50	26	44
Chelsea	23	11	10	2	34	19	43
Aston Villa	23	12	7	4	35	22	43
Arsenal	23	11	9	3	24	11	42
Leeds United	23	9	9	5	36	23	36
Liverpool	23	10	5	8	44	28	35
Wimbledon	23	9	8	6	29	33	35
Derby County	23	8	10	5	23	20	34
West Ham United	23	9	6	8	25	31	33
Middlesbrough	23	7	11	5	32	28	32
Tottenham Hotspur	23	7	9	7	29	31	30
Leicester City	23	7	9	7	25	27	30
Newcastle United	23	7	7	9	28	32	28
Sheffield Wednesday	23	7	5	11	25	23	26
Everton	23	5	9	9	13	25	24
Coventry City	23	6	5	12	23	32	23
Blackburn Rovers	23	5	7	11	22	30	22
Southampton	23	5	5	13	23	46	20
Charlton Athletic	23	3	8	12	26	37	17
Nottingham Forest	23	3	7	13	19	41	16

FEBRUARY

WEDNESDAY 3	v DERBY COUNTY	H
SATURDAY 6	v NOTTINGHAM FOREST	A
SUNDAY 14	v FULHAM	H
WEDNESDAY 17	v ARSENAL	H
SATURDAY 20	v COVENTRY CITY	A
SATURDAY 27	v SOUTHAMPTON	H

FA CARLING PREMIERSHIP
Wednesday 3 February, 1999

MANCHESTER UNITED 1

YORKE 65

1. Peter SCHMEICHEL
2. Gary NEVILLE
3. Denis IRWIN
16. Roy KEANE

6. Jaap STAM
18. Paul SCHOLES
8. Nicky BUTT
20. Ole Gunnar SOLSKJAER
19. Dwight YORKE
11. Ryan GIGGS

SUBSTITUTES

4. David MAY
7. David BECKHAM
9. Andy COLE

15. Jesper BLOMQVIST (11) 11

MATCH REPORT

Nicky Butt tries to pick his way through the Derby defence

Derby County faced United with a demanding tactical conundrum. For much of the match the Reds were confronted with a 3-6-1 formation in which the midfield was so chronically crowded that scoring opportunities were few and far between.

Thus throughout a frustrating first period, the home side were reduced mainly to speculative long-range efforts, by far

Old Trafford • 8.00pm • Attendance 55,174
Referee Steve Lodge, Barnsley

0 DERBY COUNTY

1. Russell HOULT
2. Horatio CARBONARI
7. Spencer PRIOR
4. Darryl POWELL
5. Tony DORIGO
6. Igor STIMAC
16. Jacob LAURSEN
14. Lars BOHINEN
9. Paulo WANCHOPE
18. Lee CARSLEY
11. Kevin HARPER

SUBSTITUTES

3. Stefan SCHNOOR
12. Malcolm CHRISTIE
24. Deon BURTON (11) 71
26. Jonathan HUNT (4) 80
29. Richard KNIGHT

the best of which was an explosive 30-yarder from Stam after four minutes which Hoult scrambled to repel.

In days gone by United might have reacted with a gung-ho cavalry charge, exposing themselves to dangerous counter-attacks. But now the team is patient and their controlled approach limited Derby to one serious first-half goal attempt, when Wanchope shot into the side netting.

However, as the second half progressed without a breakthrough, anxiety began to mount among the fans and the relief was palpable when Butt's arced pass found Yorke free in the box to slip a deft shot past Hoult.

Thereafter the visitors had to vary their gameplan, which gave the Reds more room, and Yorke seemed certain to double his tally from a Blomqvist cross, only for Hoult to pull off a fine save.

Wanchope came worryingly close to claiming parity near the end, but the evening's main concern was a hamstring injury suffered by Giggs, which threatened to sideline the Welshman for several weeks.

Paul Scholes congratulates Dwight Yorke on the winning goal

FA CARLING PREMIERSHIP

Saturday 6 February, 1999

NOTTINGHAM FOREST 1

ROGERS 6

1. Dave BEASANT
30. John HARKES
3. Alan ROGERS
5. Craig ARMSTRONG
20. Carlton PALMER
6. John Olav HJELDE
7. Steve STONE
8. Scot GEMMILL
40. Pierre VAN HOOIJDONK
10. Andy JOHNSON
19. Jean-Claude DARCHEVILLE

SUBSTITUTES

11. Chris BART-WILLIAMS
13. Mark CROSSLEY
14. Dougie FREEDMAN (19) 26
25. Jesper MATTSSON (8) 57
31. Hugo PORFIRIO (15) 74

MATCH REPORT

Such an extravagant scoreline was remarkable in itself, representing United's most convincing away win since the days when they were known as Newton Heath, but even more astounding was the performance of Ole Gunnar Solskjaer. Rising from the bench to replace Yorke, the quicksilver Norwegian plundered four goals in a ten-minute spell which moved Alex Ferguson to remark, with wicked understatement: 'The boy's not a bad substitute!'

Poor Forest, rooted to the foot of the table, were simply demolished by the precision, speed and inspiration of the

Ole Gunnar Solskjaer scores his second and United's sixth goal

City Ground • 3.00pm • Attendance 30,025
Referee Paul Alcock, Redhill

8 MANCHESTER UNITED

2, 67 YORKE
7, 50 COLE
80, 88, 90, 90 SOLSKJAER

1. Peter SCHMEICHEL
2. Gary NEVILLE
12. Phil NEVILLE
16. Roy KEANE
5. Ronny JOHNSEN
6. Jaap STAM
7. David BECKHAM
18. Paul SCHOLES
9. Andy COLE
19. Dwight YORKE
15. Jesper BLOMQVIST

SUBSTITUTES

4. David MAY
8. Nicky BUTT (15) 76
13. John CURTIS (16) 72
17. Raimond VAN DER GOUW
20. Ole Gunnar SOLSKJAER (19) 72

visitors' sparkling football. The annihilation was begun by Yorke after two minutes, then Rogers restored parity for all of 60 seconds before Cole put United back in front. Each of the Reds' first-choice marksmen added another strike before Yorke was withdrawn after 72 minutes, good-naturedly bemoaning the loss of a hat-trick opportunity, to be replaced by Solskjaer.

Yet for all the prolific exploits of strikers Cole, Yorke and Solskjaer, the most influential architect of Forest's eclipse was David Beckham, whose distribution had never been more majestically accurate or perfectly weighted. Keane, too, was a tower of strength against his former team, his power offering the ideal counterpoint to the Englishman's delicacy.

Meanwhile Forest's former United boss, Ron Atkinson, could still raise a laugh. Quizzed after the match about Solskjaer, he quipped: 'Good job they didn't put him on earlier or we'd really have been in trouble!'

Disappointed Forest fans leave the stadium... the scoreboard behind shows the reason for their gloom

FA CUP (Sponsored by AXA) • Fifth Round
Sunday 14 February, 1999

MANCHESTER UNITED 1

COLE 26

1. Peter SCHMEICHEL
2. Gary NEVILLE
3. Denis IRWIN
12. Phil NEVILLE
21. Henning BERG
6. Jaap STAM
7. David BECKHAM
8. Nicky BUTT
9. Andy COLE
19. Dwight YORKE
20. Ole Gunnar SOLSKJAER

SUBSTITUTES

4. David MAY
5. Ronny JOHNSEN (9) 88
15. Jesper BLOMQVIST (20) 68
17. Raimond VAN DER GOUW
34. Jonathan GREENING (3) h-t

MATCH REPORT

With the brouhaha over the appointment of a new England coach at its peak, it was hardly surprising that centre stage at a rainswept Old Trafford was occupied by the heir apparent, Fulham's chief operating officer. In the event, Kevin Keegan's Second Division pacesetters didn't let him down, offering enterprising resistance to a United side which claimed a quarter-final place without approaching their best form.

Indeed, all they had to show for their efforts against the plucky, below-strength Londoners was a single goal, turned into the net after 26 minutes by Cole – courtesy of a significant deflection from Coleman's thigh – following an adroit cutback from the bustling Solskjaer.

Though Fulham came close to equalising almost immediately, when Lehmann was foiled only by Gary Neville's last-ditch block, for the remainder of the first half it seemed inevitable that United would swamp the underdogs.

Not so. Fulham battled prodigiously to keep the predators at bay and even fashioned one fabulous opportunity to level the scores, only for Schmeichel

Peter Schmeichel keeps the ball under pressure from Fulham's Barry Hayles

Old Trafford • 2.00pm • Attendance 54,798
Referee Jeff Winter, Stockton

0 FULHAM

11. Maik TAYLOR
2. Steve FINNAN
3. Rufus BREVETT
4. Neil SMITH
5. Chris COLEMAN
6. Kit SYMONS
7. Wayne COLLINS
8. John SALAKO
9. Dirk LEHMANN
10. Steve HAYWARD
11. Barry HAYLES

SUBSTITUTES

12. Matthew BRAZIER
13. Andre ARENDSE
14. Paul TROLLOPE (8) 74
15. Gus UHLENBEEK (7) 87
16. Kevin BETSY (9) 59

to drop smartly on Salako's 67th-minute shot. The air of complacency which hung over the home team did not disperse until the closing minutes, when a wave of attacks threatened to distort a scoreline which was an accurate reflection of the action.

Jesper Blomqvist looks for a way through the Fulham defence

FA CARLING PREMIERSHIP
Wednesday 17 February, 1999

MANCHESTER UNITED 1

COLE 61

1. Peter SCHMEICHEL
2. Gary NEVILLE
12. Phil NEVILLE
16. Roy KEANE
5. Ronny JOHNSEN
6. Jaap STAM
7. David BECKHAM
8. Nicky BUTT
9. Andy COLE
19. Dwight YORKE
15. Jesper BLOMQVIST

SUBSTITUTES

11. Ryan GIGGS (8) 77
17. Raimond VAN DER GOUW
18. Paul SCHOLES (15) 61
20. Ole Gunnar SOLSKJAER
24. Wesley BROWN

MATCH REPORT

United fans could hardly complain in the light of recent bounty. But, faced by the ominously improving Champions, it was a bad night for the home marksmen to be afflicted with profligacy in front of goal.

In fairness, Cole could be exonerated. After all, he netted the equaliser with a neat close-range header from Phil Neville's delightfully curled left-wing cross, he tested Seaman with several more smart efforts and caused Arsenal persistent problems with his sprightly movement.

For Yorke, however, it was a rare evening of unremitting frustration. After spurning an acceptable early chance with his head, he missed a penalty – awarded on the half-hour after Parlour floored Johnsen in the corner of the box – and thereafter appeared to lack the irrepressible confidence that had been his hallmark. To complete his anguish the Tobagan was booked and then saw Seaman deflect a late point-blank stab set up by a sublime turn from substitute Giggs and a deft touch from Cole.

In addition, Keane twice failed to register when well placed, and it was scant consolation for the Old Trafford faithful to reflect that it was mightily unusual for the Gunners' niggardly rearguard to concede so many clear-cut openings.

It must be admitted, though, that the visitors, while fashioning few scoring opportunities themselves, had looked the better balanced team at times and in new striker Nwankwu Kanu had acquired an unorthodox but potentially lethal performer. He it was who charmed his way past Stam before the

Old Trafford • 8.00pm • Attendance 55,171
Referee Gary Willard, Worthing

1 ARSENAL

48 ANELKA

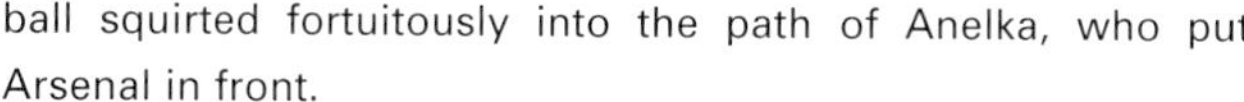

ball squirted fortuitously into the path of Anelka, who put Arsenal in front.

In the end, despite an impressive late assault by United which came tantalisingly close to yielding a crucial victory, the title race remained wide open.

1. David SEAMAN
2. Lee DIXON
3. Nigel WINTERBURN
4. Patrick VIEIRA
5. Steve BOULD
6. Tony ADAMS
15. Ray PARLOUR
25. Nwankwu KANU
9. Nicolas ANELKA
16. Stephen HUGHES
11. Marc OVERMARS

SUBSTITUTES

7. Nelson VIVAS (3) 77
13. Alex MANNINGER
18. Gilles GRIMANDI
19. Remi GARDE (25) 62
27. Kaba DIAWARA (11) 84

Andy Cole forces his way past Arsenal's Steve Bould

COVENTRY CITY 0

1. Marcus HEDMAN
2. Roland NILSSON
3. David BURROWS
4. Paul WILLIAMS
5. Richard SHAW
12. Paul TELFER
7. Darren HUCKERBY
8. Noel WHELAN
26. Stephen FROGGATT
10. Gary McALLISTER
11. George BOATENG

SUBSTITUTES

9. Muhamed KONJIC
14. Trond SOLTVEDT (3) 86
16. Steve OGRIZOVIC
28. John ALOISI (8) 65
30. Barry QUINN

MATCH REPORT

This was not a classic United performance; far from it. But, as Alex Ferguson admitted cheerfully afterwards, sometimes results have to be 'ground out'. Certainly, that's how it was against a beleaguered Coventry side who defended with commendable spirit and concentration, while creating several opportunities to earn much-needed points in their now-traditional scrap to avoid relegation.

Suffice it to say that the Red Devils' outstanding performer was Schmeichel, who made several classy saves, notably a full-length parry from a howitzer dispatched by the excellent Boateng as the Sky Blues enjoyed their most fluent period, shortly before the break.

Ole Gunnar Solskjaer fails to beat Coventry keeper Marcus Hedman

Highfield Road • 3.00pm • Attendance 22,596
Referee Dermot Gallagher, Banbury

1 MANCHESTER UNITED

79 GIGGS

1. Peter SCHMEICHEL
2. Gary NEVILLE
3. Denis IRWIN
16. Roy KEANE
5. Ronny JOHNSEN
6. Jaap STAM
7. David BECKHAM
18. Paul SCHOLES
9. Andy COLE
19. Dwight YORKE
11. Ryan GIGGS

SUBSTITUTES

12. Phil NEVILLE (19) 87
15. Jesper BLOMQVIST
17. Raimond VAN DER GOUW
20. Ole Gunnar SOLSKJAER (9) 74
21. Henning BERG (6) h-t

Roy Keane fights off Paul Telfer and keeps possession of the ball

Come the second half, the League leaders began to exert steady pressure, eventually prevailing through a devastating example of lightning counter-attacking. After catching a McAllister centre, Schmeichel bowled the ball half the length of the pitch to Yorke. The move flowed on through Giggs and the increasingly influential Beckham, whose cross skimmed Shaw's head and reached the far post. There it was met by the sprinting Welshman, still nimble near the end of his first full match after a hamstring injury, and he scored with a slightly mishit shot which Shaw helped over the line. Thus, in the blink of an eye, it was all over.

FA CARLING PREMIERSHIP
Saturday 27 February, 1999

MANCHESTER UNITED 2

KEANE 80
YORKE 84

1. Peter SCHMEICHEL
2. Gary NEVILLE
12. Phil NEVILLE
18. Paul SCHOLES
5. Ronny JOHNSEN
21. Henning BERG
7. David BECKHAM
8. Nicky BUTT
20. Ole Gunnar SOLSKJAER
19. Dwight YORKE
11. Ryan GIGGS

SUBSTITUTES

3. Denis IRWIN (12) 79
9. Andy COLE (20) 68
15. Jesper BLOMQVIST
16. Roy KEANE (8) h-t
24. Wesley BROWN

MATCH REPORT

The Red Devils were fortunate to prevail against the relegation-haunted Saints in a largely frustrating contest which came to life in the final quarter of an hour. True, after the visitors had held their own during a humdrum first half, United had poured forward ceaselessly during the second period, their momentum increased significantly by the introduction of Keane from the substitutes' bench.

However, with 75 minutes gone there was nothing to show for all the pressure and Southampton came close to sneaking the lead when Beattie stole into the penalty area and nodded an inswinging corner against Schmeichel's bar.

It was a fright to which the Reds reacted by netting twice in four minutes, though both goals owed something to deflections. First Keane shot powerfully following a Beckham corner and the ball ricocheted into goal off a Southampton boot or two, then Yorke was freed beautifully by Beckham and shot home past Jones via a defender.

Even then the Saints rallied and when Schmeichel pushed out Le Tissier's low drive Beattie was presented with an open goal, but managed only to hit the angle of post and bar when it seemed easier to score. Then, deep in added time, Le Tissier was given yards of free space to head a consolation goal past Schmeichel from a Dodd free-kick. For nervous home fans, the final whistle came as a considerable relief.

Roy Keane is buried under a pile of players after putting United in the lead

Old Trafford • 3.00pm • Attendance 55,316
Referee Peter Jones, Loughborough

1 SOUTHAMPTON

90 LE TISSIER

1. Paul JONES
2. Jason DODD
33. Patrick COLLETER
4. Chris MARSDEN
5. Claus LUNDEKVAM
6. Kenneth MONKOU
22. David HUGHES
8. Matthew OAKLEY
16. James BEATTIE
10. Egil OSTENSTAD
18. Wayne BRIDGE

SUBSTITUTES

7. Matthew LE TISSIER (10) 68
13. Neil MOSS
15. Francis BENALI (6) 51
23. Scott HILEY
32. Shayne BRADLEY

Henning Berg outruns Southampton's James Beattie

FEBRUARY IN REVIEW

WEDNESDAY 3	v DERBY COUNTY	H	1-0
SATURDAY 6	v NOTTINGHAM FOREST	A	8-1
SUNDAY 14	v FULHAM	H	1-0
WEDNESDAY 17	v ARSENAL	H	1-1
SATURDAY 20	v COVENTRY CITY	A	1-0
SATURDAY 27	v SOUTHAMPTON	H	2-1

PLAYER IN THE FRAME

Ole Gunnar Solskjaer

Ole's four goals in 11 minutes as a substitute at the City Ground, Nottingham, was the most eye-catching individual performance of another highly successful month for the Red Devils. It was the crowning moment of a bountiful, if frequently frustrating campaign for the amiable Norwegian marksman, who spends far more time on the bench than he would like.

FA CARLING PREMIERSHIP

UP TO AND INCLUDING WEDNESDAY 3 MARCH 1999

	P	W	D	L	F	A	Pts
MANCHESTER UNITED	**28**	**16**	**9**	**3**	**63**	**29**	**57**
Chelsea	27	14	11	2	41	22	53
Arsenal	27	13	11	3	35	13	50
Leeds United	27	12	9	6	41	26	45
Aston Villa	27	12	8	7	38	31	44
Wimbledon	27	10	10	7	32	37	40
West Ham United	27	11	7	9	31	38	40
Liverpool	27	11	6	10	50	34	39
Derby County	27	9	11	7	26	25	38
Tottenham Hotspur	27	8	12	7	33	32	36
Sheffield Wednesday	27	10	5	12	35	27	35
Newcastle United	27	9	8	10	35	36	35
Middlesbrough	27	7	12	8	34	39	33
Leicester City	26	7	9	10	26	36	30
Everton	27	6	10	11	20	29	28
Charlton Athletic	27	6	9	12	31	37	27
Coventry City	27	7	6	14	28	38	27
Blackburn Rovers	27	6	8	13	27	38	26
Southampton	27	6	8	13	27	38	26
Nottingham Forest	27	6	5	16	26	53	23

MARCH

WEDNESDAY 3	v INTERNAZIONALE MILAN	H
SUNDAY 7	v CHELSEA	H
WEDNESDAY 10	v CHELSEA	A
SATURDAY 13	v NEWCASTLE UNITED	A
WEDNESDAY 17	v INTERNAZIONALE MILAN	A
SUNDAY 21	v EVERTON	H

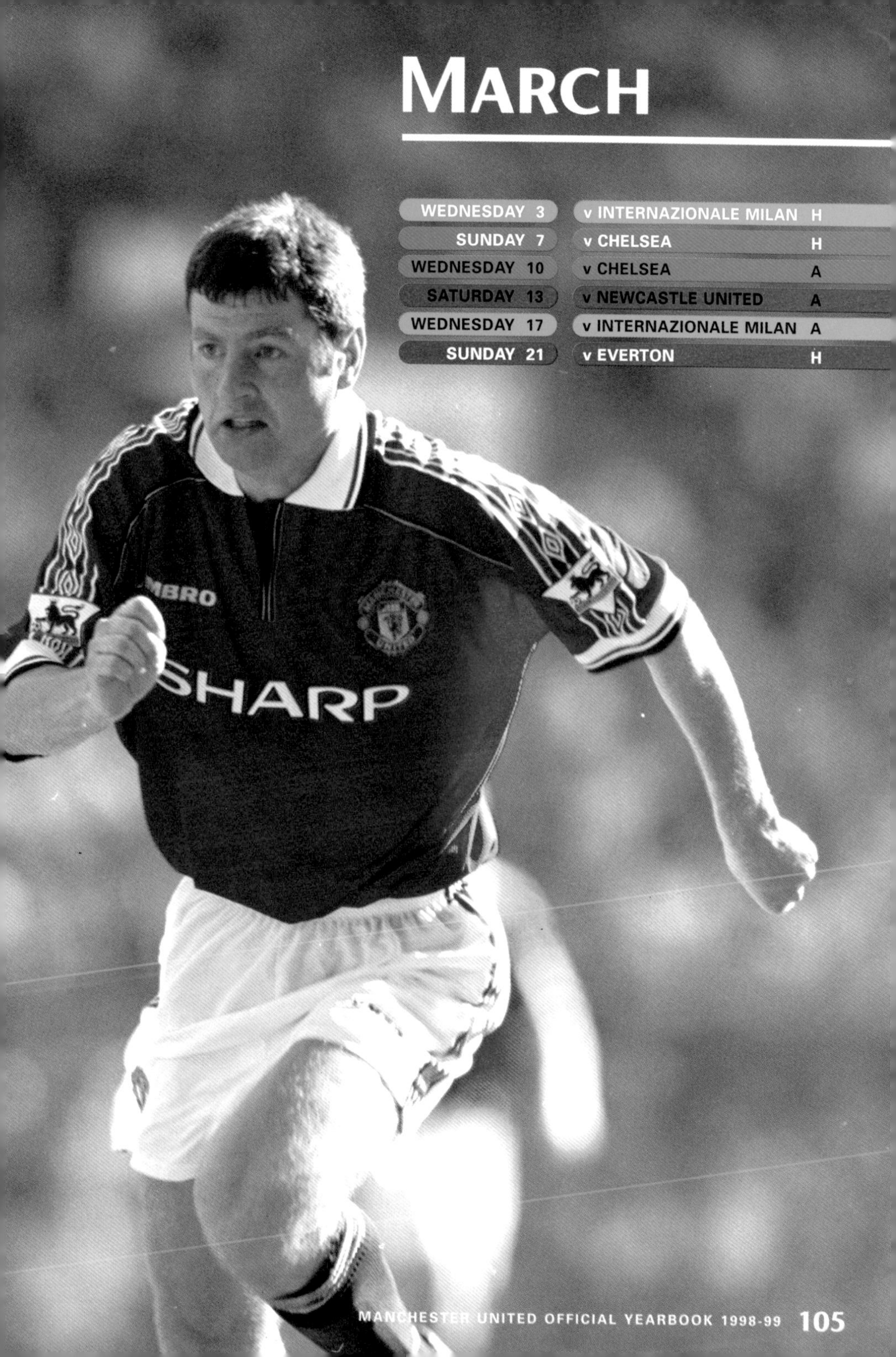

UEFA CHAMPIONS LEAGUE • Quarter-Final, First Leg
Wednesday 3 March, 1999

MANCHESTER UNITED 2

YORKE 6, 45

1. Peter SCHMEICHEL
2. Gary NEVILLE
3. Denis IRWIN
16. Roy KEANE
5. Ronny JOHNSEN
6. Jaap STAM
7. David BECKHAM
18. Paul SCHOLES
9. Andy COLE
19. Dwight YORKE
11. Ryan GIGGS

SUBSTITUTES

8. Nicky BUTT (18) 69
12. Phil NEVILLE
15. Jesper BLOMQVIST
17. Raimond VAN DER GOUW
20. Ole Gunnar SOLSKJAER
21. Henning BERG (5) h-t
30. Wesley BROWN

MATCH REPORT

Dwight Yorke heads in his and United's second goal on half-time

The Red Devils completed a richly entertaining if unremittingly tense night's work against the star-studded Italians, who never came to terms with the deadly combination of Beckham and Yorke. Twice, at either end of the first half, the sumptuously talented England midfielder delivered exquisite first-time crosses for the effervescent Tobagan to rise unopposed and head priceless goals which rendered the imminent trip to San Siro considerably less daunting.

United had golden opportunities to enhance their advantage further, with Giggs missing one glorious opening with a header,

Old Trafford • 7.45pm • Attendance 54,430
Referee Hellmut Krug, Germany

0 INTERNAZIONALE MILAN

1. Gianluca PAGLIUCA
2. Giuseppe BERGOMI
3. Francesco COLONNESE
4. Javier ZANETTI
5. Fabio GALANTE
6. Youri DJORKAEFF
15. Benoit CAUET
8. Aron WINTER
18. Ivan ZAMORANO
10. Roberto BAGGIO
14. Diego SIMEONE

SUBSTITUTES

11. Nicola VENTOLA (18) 68
13. ZE ELIAS
16. Taribo WEST
21. Andrea PIRLO
22. Sebastien FREY
25. Mauro MILANESE
27. GILBERTO

while Stam nodded narrowly wide and Cole had two goalbound efforts blocked by desperate Inter defenders.

Against that, Simeone netted with a powerful second-half header only for the 'goal' to be disallowed, somewhat harshly, for pushing, while Schmeichel, who was back to his near-omnipotent best, pulled off fabulous saves from Zamorano and Ventola. Then, deep into stoppage time, after the United keeper had blocked brilliantly from Colonnese, Berg cleared the follow-up shot off his line when a goal had seemed inevitable.

Overall, then, the hosts could be well satisfied. They had reaped the benefit from a series of enthralling attacks and, perhaps more significantly, they had denied Baggio and company what they had most craved, the luxury of an away goal.

There were plenty of splendid individual displays to savour. Beckham could be congratulated whole-heartedly for sparkling so vividly while retaining his cool when faced with the provocative Simeone, the Argentinian with whom he had clashed calamitously during the World Cup, while Yorke and Schmeichel both excelled. But, as so often, the performance at the heart of the Reds' success was that of the majestic Keane, an inspiration from first to last.

Peter Schmeichel celebrates victory and a brilliant personal performance

FA CUP (Sponsored by AXA) • Sixth Round
Sunday 7 March, 1999

MANCHESTER UNITED 0

1. Peter SCHMEICHEL
2. Gary NEVILLE
3. Denis IRWIN
16. Roy KEANE
24. Wesley BROWN
21. Henning BERG
7. David BECKHAM
18. Paul SCHOLES
20. Ole Gunnar SOLSKJAER
12. Phil NEVILLE
15. Jesper BLOMQVIST

SUBSTITUTES

9. Andy COLE (20) 82
10. Teddy SHERINGHAM (15) 82
13. John CURTIS
17. Raimond VAN DER GOUW
19. Dwight YORKE (12) 73

MATCH REPORT

Mere figures rarely paint an accurate picture of a football match, but the fact that United made 24 attempts on goal, compared with only four by Chelsea, points to the incontrovertible conclusion that the Reds should have progressed to the FA Cup semi-finals. However, a further revealing statistic is that only five of the home side's efforts were on target, offering considerable illumination regarding the blank scoreline.

That said, the nature of the game was altered radically by the sending off of Di Matteo just before the interval for a second bookable offence. Until then, while United had shaded exchanges, the contest remained essentially equal. Thereafter, until Scholes was dismissed under similar circumstances after 85 minutes, the Reds had assumed virtual dominance without ever looking at their incisive best.

Scholes alone might have scored four, Gary Neville glided a header against the post from Beckham's delectable cross and the England midfielder was guilty of skying a presentable opportunity over the bar. Meanwhile De Goey, the Chelsea keeper, was in magnificent form, as was centre-half Desailly, while United's prolific goal-scoring duo, Yorke and Cole, spent most of the afternoon on the substitutes' bench.

Looking for pluses at the end of a frustrating afternoon, three Reds adapted well to slightly unusual roles. Solskjaer ploughed a lone furrow up front, Phil Neville performed an admirable marking job on the dangerous Zola and Brown proved a cool and able deputy at centre-half for the suspended Stam.

Old Trafford • 2.00pm • Attendance 54,587
Referee Paul Durkin, Portland

0 CHELSEA

1. Ed DE GOEY
2. Dan PETRESCU
14. Graeme LE SAUX
17. Albert FERRER
21. Bernard LAMBOURDE
6. Marcel DESAILLY
7. Bjarne GOLDBAEK
16. Roberto DI MATTEO
19. Tore Andre FLO
25. Gianfranco ZOLA
28. Jody MORRIS

SUBSTITUTES

13. Kevin HITCHCOCK
18. Andy MYERS (25) 80
22. Mark NICHOLLS
24. Eddie NEWTON (2) h-t
32. Mikael FORSSELL (19) 61

Dwight Yorke attempts an overhead kick without success

FA CUP (Sponsored by AXA) • Sixth Round Replay
Wednesday 10 March, 1999

CHELSEA 0

1. Ed DE HOEY
14. Graeme LE SAUX
3. Celestine BABAYARO
21. Bernard LAMBOURDE
5. Frank LEBOEUF
6. Marcel DESAILLY
28. Jody MORRIS
16. Roberto DI MATTEO
19. Tore Andre FLO
25. Gianfranco ZOLA
11. Dennis WISE

SUBSTITUTES

7. Bjarne GOLDBAEK (28) 72
13. Kevin HITCHCOCK
18. Andy MYERS (5) h-t
24. Eddie NEWTON
32. Mikael FORSSELL (19) 72

MATCH REPORT

The composed and efficient Reds quelled a prolonged Chelsea offensive to emerge triumphant from a compellingly fascinating contest, the difference between two splendid teams being the inspired opportunism of Dwight Yorke and the commanding presence of Peter Schmeichel.

Dwight Yorke dances after scoring a crucial goal four minutes into the match

Stamford Bridge • 7.45pm • Attendance 33,075
Referee Paul Durkin, Portland

2 MANCHESTER UNITED

4, 59 YORKE

1. Peter SCHMEICHEL
2. Gary NEVILLE
3. Denis IRWIN
16. Roy KEANE
21. Henning BERG
6. Jaap STAM
7. David BECKHAM
18. Paul SCHOLES
9. Andy COLE
19. Dwight YORKE
11. Ryan GIGGS

SUBSTITUTES

12. Phil NEVILLE (9) 71
15. Jesper BLOMQVIST (11) 76
17. Raimond VAN DER GOUW
20. Ole Gunnar SOLSKJAER (19) 85
24. Wesley BROWN

United began brightly and their seemingly startled hosts conceded a crucial early goal when Leboeuf made a sluggish clearance from a Beckham free-kick, Cole nodded on and Yorke swivelled to volley past De Goey from eight yards.

Thus jolted, the Blues reacted positively and mounted a spell of sustained pressure, the highlight of which arrived on 21 minutes when Di Matteo sent Zola through on Schmeichel, only for the Dane to stretch out a leg and block the Italian's shot.

Thereafter Chelsea continued to buzz and create half-chances but United were not seriously extended again until the 55th minute when Wise was in the act of netting from Babayaro's teasing cross, only for Flo to inadvertently block his skipper's shot on the line.

Soon after that United took control when the persistence of Cole unsettled Desailly and the ball ran loose to Yorke, who delivered an instant chip with the outside of his right foot which cleared De Goey to nestle in the net. It was a moment of blinding brilliance, a truly classic goal, which seemed likely to settle the match.

With more than half an hour remaining, though, the Blues were still dangerous and they pushed forward gamely, Schmeichel being forced to save superbly from Morris while Lambourde, Di Matteo and Forssell missed acceptable chances.

But as the final minutes ticked away, the Reds assumed dominance, and Chelsea were left to reflect on their fourth FA Cup defeat in six seasons at the hands of United.

FA CARLING PREMIERSHIP
Saturday 13 March, 1999

NEWCASTLE UNITED 1

SOLANO 16

1. Shay GIVEN
2. Warren BARTON
16. Laurent CHARVET
4. Didier DOMI
34. Nikolaos DABIZAS
15. George GEORGIADIS
12. Dietmar HAMANN
24. Nolberto SOLANO
9. Alan SHEARER
14. Temuri KETSBAIA
11. Gary SPEED

SUBSTITUTES

7. Robert LEE (15) h-t
10. Silvio MARIC (2) 84
13. Steve HARPER
18. Louis SAHA (14) 62
38. Andrew GRIFFIN

MATCH REPORT

Andy Cole's habit of scoring goals at St James' Park was not terminated by his transfer from Newcastle to Manchester United. This latest brace, which lifted the England marksman's Tyneside total to half a century, earned the Red Devils a precious victory and preserved their four-point lead at the top of the Premiership table.

Dwight Yorke shields the ball from Newcastle's Warren Barton

St James' Park • 3.00pm • Attendance 36,776
Referee David Elleray, Harrow-on-the-Hill

2 MANCHESTER UNITED

25, 51 COLE

1. Peter SCHMEICHEL
2. Gary NEVILLE
3. Denis IRWIN
16. Roy KEANE
21. Henning BERG
6. Jaap STAM
7. David BECKHAM
18. Paul SCHOLES
9. Andy COLE
19. Dwight YORKE
11. Ryan GIGGS

SUBSTITUTES

5. Ronny JOHNSEN (11) 74
12. Phil NEVILLE (18) 87
15. Jesper BLOMQVIST
17. Raimond VAN DER GOUW (1) h-t
20. Ole Gunnar SOLSKJAER

The visitors, who fielded an unchanged starting line-up for the first time in ten games, began briskly only to be jolted from their promising rhythm after a quarter of an hour. When Stam fouled Hamann some 25 yards out, the Manchester defence might have expected the German to launch one of his trademark howitzers. Instead they were undone by Peruvian skipper Solano, who curled a glorious right-footer into Schmeichel's net via his left-hand post.

The Reds reacted with characteristic calm, continuing to play progressive football, and soon they were rewarded. Gary Neville launched a long throw into the Magpies' goalmouth, Berg nodded it on, Yorke touched it to Cole, who buried his shot gleefully from close range.

From that moment Alex Ferguson's men asserted themselves ever more insistently and Cole's second arrived early in the second half.

Thereafter van der Gouw, on as a substitute for flu-victim Schmeichel, did not have a save to make and the points were secured as comfortably as a single-goal margin could allow.

Paul Scholes and Dwight Yorke congratulate Andy Cole on two goals against his old club

UEFA CHAMPIONS LEAGUE • Quarter-Final, Second Leg
Wednesday 17 March, 1999

INTERNAZIONALE MILAN 1

VENTOLA 63

1. Gianluca PAGLIUCA
2. Giuseppe BERGOMI
3. Francesco COLONNESE
4. Javier ZANETTI
16. Taribo WEST
24. Mickael SILVESTRE
15. Benoit CAUET
18. Ivan ZAMORANO
9. RONALDO
10. Roberto BAGGIO
14. Diego SIMEONE

SUBSTITUTES

5. Fabio GALANTE
6. Youri DJORKAEFF
8. Aron WINTER
11. Nicola VENTOLA (9) 60
13. ZE ELIAS (14) 32
17. Francesco MORIERO (2) 69

MATCH REPORT

It was a test of character as much as ability and the Reds were not found wanting. When Inter scored half an hour from the end of a compellingly dramatic contest, thus leaving the tie exquisitely but agonisingly balanced, United responded with a mature mixture of fortitude and flair which earned them overall triumph and a place in the next round.

For most of the game, the visitors came under steady pressure and Schmeichel, Stam and Berg, enjoying arguably his finest performance in a red shirt, emerged as heroic figures. Perhaps the most glowing tribute, however, should be reserved for the French referee, Gilles Veissiere, who was left unmoved

Paul Scholes scores the equaliser for United...

Giuseppe Meazza Stadium • 8.45pm • Attendance 79,528
Referee Gilles Veissiere, France

1 MANCHESTER UNITED

88 SCHOLES

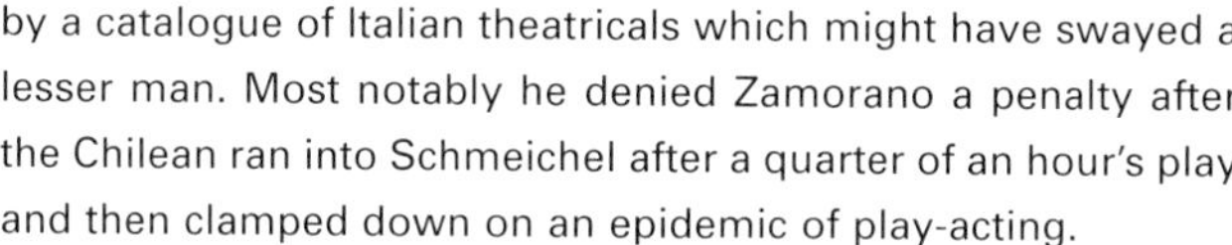

1. Peter SCHMEICHEL
2. Gary NEVILLE
3. Denis IRWIN
16. Roy KEANE
5. Ronny JOHNSEN
6. Jaap STAM
7. David BECKHAM
21. Henning BERG
9. Andy COLE
19. Dwight YORKE
11. Ryan GIGGS

SUBSTITUTES

10. Teddy SHERINGHAM
12. Phil NEVILLE (11) 82
15. Jesper BLOMQVIST
17. Raimond VAN DER GOUW
18. Paul SCHOLES (5) 77
20. Ole Gunnar SOLSKJAER
30. Wesley BROWN

by a catalogue of Italian theatricals which might have swayed a lesser man. Most notably he denied Zamorano a penalty after the Chilean ran into Schmeichel after a quarter of an hour's play and then clamped down on an epidemic of play-acting.

That said, Inter fashioned plenty of genuine chances, the pick of which was Zanetti's shot against a post. Then there was an explosive burst by the half-fit Ronaldo, which culminated in Schmeichel pulling off a wonderful reflex save, and a succession of crucial last-ditch challenges from the sterling Berg. In reply, Cole blazed a first time shot over the bar after being set up by Johnsen.

United survived until midway into the second half when Keane fell victim to an unlucky bounce and the substitute, Ventola, scored from close range. Thereafter, urged on by their fanatical home fans, Inter started to swarm all over United in search of the equaliser. They created yet more openings, the best being squandered by substitute Ze Elias after 82 minutes. The clock had seemed to crawl for six more minutes when Scholes dispelled the tension, netting clinically from eight yards after Cole had nodded into his path following a steepling cross from Gary Neville. Suddenly, as if by magic, the stadium began to empty, leaving the Red Army to their ecstatic celebrations.

United were jubilant and delighted to be in the semi-finals of the Champions League for the second time in three years.

...and Roy Keane leads the celebrations

MANCHESTER UNITED 3

1. Peter SCHMEICHEL
2. Gary NEVILLE
12. Phil NEVILLE
21. Henning BERG
5. Ronny JOHNSEN
6. Jaap STAM
7. David BECKHAM
8. Nicky BUTT
9. Andy COLE
19. Dwight YORKE
20. Ole Gunnar SOLSKJAER

SUBSTITUTES

10. Teddy SHERINGHAM (9) 71
13. John CURTIS (20) 90
17. Raimond VAN DER GOUW
24. Wesley BROWN
34. Jonathan GREENING (7) 71

SOLSKJAER 55
G. NEVILLE 64
BECKHAM 67

MATCH REPORT

There were extenuating circumstances, with United perhaps jaded by their midweek exertions in Milan, but nothing could alter the stark truth that the first half of this clash between the two ancient north-western rivals was utterly dire, an arid interlude best forgotten by all who witnessed it.

True, the relegation-haunted Blues made it difficult for their hosts, massing their forces behind the ball, yet still they managed the most meaningful attacking action of the opening 45 minutes, when a free-kick from Materazzi forced Schmeichel to save sharply.

After the break, for all those of the Red persuasion, it was as though the sun had come out from behind the clouds. Suddenly United displayed some of their characteristic zip and imagination, and the Merseysiders were duly swamped by three goals in 12 minutes.

First Gary Neville fed Solskjaer on the edge of the box and the Norwegian completed a slick one-two with Yorke before drilling an emphatic low shot past the helpless Myhre. Then Yorke shrugged off the attentions of Hutchison and ran at the Everton defence before slipping the ball to Gary Neville, who netted coolly from a narrow angle. It was only the second senior strike of his Old Trafford career. The points were effectively wrapped up by Beckham, who curled home a 25-yard free-kick, his first goal since early November.

Hutchison replied with a bullet-like free-kick while Schmeichel was still organising his defensive wall, but the Reds

Old Trafford • 3.00pm • Attendance 55,182
Referee Mike Riley, Leeds

1 EVERTON

81 HUTCHISON

1. Thomas MYHRE
18. David WEIR
3. Michael BALL
4. Olivier DACOURT
12. Craig SHORT
6. David UNSWORTH
32. John O'KANE
15. Marco MATERAZZI
26. Ibrahima BAKAYOKO
10. Don HUTCHISON
14. Tony GRANT

SUBSTITUTES

5. Dave WATSON
22. Peter DEGN (14) 68
29. Danny CADAMARTERI (26) 5
34. Francis JEFFERS (32) 61
35. Steve SIMONSEN

might have added further goals, the lively Greening, on in place of Beckham, rapping an upright and then dragging wide from close range in front of the posts.

David Beckham celebrates his first goal since November

MARCH IN REVIEW

WEDNESDAY 3	v INTERNAZIONALE MILAN	H	2-0
SUNDAY 7	v CHELSEA	H	0-0
WEDNESDAY 10	v CHELSEA	A	2-0
	v NEWCASTLE UNITED	A	2-1
WEDNESDAY 17	v INTERNAZIONALE MILAN	A	1-1
SATURDAY 21	v EVERTON	H	3-1

PLAYER IN THE FRAME

Dwight Yorke

The multi-talented Tobagan continued to justify his £12.6 million fee with a brace of goals in each of two compelling team performances which ensured that United stayed in both major cup competitions. First came two headers from Beckham crosses at home to Internazionale of Milan, and then a volley and an exquisite first-time chip to knock Chelsea out of the FA Cup at Stamford Bridge.

FA CARLING PREMIERSHIP

UP TO AND INCLUDING MONDAY 22 MARCH 1999

	P	W	D	L	F	A	Pts
MANCHESTER UNITED	**30**	**18**	**9**	**3**	**68**	**31**	**63**
Arsenal	30	16	11	3	42	20	59
Chelsea	29	15	11	3	44	23	56
Leeds United	30	15	9	6	49	27	54
West Ham United	30	13	7	10	34	39	46
Aston Villa	30	12	8	10	39	37	44
Derby County	30	11	11	8	32	32	44
Wimbledon	30	10	10	10	34	44	40
Liverpool	28	11	6	11	52	37	39
Tottenham Hotspur	29	9	12	8	34	34	39
Middlesbrough	29	9	12	8	39	40	39
Newcastle United	30	10	8	12	38	41	38
Sheffield Wednesday	30	10	5	15	35	33	35
Leicester City	28	8	10	10	28	37	34
Coventry City	30	8	7	15	31	37	31
Everton	30	7	10	13	23	35	31
Blackburn Rovers	30	7	9	14	32	42	30
Southampton	30	8	5	17	28	56	29
Charlton Athletic	29	6	10	13	33	50	28
Nottingham Forest	30	4	8	18	27	59	20

WEDNESDAY 7	v JUVENTUS	H
SUNDAY 11	v ARSENAL	A
WEDNESDAY 14	v ARSENAL	A
SATURDAY 17	v SHEFFIELD WEDNESDAY	H
WEDNESDAY 21	v JUVENTUS	A
SUNDAY 25	v LEEDS UNITED	A

WIMBLEDON 1

EUELL 5

1. Neil SULLIVAN
16. Michael HUGHES
3. Alan KIMBLE
4. Chris PERRY
5. Dean BLACKWELL
6. Ben THATCHER
7. Ceri HUGHES
8. Robbie EARLE
29. John HARTSON
20. Jason EUELL
11. Marcus GAYLE

SUBSTITUTES

10. Andy ROBERTS (7) 83
12. Neal ARDLEY (3) 81
13. Paul HEALD
23. Carl CORT (29) 68
26. Gareth AINSWORTH

MATCH REPORT

Jesper Blomqvist tangles with Michael Hughes in a midfield battle

A sustained, sometimes frenzied second-half assault failed to yield Manchester United the three points they needed to plump up a six-point cushion at the Premiership summit.

In truth, it might have been worse for the Reds, who had fallen behind after only five minutes when Gary Neville misjudged a header which was intended to reach Schmeichel,

Selhurst Park • 3.00pm • Attendance 26,121
Referee Graham Barber, Pyrford

1 MANCHESTER UNITED

44 BECKHAM

1. Peter SCHMEICHEL
2. Gary NEVILLE
3. Denis IRWIN
16. Roy KEANE
5. Ronny JOHNSEN
21. Henning BERG
7. David BECKHAM
18. Paul SCHOLES
9. Andy COLE
19. Dwight YORKE
15. Jesper BLOMQVIST

SUBSTITUTES

8. Nicky BUTT
11. Ryan GIGGS
12. Phil NEVILLE
17. Raimond VAN DER GOUW
20. Ole Gunnar SOLSKJAER (15) 73

enabling Euell to push the ball around the stranded keeper and turn it into the unguarded net.

Before the interval Euell might have doubled his tally with a ferocious shot from 12 yards but was foiled by a fabulous Schmeichel save, then Gayle shot wildly when well placed and Ceri Hughes missed with a close-range header.

However, United had been making chances too and, with half-time approaching, Beckham made one count, volleying into the corner of the net from seven yards after an Irwin cross had been deflected into his path by Blackwell.

During the second period the visitors exerted almost total territorial dominance, and but for the excellence of the Dons' rearguard, in which Sullivan and Perry were especially outstanding, the bombardment must have paid off.

Yorke, Beckham, Blomqvist, Scholes, Cole and Keane all went close to snatching a winner, but Wimbledon held firm until the final whistle and United had to be content with stretching their unbeaten run to 20 matches.

Roy Keane almost beats Dons' keeper Neil Sullivan to the ball to steal the points for United

MANCHESTER UNITED 1

GIGGS 90

1. Peter SCHMEICHEL
2. Gary NEVILLE
3. Denis IRWIN
16. Roy KEANE
21. Henning BERG
6. Jaap STAM
7. David BECKHAM
18. Paul SCHOLES
9. Andy COLE
19. Dwight YORKE
11. Ryan GIGGS

SUBSTITUTES

5. Ronny JOHNSEN (21) h-t
8. Nicky BUTT
10. Teddy SHERINGHAM (19) 79
12. Phil NEVILLE
15. Jesper BLOMQVIST
17. Raimond VAN DER GOUW
20. Ole Gunnar SOLSKJAER

MATCH REPORT

A spirited late United barrage produced a precious equaliser by Giggs in stoppage time, but only after the hosts had been outplayed for an hour by a Juventus side which oozed quality. The Italians had stars all over the pitch, but it was the midfield majesty of the Frenchman Zidane and the Dutchman Davids which enchanted neutrals and punctured the optimism of the hitherto-confident home multitude.

The Reds started at a sprightly tempo but it was a false dawn. Soon Juve's fluid movement and penetrative passing earned them the ascendancy and Schmeichel had to be at his best to parry an Inzaghi shot after 15 minutes. Then Beckham scraped a post with a sumptuously flighted free-kick but that proved an isolated highlight for Alex Ferguson's men, who deservedly fell behind three minutes later. Di Livio and Zidane combined cleverly on the left before Davids threaded a cute pass to the unmarked Conte, who netted with a low cross-shot.

The pattern of Italian dominance punctuated by occasional United probes – notably Cole's header over the bar – continued until the interval, by which time Conte, Pessotto and Inzaghi had all spurned inviting chances to stretch the lead.

It wasn't until the mid-point of the second half that the Mancunians began to impose themselves, with Giggs and Keane testing keeper Peruzzi, then Scholes prodding wide from 12 yards as penalty appeals for handball were ignored.

Now Sheringham replaced the disappointing Yorke and a pulsating final assault gathered momentum. It seemed to have

Old Trafford • 7.45pm • Attendance 54,487
Referee Manuel Diaz Vega, Spain

1 JUVENTUS

25 CONTE

1. Angelo PERUZZI
17. Gianluca PESSOTTO
3. Zoran MIRKOVIC
4. Paolo MONTERO
13. Mark IULIANO
14. Didier DESCHAMPS
7. Angelo DI LIVIO
8. Antonio CONTE
9. Filippo INZAGHI
26. Edgar DAVIDS
21. Zinedine ZIDANE

SUBSTITUTES

2. Ciro FERRARA (4) 68
12. Michelangelo RAMPULLA
15. Alessandro BIRINDELLI
16. Nicola AMORUSO
19. Igor TUDOR
20. Alessio TACCHINARDI (7) 77
34. Juan ESNAIDER (9) 88

borne fruit after 86 minutes when the substitute netted with a deft header from a Keane shot, but it was ruled out for marginal offside. Scholes and Cole missed further chances before Juve failed to clear Beckham's overhead cross and Giggs half-volleyed high into the net from four yards to throw the plucky Reds a desperately needed lifeline.

Ryan Giggs drives the ball into the net in the last minute to give United a precious lifeline to take with them to Turin

FA CUP (Sponsored by AXA) • Semi-Final
Sunday 11 April, 1999

ARSENAL 0

1. David SEAMAN
2. Lee DIXON
3. Nigel WINTERBURN
4. Patrick VIEIRA
14. Martin KEOWN
6. Tony ADAMS
7. Nelson VIVAS
15. Ray PARLOUR
9. Nicolas ANELKA
10. Dennis BERGKAMP
11. Marc OVERMARS

SUBSTITUTES

5. Steve BOULD
8. Fredrik LJUNGBERG (11) 90
18. Gilles GRIMANDI
24. John LUKIC
25. Nwankwu KANU (9) 100

MATCH REPORT

United had the best of a thunderous semi-final clash, fashioning more chances than Arsenal but failing to take them, even after the FA Cup holders were reduced to ten men by the dismissal of Vivas early in the first period of extra time.

The most controversial moment of a typically taut encounter between two well-matched sides came after 38 minutes, when Giggs bewitched Dixon before crossing for Yorke to nod into the path of Keane. The Reds' skipper netted with a savage half-volley from 12 yards, only for the strike to be ruled out because of an earlier offside decision against the Tobagan. United's players were not amused, contending that Yorke was not interfering with play at the time, and Irwin was booked in the ensuing mass protest.

For all that, Arsenal had enjoyed the more convincing start and it had been against the run of play when the first clear-cut opening fell to Giggs, who blasted over after being set up by Cole. Then Schmeichel saved a header from Adams and a fierce shot from Bergkamp before Keane's disallowed effort appeared to stimulate a prolonged period of United superiority.

Yorke shot feebly when well placed shortly before the break, the unmarked Cole failed to connect with a Gary Neville cross after 47 minutes and the same player finished lamely with his unfavoured left foot after a lovely pass from Giggs. As normal time ebbed away Keane went close with a header and Beckham with a free-kick, while for Arsenal Anelka ballooned over the bar.

Four minutes into extra time, Vivas departed after elbowing

Villa Park • 12.30pm • Attendance 39,217
Referee David Elleray, Harrow-on-the-Hill

0 MANCHESTER UNITED

after extra time

1. Peter SCHMEICHEL
2. Gary NEVILLE
3. Denis IRWIN
16. Roy KEANE
5. Ronny JOHNSEN
6. Jaap STAM
7. David BECKHAM
8. Nicky BUTT
9. Andy COLE
19. Dwight YORKE
11. Ryan GIGGS

SUBSTITUTES

12. Phil NEVILLE (3) 85
15. Jesper BLOMQVIST
17. Raimond VAN DER GOUW
18. Paul SCHOLES (9) 113
20. Ole Gunnar SOLSKJAER (11) 99

Butt and United set about dismantling a blanket defence, a task which proved beyond them. However, both teams came near to late victory, Schmeichel saving brilliantly at the feet of Ljungberg, then Yorke miscuing from a fairly narrow angle.

Nicky Butt and Arsenal's Tony Adams both look for the ball in vain

FA Cup (Sponsored by AXA) • Semi-Final Replay
Wednesday 14 April, 1999

Arsenal 1

BERGKAMP 69

1. David SEAMAN
2. Lee DIXON
3. Nigel WINTERBURN
4. Patrick VIEIRA
14. Martin KEOWN
6. Tony ADAMS
15. Ray PARLOUR
8. Fredrik LJUNGBERG
9. Nicolas ANELKA
10. Dennis BERGKAMP
17. Emmanuel PETIT

SUBSTITUTES

5. Steve BOULD (17) 119
7. Nelson VIVAS
11. Marc OVERMARS (8) 62
24. John LUKIC
25. Nwankwu KANU (15) 104

MATCH REPORT

In an epic rollercoaster of a contest graced by one of the truly great FA Cup goals, United came back from the brink of seemingly inevitable defeat to reach their fifteenth FA Cup Final.

The excitement was unremitting. There was an exquisite goal by Beckham, bent past Seaman from 20 yards after a lay-off by Sheringham; an equaliser by Bergkamp, deflected in off the magnificent Stam; a correctly disallowed strike by Anelka shortly afterwards, then the sending off of Keane for a second bookable offence – and all that was before the real drama began!

Following the 73rd-minute dismissal of their skipper, ten-man United began an heroic rearguard action which was to encompass a penalty save by Schmeichel from Bergkamp in the 90th minute, an extra-time injury to the Dane which severely hampered his movement, and a Giggs winner which will be enshrined in Red Devil folklore, both for its sheer artistry and for earning victory against overwhelming odds.

The game's ebb and flow unfolded thus: United's more enterprising start was rewarded by Beckham's strike, then Alex Ferguson's men missed a succession of chances before Arsenal finished the half strongly. In the second period Solskjaer (twice) and Blomqvist for United and Anelka for Arsenal all spurned inviting openings before Bergkamp's lucky leveller. Then, after Keane's premature departure, it seemed the Gunners must prevail, but Schmeichel brilliantly repelled the Dutchman's spot-kick – awarded for Phil Neville's trip on Parlour – and the Londoners began extra time in deflated mode.

Villa Park • 7.45pm • Attendance 30,223
Referee David Elleray, Harrow-on-the-Hill

2 MANCHESTER UNITED

after extra time

17 BECKHAM
109 GIGGS

1. Peter SCHMEICHEL
2. Gary NEVILLE
12. Phil NEVILLE
16. Roy KEANE
5. Ronny JOHNSEN
6. Jaap STAM
7. David BECKHAM
8. Nicky BUTT
20. Ole Gunnar SOLSKJAER
10. Teddy SHERINGHAM
15. Jesper BLOMQVIST

SUBSTITUTES

3. Denis IRWIN
11. Ryan GIGGS (15) 61
17. Raimond VAN DER GOUW
18. Paul SCHOLES (10) 76
19. Dwight YORKE (2) 91

They pushed forward but never convincingly, leaving the stage to Ryan Giggs. Seizing possession in his own half, the United substitute danced 70 yards, leaving five defenders in his wake before cracking a venomous shot over Seaman's head from six yards. It was a breathtaking climax to a pulsating encounter.

Ryan Giggs leaves the Arsenal defence in his wake and cracks the ball past David Seaman for his magnificent extra-time winner

MANCHESTER UNITED 3

17. Raimond VAN DER GOUW
2. Gary NEVILLE
12. Phil NEVILLE
16. Roy KEANE
24. Wesley BROWN
6. Jaap STAM
18. Paul SCHOLES
8. Nicky BUTT
20. Ole Gunnar SOLSKJAER
10. Teddy SHERINGHAM
15. Jesper BLOMQVIST

SUBSTITUTES

3. Denis IRWIN (15) 75
4. David MAY (6) 63
7. David BECKHAM
19. Dwight YORKE
34. Jonathan GREENING (16) 63

SOLSKJAER 34
SHERINGHAM 45
SCHOLES 62

MATCH REPORT

After the high-octane intensity of recent games, this efficient but distinctly undemanding home victory offered United a much-needed breather as the season moved towards its frenetic climax.

True, Sheffield Wednesday opened enterprisingly and there were two characteristically spectacular goal-attempts from the

Teddy Sheringham heads United into a 2-0 lead on the stroke of half-time after getting on the end of a cross from Ole Gunnar Solskjaer

Old Trafford • 3.00pm • Attendance 55,270
Referee Neal Barry, Scunthorpe

0 SHEFFIELD WEDNESDAY

33. Pavel SRNICEK
2. Peter ATHERTON
20. Andy HINCHCLIFFE
4. Wim JONK
22. Emerson THOME
6. Des WALKER
26. Niclas ALEXANDERSSON
8. Benito CARBONE
32. Danny SONNER
10. Andy BOOTH
25. Petter RUDI

SUBSTITUTES

1. Kevin PRESSMAN
12. Philip SCOTT (26) 55
17. Lee BRISCOE
18. Dejan STEFANOVIC
21. Richard CRESSWELL (10) 71

were two characteristically spectacular goal-attempts from the gifted Carbone, one a long-range curler which brought a fine save from van der Gouw and the other an extravagant 25-yard volley which missed the target.

But soon the Reds assumed imperious control, especially in the midfield, and it seemed only a matter of time before they took the lead, and so it proved. After Srnicek in the Wednesday goal had expertly denied Keane, Sheringham (twice) and Scholes, the breakthrough came after 34 minutes when Keane turned a Blomqvist cross to Sheringham, whose clever back-flick was volleyed into the net by the predatory Solskjaer from eight yards.

Eleven minutes later Solskjaer returned the favour. Picking up the ball in a wide position he delivered a centre worthy of the rested Beckham, which Sheringham met with a precise glancing header, the ball entering the net off the foot of a post. It was the 250th senior goal of the Londoner's career.

The points were sewn up shortly after the break when Scholes was found by Keane, the England midfielder exchanging passes with the on-form Sheringham before netting with a low cross shot which took a slight deflection.

Now, with United utterly dominant over near-supine opponents, Stam and Keane, then Blomqvist, were withdrawn with more arduous labours in prospect.

Jesper Blomqvist tussles for the ball in midfield, control of which eventually earned United an easy victory

UEFA CHAMPIONS LEAGUE • Semi-Final, Second Leg
Wednesday 21 April, 1999

JUVENTUS 2

INZAGHI 6, 11

1. Angelo PERUZZI
2. Ciro FERRARA
15. Alessandro BIRINDELLI
17. Gianluca PESSOTTO
13. Mark IULIANO
14. Didier DESCHAMPS
7. Angelo DI LIVIO
8. Antonio CONTE
9. Filippo INZAGHI
26. Edgar DAVIDS
21. Zinedine ZIDANE

SUBSTITUTES

4. Paolo MONTERO (13) h-t
11. Daniel FONSECA (7) 80
16. Nicola AMORUSO (15) h-t
19. Igor TUDOR
20. Alessio TACCHINARDI
34. Juan ESNAIDER

MATCH REPORT

For the second time in a week, United rose to supreme heights to triumph in a semi-final which had seemed to be lost, and in doing so they completed one of the most stirring comebacks in European football history.

Two down after 11 minutes to a Juventus side renowned for virtual impregnability on their own soil, the Reds refused to bow

At full stretch, Dwight Yorke flings himself at a cross from Andy Cole to pull the scores level after 34 minutes

Stadio Delle Alpi •7.45pm • Attendance 60,806
Referee Urs Meier, Switzerland

3 MANCHESTER UNITED

24 KEANE
34 YORKE
84 COLE

1. Peter SCHMEICHEL
2. Gary NEVILLE
3. Denis IRWIN
16. Roy KEANE
5. Ronny JOHNSEN
6. Jaap STAM
7. David BECKHAM
8. Nicky BUTT
9. Andy COLE
19. Dwight YORKE
15. Jesper BLOMQVIST

SUBSTITUTES

4. David MAY
10. Teddy SHERINGHAM
12. Phil NEVILLE
17. Raimond VAN DER GOUW
18. Paul SCHOLES (15) 68
20. Ole Gunnar SOLSKJAER
30. Wesley BROWN

the knee. Instead they pulled level by the 34th minute, then rapped the Juve woodwork twice and dominated large swathes of the action before claiming a richly deserved victory six minutes from time.

Such a scenario had seemed unthinkable after Zidane had created two early goals for Inzaghi, the first bundled in at the far post as the quicksilver marksman eluded Gary Neville, the second resulting from a freak ricochet from the boot of Stam which sent the ball ballooning over the hapless Schmeichel.

At this stage, the spectre of humiliation loomed large, but United fought back with a vengeance. Gradually they mounted a series of coherent attacks, they might have had a penalty when Yorke was impeded, then Keane netted with a princely glancing header from a raking Beckham corner. Game on.

The Reds assumed the ascendancy, but Juventus remained dangerous and Stam headed off his own line before Yorke equalised with an adroit header from a Cole cross. Thereafter there were chances at both ends but United came closest when Yorke hit a post on 38 minutes, then Irwin did the same after 71.

A 2-2 draw would have been enough to reach the final, but Cole put the issue beyond doubt when he slid home from a narrow angle after Yorke had been felled while bursting past the keeper.

Sadly, bookings for Keane and Scholes ruled them out of the reckoning for Barcelona, but time enough to worry about that later. This was a night for pride, joy and celebration.

LEEDS UNITED 1

HASSELBAINK 32

1. Nigel MARTYN
40. Matthew JONES
20. Ian HARTE
25. Jonathan WOODGATE
5. Lucas RADEBE
37. Stephen McPHAIL
23. David BATTY
39. Alan SMITH
9. Jimmy Floyd HASSELBAINK
19. Harry KEWELL
11. Lee BOWYER

SUBSTITIUTES

6. David WETHERALL (25) 59
8. Clyde WIJNHARD (9) 87
10. Bruno RIBEIRO
18. Gunnar HALLE
36. Paul ROBINSON

MATCH REPORT

The Reds' seemingly bottomless pit of resilience kept them in contention after Leeds' voraciously hungry young side dominated the first half. Yet Alex Ferguson's men bounced back to shade the second period and would have claimed all three points had Yorke not miscued spectacularly with the last kick of the game.

The visitors' afternoon got off to an unpromising start when Stam aggravated an injury during the pre-match kick-in and had to be withdrawn, being replaced by May. Their hosts began with a flourish, the outstanding Kewell crossing for the unmarked Bowyer to head over after two minutes, then Smith hammering goalwards from close range, only to be denied by an archetypal Schmeichel block.

Gradually the Reds gained a foothold and came close to scoring in a frantic goalmouth scramble, but as the half progressed Leeds created a succession of chances, the best of which Smith pulled wide after 29 minutes.

However it came as no surprise when they took the lead, a sloppy Butt pass allowing Kewell to feed Hasselbaink, who beat the charging Schmeichel from 12 yards, the ball entering the net off the near post.

Andy Cole stretches out a leg to equalise 10 minutes after half-time

Elland Road • 11.30am • Attendance 40,255
Referee Dermot Gallagher, Banbury

1 MANCHESTER UNITED

55 COLE

1. Peter SCHMEICHEL
2. Gary NEVILLE
3. Denis IRWIN
4. David MAY
24. Wesley BROWN
16. Roy KEANE
7. David BECKHAM
8. Nicky BUTT
9. Andy COLE
19. Dwight YORKE
15. Jesper BLOMQVIST

SUBSTITUTES

10. Teddy SHERINGHAM (15) 76
12. Phil NEVILLE (3) 71
13. John CURTIS
17. Raimond VAN DER GOUW
18. Paul SCHOLES (7) 84

Shortly before the interval Kewell almost doubled the lead with a header, then Yorke might have equalised but nodded wide as the Mancunians began a positive response which continued into the second period. The sustained improvement bore fruit when Butt's header from a Keane cross was parried by Martyn, only for Cole to poke home from four yards.

Subsequently, opportunities were created and spurned by both sides, Yorke missing the best of them following a delightful one-two interchange with Sheringham deep inside stoppage time. With Arsenal on the rampage, the Tobagan's inaccuracy seemed ominously significant.

Dwight Yorke narrowly misses with the last kick of the match

April in Review

SATURDAY 3	v WIMBLEDON	A	1-1
WEDNESDAY 7	v JUVENTUS	H	1-1
SUNDAY 11	v ARSENAL	A	0-0
WEDNESDAY 14	v ARSENAL	A	2-1
SATURDAY 17	v SHEFFIELD WEDNESDAY	H	3-0
WEDNESDAY 21	v JUVENTUS	A	3-2
SUNDAY 25	v LEEDS UNITED	A	1-1

PLAYER IN THE FRAME

Jaap Stam

Jaap looked better and better as the campaign progressed and by April he was living up to his pre-season billing as the complete central defender. In both legs of two semi-finals, against Juventus in the Champions League and Arsenal in the replayed FA Cup encounter, the Dutchman was a veritable colossus.

FA Carling Premiership

UP TO AND INCLUDING SUNDAY 25 APRIL 1999

	P	W	D	L	F	A	Pts
Arsenal	34	19	12	3	54	15	69
Manchester United	**33**	**19**	**11**	**3**	**73**	**33**	**68**
Chelsea	34	17	14	3	49	26	65
Leeds United	34	16	12	6	54	30	60
Aston Villa	35	15	10	10	47	39	55
West Ham United	35	15	9	11	41	42	54
Middlesbrough	35	12	14	9	47	48	50
Derby County	34	12	12	10	37	41	48
Liverpool	34	13	8	13	60	44	47
Tottenham Hotspur	34	11	13	10	41	40	46
Leicester City	34	11	13	10	36	41	46
Newcastle United	35	11	11	13	46	51	44
Wimbledon	35	10	12	13	39	56	42
Sheffield Wednesday	35	11	7	17	39	40	40
Everton	35	10	10	15	35	42	40
Coventry City	35	10	7	18	35	48	37
Blackburn Rovers	34	7	11	16	36	49	32
Charlton Athletic	35	7	11	17	37	52	32
Southampton	35	8	8	19	31	63	32
Nottingham Forest	35	4	9	22	30	68	21

May

SATURDAY 1	v ASTON VILLA	H
WEDNESDAY 5	v LIVERPOOL	A
SATURDAY 8	v MIDDLESBROUGH	A
WEDNESDAY 12	v BLACKBURN ROVERS	A
SUNDAY 16	v TOTTENHAM HOTSPUR	H
SATURDAY 22	v NEWCASTLE UNITED WEMBLEY	
WEDNESDAY 26	v BAYERN MUNICH NOU CAMP STADIUM	

FA Carling Premiership
Saturday 1 May, 1999

MANCHESTER UNITED 2

WATSON (o.g.) 20
BECKHAM 47

1. Peter SCHMEICHEL
2. Gary NEVILLE
3. Denis IRWIN
4. David MAY
5. Ronny JOHNSEN
18. Paul SCHOLES
7. David BECKHAM
8. Nicky BUTT
19. Dwight YORKE
10. Teddy SHERINGHAM
15. Jesper BLOMQVIST

SUBSTITUTES

12. Phil NEVILLE (15) 63
17. Raimond VAN DER GOUW
24. Wesley BROWN (4) 79
33. Mark WILSON
34. Jonathan GREENING

MATCH REPORT

United delivered some enterprising football and there was a Beckham 'special' to savour, yet the afternoon ended with Old Trafford racked by gnawing tension as Alex Ferguson's team inched another step closer to their dream of a hitherto unattained treble.

The hosts opened with a controlled onslaught and came close to an early breakthrough when Blomqvist crossed, Sheringham knocked the ball into the six-yard box and Scholes' diving header was saved by Oakes. Soon after that the keeper was bypassed by a Beckham free-kick only for Southgate to head off the line.

The pressure continued to mount and the Villa rearguard finally cracked when Blomqvist dispatched a rare right-foot centre, Scholes turned it back across goal and Watson ran it it over his own line.

Now the visitors responded with some aggression and they equalised when the dangerous Stone crossed from the right and, with the United defence looking for the offside flag, Joachim netted via a slight deflection off May.

United poured forward again and went ahead immediately after the interval when Beckham's 25-yard free-kick described a perfect arc from boot to top right-hand corner of Oakes' goal. Mysteriously, no defensive wall was deemed necessary. However, even though there was no barricade in his way the Villa goalkeeper hardly saw the ball, such was the power, speed and accuracy of Beckham's shot.

Old Trafford • 3.00pm • Attendance 55,189
Referee Keith Burge, Tonypandy

1 ASTON VILLA

34 JOACHIM

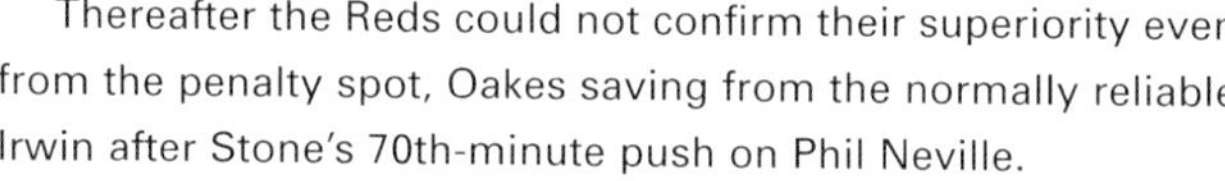

Thereafter the Reds could not confirm their superiority even from the penalty spot, Oakes saving from the normally reliable Irwin after Stone's 70th-minute push on Phil Neville.

No doubt sensing their opponents' growing nervousness, Villa now threw themselves into a late quest for parity and United were reduced to hanging on. They did so, but in the end it was far too close for comfort.

13. Michael OAKES
26. Steve STONE
3. Alan WRIGHT
4. Gareth SOUTHGATE
34. Colin CALDERWOOD
6. Steve WATSON
7. Ian TAYLOR
8. Mark DRAPER
14. Dion DUBLIN
10. Paul MERSON
12. Julian JOACHIM

SUBSTITUTES

5. Ugo EHIOGU
11. Alan THOMPSON (8) 67
15. Gareth BARRY
22. Darius VASSELL (14) 76
39. Peter ENCKELMAN

Aston Villa's Steve Watson watches in horror as the ball deflects off his leg and into the net to give United the lead

FA CARLING PREMIERSHIP
Wednesday 5 May, 1999

LIVERPOOL 2

REDKNAPP (penalty) 70
INCE 89

- 19. Brad FRIEDEL
- 23. Jamie CARRAGHER
- 21. Dominic MATTEO
- 4. Rigobert SONG
- 5. Steve STAUNTON
- 6. Phil BABB
- 7. Steve McMANAMAN
- 8. Oyvind LEONHARDSEN
- 13. Karlheinz RIEDLE
- 17. Paul INCE
- 11. Jamie REDKNAPP

SUBSTITUTES

- 1. David JAMES
- 15. Patrik BERGER (4) 57
- 18. Jean Michel FERRI
- 20. Stig Inge BJORNEBYE
- 25. David THOMPSON (5) 79

MATCH REPORT

It is both useless and unseemly to bleat, but the truth is that Manchester United were unfortunate to drop two precious points at Anfield. Seemingly in comfortable control and two goals to the good with some 20 minutes left, they were victims of a controversial penalty decision when Blomqvist was adjudged to have upended Leonhardsen and Redknapp netted from the spot.

Still the visitors did not appear unduly perturbed, but then five minutes later Irwin received his second yellow card of the night for allegedly kicking the ball away, an interpretation of the event which seemed harsh, to say the least.

Thus reduced to ten men, United came under severe pressure but looked likely to hold out until the 89th minute when a goalmouth scramble climaxed with Ince prodding past Schmeichel. It might have been even worse as the unmarked Carragher squandered a free eight-yard header deep into stoppage time. Thus Alex Ferguson's men were spared their first defeat of the year, but enormous damage had already been inflicted to their title hopes.

Dwight Yorke heads a far post cross past Brad Friedel to put United in front

Anfield • 8.00pm • Attendance 44,702
Referee David Elleray, Harrow-on-the-Hill

2 MANCHESTER UNITED

22 YORKE
57 IRWIN (penalty)

1. Peter SCHMEICHEL
2. Gary NEVILLE
3. Denis IRWIN
16. Roy KEANE
5. Ronny JOHNSEN
6. Jaap STAM
7. David BECKHAM
18. Paul SCHOLES
9. Andy COLE
19. Dwight YORKE
15. Jesper BLOMQVIST

SUBSTITUTES

4. David MAY
8. Nicky BUTT (9) 77
10. Teddy SHERINGHAM
12. Phil NEVILLE (15) 77
17. Raimond VAN DER GOUW

Denis Irwin makes it 2-0 from the penalty spot after 57 minutes

The match had been played at breakneck pace with Liverpool piling forward boldly but without penetration, and United went ahead with a beautifully worked goal, Beckham exchanging passes with Keane before delivering a soaring cross which Yorke headed beyond Friedel at the far post.

A similar move involving the same players almost doubled the lead after 43 minutes, but Friedel saved smartly. Early in the second half Ince missed the hosts' first clear opening, then United scored again, Irwin converting a penalty after Carragher, straining to cope with a high bounce, had kicked Blomqvist in the stomach. About that award, at least, there was not the slightest doubt.

FA CARLING PREMIERSHIP
Sunday 9 May, 1999

MIDDLESBROUGH 0

1. Mark SCHWARZER
28. Robbie STOCKDALE
3. Dean GORDON
4. Steve VICKERS
31. Jason GAVIN
6. Gary PALLISTER
7. Robbie MUSTOE
22. Mark SUMMERBELL
19. Hamilton RICARD
10. Brian DEANE
16. Andy TOWNSEND

SUBSTITUTES

13. Marlon BERESFORD
15. Neil MADDISON
18. Andy CAMPBELL (31) 72
20. Alun ARMSTRONG
24. Steve BAKER

MATCH REPORT

Having slipped three points adrift of Arsenal in the title race, United were in desperate need of victory on Teesside, preferably by a margin that would massage their goal difference. In a full-blooded but scrappy encounter, they attained the first objective but not the second, leaving them on top of the table but only by virtue of having scored more goals than the Gunners.

The visitors began the match oozing with urgency and their comprehensive domination appeared to bear fruit after 15 minutes when a Keane scorcher was spilled by Schwarzer and Sheringham netted the rebound. However, the strike was ruled out for offside, although later television evidence proved it had been perfectly legal.

United continued to press and Yorke and Blomqvist spurned chances before the contest became more even following the withdrawal through injury of the influential Keane. Summerbell shaved Schmeichel's post with a cross-shot and Gordon scooped over, but it was Alex Ferguson's side who took a deserved lead in first-half stoppage time. A Beckham cross was cleared, Butt dinked it back in, Sheringham nodded to Yorke and the

Paul Scholes gets in a shot despite being the filling in a Middlesbrough sandwich

Riverside Stadium • 4.00pm • Attendance 34,665
Referee Graham Barber, Pyrford

1 MANCHESTER UNITED

45 YORKE

- 1. Peter SCHMEICHEL
- 2. Gary NEVILLE
- 3. Denis IRWIN
- 4. David MAY
- 16. Roy KEANE
- 6. Jaap STAM
- 7. David BECKHAM
- 18. Paul SCHOLES
- 19. Dwight YORKE
- 10. Teddy SHERINGHAM
- 15. Jesper BLOMQVIST

SUBSTITUTES

- 8. Nicky BUTT (16) 25
- 9. Andy COLE (15) 66
- 12. Phil NEVILLE (18) 90
- 17. Raimond VAN DER GOUW
- 24. Wesley BROWN

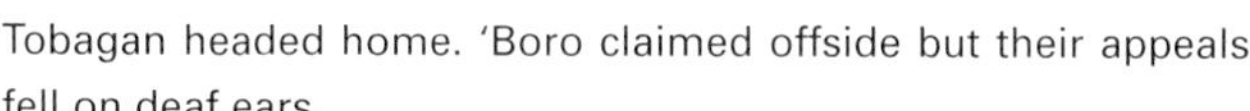

Tobagan headed home. 'Boro claimed offside but their appeals fell on deaf ears.

During a tense second half there were opportunities at either end, but generally United held sway though they failed to make the most of many promising positions, with Blomqvist especially hesitant.

The final whistle brought relief to United, albeit tinged with regret that their goal difference was merely equal to Arsenal's. A nail-biting week lay ahead.

Once again Dwight Yorke comes to the rescue by heading the winner right on half time

FA Carling Premiership
Wednesday 12 May, 1999

Blackburn Rovers 0

13. John FILAN
20. Gary CROFT
3. Callum DAVIDSON
15. Lee CARSLEY
5. Darren PEACOCK
6. Stephane HENCHOZ
31. Keith GILLESPIE
27. David DUNN
32. Ashley WARD
33. Matt JANSEN
11. Jason WILCOX

SUBSTITUTES

1. Tim FLOWERS
10. Kevin DAVIES
12. Damien DUFF
16. Marlon BROOMES
19. Damien JOHNSON (31) 81

MATCH REPORT

The goal attempts totalled 18-4 in United's favour, but on a night of intense and poignant emotion, the Reds simply did not play well enough to overcome a spirited Blackburn side.

Alas for Rovers boss Brian Kidd, who deserves immense credit for his part in the Old Trafford success story of the 1990s, this untidy goalless draw was not enough to keep his new team in the top flight.

The hosts opened in lively fashion but it was the visitors who mounted the first spell of sustained pressure and nearly went ahead after ten minutes when Beckham dispatched a wickedly curling cross to Giggs, whose header cannoned off the far post only for Cole to miscue from the rebound.

Ryan Giggs tries to find an opening, but without success

Ewood Park • 8.00pm • Attendance 30,436
Referee Mike Reed, Birmingham

0 MANCHESTER UNITED

1. Peter SCHMEICHEL
2. Gary NEVILLE
3. Denis IRWIN
12. Phil NEVILLE
5. Ronny JOHNSEN
6. Jaap STAM
7. David BECKHAM
8. Nicky BUTT
9. Andy COLE
19. Dwight YORKE
11. Ryan GIGGS

SUBSTITUTES

4. David MAY (6) h-t
10. Teddy SHERINGHAM (9) 71
17. Raimond VAN DER GOUW
18. Paul SCHOLES (12) 76
20. Ole Gunnar SOLSKJAER

Even Dwight Yorke failed to find a way through a resolute Rovers defence

Blackburn, facing a win-or-bust scenario, worked hard but it was United who continued to look the more dangerous and a Yorke 20-yarder brought an acrobatic save from Filan, then Cole and Johnsen both wasted splendid openings before the interval.

In the second half Rovers, spurred on by a passionate crowd, lifted their tempo and battled desperately for the goal that would preserve their hopes of avoiding relegation. The most inviting opportunity fell to Ward after 83 minutes. However, with the keeper off his line and stranded, the Blackburn striker failed to hit the target from 16 yards.

Meanwhile United failed to exploit the defensive gaps left by their opponents' increasing need to drive forward, leaving the Reds requiring victory in their last-day encounter with Spurs at Old Trafford to make sure of the title.

FA CARLING PREMIERSHIP
Sunday 16 May, 1999

MANCHESTER UNITED 2

BECKHAM 43
COLE 48

1. Peter SCHMEICHEL
2. Gary NEVILLE
3. Denis IRWIN
4. David MAY
5. Ronny JOHNSEN
16. Roy KEANE
7. David BECKHAM
18. Paul SCHOLES
19. Dwight YORKE
10. Teddy SHERINGHAM
11. Ryan GIGGS

SUBSTITUTES

8. Nicky BUTT (18) 70
9. Andy COLE (10) h-t
12. Phil NEVILLE (11) 80
17. Raimond VAN DER GOUW
20. Ole Gunnar SOLSKJAER

MATCH REPORT

It was the fifth Championship triumph of Alex Ferguson's reign, but the first to be clinched at Old Trafford, and the Theatre of Dreams partied accordingly.

Beautiful goals from Beckham and Cole furnished United with the three points they needed to claim their crown, but not before Spurs had temporarily silenced the fretful multitude by taking the lead.

As the season reached an almost unbearably tense climax, the drama was unremitting from first whistle to last. After four minutes Yorke nearly scored at the near post following a Giggs

Andy Cole lifts the ball over Ian Walker and into the Spurs' net to give United their fifth Championship under Alex Ferguson...

Old Trafford • 4.00pm • Attendance 55,189
Referee Graham Poll, Tring

1 TOTTENHAM HOTSPUR

25 FERDINAND

1. Ian WALKER
2. Stephen CARR
12. Justin EDINBURGH
4. Steffen FREUND
17. John SCALES
23. Sol CAMPBELL
24. Tim SHERWOOD
18. Steffen IVERSEN
9. Darren ANDERTON
10. Les FERDINAND
14. David GINOLA

SUBSTITUTES

13. Espen BAARDSEN
20. Jose DOMINGUEZ (14) 10
22. Andy SINTON (20) 78
25. Stephen CLEMENCE
32. Luke YOUNG (17) 71

cross, then came even closer when an attempted clearance by Walker rebounded from the Tobagan against a post, only for the keeper to grasp the spinning ball on the line.

Then both Giggs and Yorke went close as United dominated, but Tottenham went ahead after 25 minutes when Iversen nodded on to Ferdinand, who won his race with Johnsen and scooped the ball cleverly over Schmeichel. Thereafter the hosts created chance after chance but Scholes, Yorke and Beckham all failed to register and Old Trafford was awash with anxiety. The atmosphere was transformed from anxious to expectant with goals either side of the break. First it was from Scholes to Giggs to Scholes to Beckham, and the England star netted with a rasping, angled drive which Walker touched but could not repel. Then Gary Neville dispatched a long pass into the penalty box and Cole controlled the ball deftly before dinking it exquisitely over Walker from six yards. Old Trafford went crazy. But that was not the end of it.

Opportunities to make the prize safe were missed and when news filtered through of an Arsenal goal at Highbury, nerve ends became frazzled. The title could have slipped away with one mistake – and Spurs battled purposefully – but there were no more goals. Thus the Reds extended their unbeaten run to 31 matches and became Champions for the twelfth time.

...and Roy Keane gets to lift the trophy in front of the Old Trafford faithful for the first time

FA CUP (Sponsored by AXA) • Final
Saturday 22 May, 1999

MANCHESTER UNITED 2

SHERINGHAM 11
SCHOLES 52

1. Peter SCHMEICHEL
2. Gary NEVILLE
12. Phil NEVILLE
4. David MAY
5. Ronny JOHNSEN
16. Roy KEANE
7. David BECKHAM
18. Paul SCHOLES
9. Andy COLE
20. Ole Gunnar SOLSKJAER
11. Ryan GIGGS

SUBSTITUTES

6. Jaap STAM (18) 76
10. Teddy SHERINGHAM (16) 9
15. Jesper BLOMQVIST
17. Raimond VAN DER GOUW
19. Dwight YORKE (9) 60

MATCH REPORT

The Red Devils dominated proceedings in the Wembley sunshine, overcoming the early loss of injured skipper Roy Keane to inflict on Newcastle a second successive Wembley defeat.

The heroes of the hour as United claimed an unprecedented third League and FA Cup double were goalscorers Teddy Sheringham and Paul Scholes. Sheringham rose from the bench to replace Keane after nine minutes, and 96 seconds later had put his team in front. From that moment Alex Ferguson's men were in charge and Scholes, who had overcome illness to play,

Paul Scholes takes a pass from Teddy Sheringham and shoots past Steve Harper in the Magpies goal to make it 2-0

Wembley Stadium • 3.00pm • Attendance 79,101
Referee Peter Jones, Loughborough

0 NEWCASTLE UNITED

13. Steve HARPER
38. Andrew GRIFFIN
16. Laurent CHARVET
4. Didier DOMI
34. Nikos DABIZAS
12. Dietmar HAMANN
7. Robert LEE
24. Nolberto SOLANO
9. Alan SHEARER
14. Temuri KETSBAIA
11. Gary SPEED

SUBSTITUTES

1. Shay GIVEN
2. Warren BARTON
10. Silvio MARIC (24) 68
17. Stephen GLASS (14) 78
20. Duncan FERGUSON (12) h-t

doubled the tally in the second half to cap a masterful personal contribution to United's treble challenge.

The Magpies had begun brightly and aggressively, a second minute tackle by Speed accounting for Keane, leaving the Reds to reshape with Sheringham up front, Solskjaer on the right flank and Beckham in central midfield. However, the black and white charge was halted by a beautifully worked opening goal, Sheringham exchanging passes sweetly with Scholes before slipping the ball expertly under Harper from 15 yards.

For the remainder of the half United had the better of the exchanges, with Solskjaer, Cole and Sheringham all going close, while at the other end Hamann brought a fine diving save from Schmeichel.

Reinforced by Duncan Ferguson, Newcastle began the second period as enterprisingly as they had the first, but again were halted by a goal. This time Solskjaer robbed a defender on the right, Sheringham laid a perfect pass into the path of Scholes, who netted with a low left-footer from the edge of the box.

Thereafter Ketsbaia rapped the outside of the post with Schmeichel stranded and Maric missed a golden 82nd minute opportunity to set up a grandstand finish, but the Reds had far more chances, the pick of which was Sheringham's delightful chip on to Harper's bar. In the end United won at a canter.

On to Barcelona.

Peter Schmeichel lifts the Cup, David May applauds

UEFA CHAMPIONS LEAGUE • Final
Wednesday 26 May, 1999

BAYERN MUNICH 1

BASLER 6

1. Oliver KAHN
2. Markus BABBEL
18. Michael TARNAT
4. Samuel Osei KUFFOUR
25. Thomas LINKE
16. Jens JEREMIES
14. Mario BASLER
21. Alexander ZICKLER
19. Carsten JANCKER
10. Lothar MATTHAUS
11. Stefan EFFENBERG

SUBSTITUTES

5. Thomas HELMER
7. Mehmet SCHOLL (21) 71
8. Thomas STRUNZ
17. Thorsten FINK (10) 80
20. Hasan SALIHAMIDZIC (14) 88
22. Bernd DREHER
24. Ali DAEI

MATCH REPORT

The final dramatic moment. Ole Gunnar Solskjaer steers the ball past Oliver Kahn to make United's dream of the treble come true

The scale of the glory, and the melodramatic manner in which it arrived, was hard to take in. Manchester United wrought a sporting miracle to devastate Bayern Munich with two stoppage-time strikes, thus transforming a contest which had appeared irretrievable.

The Germans had made the more assured start and led through an early Basler free-kick, which the flamboyant midfielder had bent around the Reds' defensive wall with Schmeichel rooted to his line. The award was controversial, Johnsen's challenge on Jancker appearing to be accidental.

Nou Camp Stadium • 8.45pm • Attendance 91,000
Referee Pierluigi Collina, Italy

2 MANCHESTER UNITED

90 SHERINGHAM
90 SOLSKJAER

1. Peter SCHMEICHEL
2. Gary NEVILLE
3. Denis IRWIN
15. Jesper BLOMQVIST
5. Ronny JOHNSEN
6. Jaap STAM
7. David BECKHAM
8. Nicky BUTT
9. Andy COLE
19. Dwight YORKE
11. Ryan GIGGS

SUBSTITUTES

4. David MAY
10. Teddy SHERINGHAM (15) 67
12. Phil NEVILLE
17. Raimond VAN DER GOUW
20. Ole Gunnar SOLSKJAER (9) 81
30. Wesley BROWN
34. Jonathan GREENING

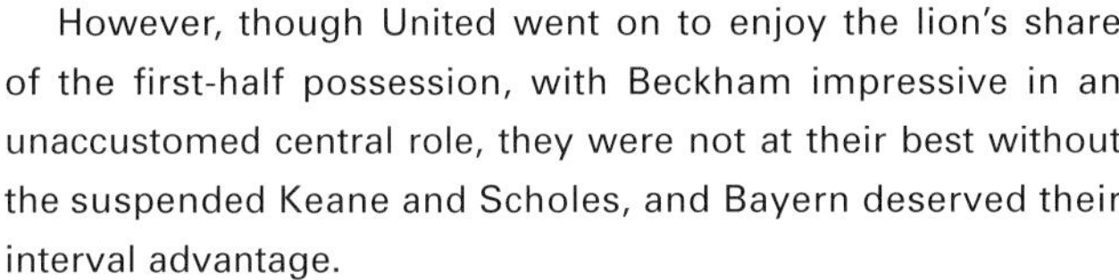

However, though United went on to enjoy the lion's share of the first-half possession, with Beckham impressive in an unaccustomed central role, they were not at their best without the suspended Keane and Scholes, and Bayern deserved their interval advantage.

Thereafter the English Champions laboured energetically but with insufficient penetration, while Bayern looked increasingly composed, and as time began to run out the Reds were hit by a series of counter-attacks. Schmeichel made saves from Effenberg and Scholl, and there were heart-stopping moments when Scholl chipped against a post on 79 minutes and Jancker's overhead volley crashed against the bar five minutes later.

Still United refused to buckle and they mounted desperate pressure which saw chances for Yorke, Sheringham and Solskjaer slip away. All that remained was added time, during which two Beckham corners set up the most astonishing resurrection ever witnessed in a major final. First a mishit Giggs shot ran to Sheringham, who steered the ball just inside a post from close range. Then, with Bayern reeling, the Londoner nodded across goal for Solskjaer to poke an incredible winner into the top corner of Kahn's net.

Manchester United had completed a fantastic treble on the 90th anniversary of Sir Matt Busby's birth. The ultimate footballing fairytale was complete.

Ronny Johnsen celebrates with United's goalscorers and their prize

MAY IN REVIEW

SATURDAY 1	v ASTON VILLA	H	2-1
WEDNESDAY 5	v LIVERPOOL	A	2-2
SATURDAY 8	v MIDDLESBROUGH	A	1-0
WEDNESDAY 12	v BLACKBURN ROVERS	A	0-0
SUNDAY 16	v TOTTENHAM HOTSPUR	H	2-1
SATURDAY 22	v NEWCASTLE UNITED WEMBLEY		2-0
WEDNESDAY 26	v BAYERN MUNICH NOU CAMP STADIUM		2-1

PLAYER IN THE FRAME

Peter Schmeichel

Farewell Peter, and thanks for everything. After overcoming a mid-season blip, the imposing Dane returned to his dominant best in the spring and it was a fitting climax to his majestic Old Trafford career when he led the Red Devils to triumph in the UEFA Champions League Final.

FA CARLING PREMIERSHIP

FINAL TABLE

	P	W	D	L	F	A	Pts
MANCHESTER UNITED	**38**	**22**	**13**	**3**	**80**	**37**	**79**
Arsenal	38	22	12	4	59	17	78
Chelsea	38	20	15	3	57	30	67
Leeds United	38	18	13	7	62	34	67
West Ham United	38	16	9	13	46	53	57
Aston Villa	38	15	10	13	51	46	55
Liverpool	38	15	9	14	68	49	54
Derby County	38	13	13	12	40	45	52
Middlesbrough	38	12	15	11	48	54	51
Leicester City	38	12	13	13	40	46	49
Tottenham Hotspur	38	11	14	13	47	50	47
Sheffield Wednesday	38	13	7	18	41	42	46
Newcastle United	38	11	13	14	48	54	46
Everton	38	11	10	17	42	47	43
Coventry City	38	11	9	18	39	51	42
Wimbledon	38	10	12	16	40	63	42
Southampton	38	11	8	19	37	64	41
Charlton Athletic	38	8	12	18	41	56	36
Blackburn Rovers	38	7	14	17	38	52	35
Nottingham Forest	38	7	9	22	35	69	30

1998–99 Season in Review

If nothing in life is absolutely perfect, Manchester United's latest and greatest campaign came pretty close. Of course, any season which yielded the unprecedented treble of European Cup, League Championship and FA Cup was, by definition, bound to be momentous. Yet sometimes trophies can be accumulated in a clinical manner which is professionally admirable but which neglects to thrill or to enchant. The Red Devils of 1998-99 could never be accused of that.

Their triumphs were achieved through a succession of truly epic contests studded by individual feats of coruscating brilliance, and is fitting for a club of United's unique tradition that their most overwhelming success should coincide with so much unforgettable derring-do. But where to begin? Try those two spellbinding 3-3 draws with Barcelona, titanic FA Cup clashes with Arsenal and Chelsea and, at least until the final stunning act at the Nou Camp, and FA Cup fightback against Liverpool that seemed impossible to outdo.

Gigg's extraordinary effort against the Gunners at Villa Park will live forever in the minds of all those privileged to witness it and for many fans that will remain the supreme highlight. But that is not to ignore a glittering selection of Beckham masterpieces, several sumptuous European interchanges between Yorke and Cole, Solskjaer's 11-minute demolition of Nottingham Forest... space precludes extending the almost endless list of precious moments which queue up to be singled out.

And then there is the manager. Refusing to be distracted by the BSkyB takeover saga, or by the unexpected loss of assistant Brian Kidd, he juggled his massively talented squad with infinite skill, occasionally with downright inspiration, to lead his team to ultimate glory.

Incredibly, within minutes of turning the erstwhile fantasy of the treble into joyous reality, Alex was already looking forward to the next challenge. And, with performers such as Keane, Giggs, Stam, Scholes, Beckham and the rest all either in their prime or on its threshold, the outlook is rosy, indeed.

For now, though, let's just savour the moment. As long as people gather together to kick a football, they will be talking about what Manchester United achieved in 1998-99.

APPEARANCES

substitute appearances shown in parenthesis

- FA CARLING PREMIERSHIP
- WORTHINGTON CUP
- FA CUP
- UEFA CHAMPIONS LEAGUE
- TOTAL

Player	FA Carling Premiership	Worthington Cup	FA Cup	UEFA Champions League	Total
SCHMEICHEL • Peter	34	0	8	13	55
NEVILLE • Gary	34	0	7	12	53
BECKHAM • David	33 (1)	0 (1)	7	12	52 (2)
KEANE • Roy	33 (2)	0	7	12	52 (2)
STAM • Jaap	30	0	6 (1)	13	49 (1)
YORKE • Dwight	32	0	5 (3)	11	48 (3)
IRWIN • Denis	26 (3)	0	6	12	44 (3)
COLE • Andy	26 (6)	0	6 (1)	10	42 (7)
SCHOLES • Paul	24 (7)	0 (1)	3 (3)	10 (2)	37(13)
GIGGS • Ryan	20 (4)	1	5 (1)	9	35 (5)
BUTT • Nicky	22 (9)	2	5	4 (4)	33(13)
NEVILLE • Phil	19 (9)	2	4 (3)	4 (2)	29(14)
BLOMQVIST • Jesper	20 (5)	0 (1)	3 (2)	6 (1)	29 (9)
JOHNSEN • Ronny	19 (3)	1	3 (2)	6 (2)	29 (7)
BERG • Henning	10 (6)	3	5	3 (1)	21 (7)
SOLSKJAER • Ole Gunnar	9(10)	3	4 (4)	1 (5)	17(19)
BROWN • Wesley	11 (3)	0 (1)	2	3 (1)	16 (5)
SHERINGHAM • Teddy	7(10)	1	1 (3)	2 (2)	11(15)
MAY • David	4 (2)	2	1	0	7 (2)
VAN DER GOUW • Raimond	4 (1)	3	0	0	7 (1)
CURTIS • John	1 (3)	3	0	0	4 (3)
GREENING • Jonathan	0 (3)	3	0 (1)	0	3 (4)
CLEGG • Michael	0	3	0	0	3
CRUYFF • Jordi	0 (5)	2	0	0 (3)	2 (8)
WILSON • Mark	0	2	0	0 (1)	2 (1)
MULRYNE • Philip	0	2	0	0	2
NEVLAND • Erik	0	0 (1)	0	0	0 (1)
NOTMAN • Alex	0	0 (1)	0	0	0 (1)
WALLWORK • Ronnie	0	0 (1)	0	0	0 (1)

GOALSCORERS

Player	FA Carling Premiership	Worthington Cup	FA Cup	UEFA Champions League	Total
YORKE • Dwight	18	0	3	8	29
COLE • Andy	17	0	2	5	24
SOLSKJAER • Ole Gunnar	12	3	1	2	18
SCHOLES • Paul	6	0	1	4	11
GIGGS • Ryan	3	0	2	5	10
BECKHAM • David	6	0	1	2	9
KEANE • Roy	2	0	0	3	5
SHERINGHAM • Teddy	2	1	1	1	5
IRWIN • Denis	2	0	1	0	3
JOHNSEN • Ronny	3	0	0	0	3
BUTT • Nicky	2	0	0	0	2
CRUYFF • Jordi	2	0	0	0	2
BLOMQVIST • Jesper	1	0	0	0	1
NEVILLE • Gary	1	0	0	0	1
NEVILLE • Philip	0	0	0	1	1
NEVLAND • Erik	0	1	0	0	1
STAM • Jaap	1	0	0	0	1
SHORT • Craig (Everton)	1 o.g.	0	0	0	1 o.g.
WATSON • Steve (Aston Villa)	1 o.g.	0	0	0	1 o.g.
Total	**80**	**5**	**12**	**31**	**128**

LEAGUE ATTENDANCES 1998-99

Home		Away	
55,316	v Southampton	44,702	v Liverpool
55,270	v Sheffield Wednesday	40,255	v Leeds United
55,265	v Wimbledon	40,079	v Everton
55,216	v Nottingham Forest	39,475	v Sheffield Wednesday
55,198	v Blackburn Rovers	39,241	v Aston Villa
55,193	v Coventry City	38,142	v Arsenal
55,189	v Aston Villa	36,776	v Newcastle United
55,189	v Tottenham Hotspur	36,079	v Tottenham Hotspur
55,182	v Everton	34,741	v Chelsea
55,181	v Liverpool	34,665	v Middlesbrough
55,180	v West Ham United	30,867	v Derby County
55,174	v Derby County	30,436	v Blackburn Rovers
55,174	v Newcastle United	30,025	v Nottingham Forest
55,172	v Leeds United	26,121	v Wimbledon
55,171	v Arsenal	26,039	v West Ham United
55,159	v Chelsea	22,596	v Coventry City
55,152	v Middlesbrough	22,091	v Leicester City
55,147	v Charlton Athletic	20,043	v Charlton Athletic
55,052	v Leicester City	15,251	v Southampton

Home		Away	
Highest	55,316 (Southampton)	Highest	44,702 (Liverpool)
Lowest	55,052 (Leicester City)	Lowest	15,251 (Southampton)
Total	1,048,580	Total	607,624
Average	55,188	Average	31,980

OLD TRAFFORD ATTENDANCES

League & Cup

Total 1,675,628

Average 54,052

Includes: 19 FA Carling Premiership games
4 FA Cup
2 Worthington Cup
6 UEFA Champions League

SUMMARY

It's been a long time since a friendly match generated so much interest and excitement at Old Trafford.

Not since the series of challenge games against the great Real Madrid in the early sixties had Old Trafford witnessed a 'European Night' atmosphere for a non-competitive game.

But this was no ordinary friendly, this was the night that Eric Cantona, the greatest Manchester United player of modern times, came back to pay homage to his adoring fans and to those who suffered in the Munich Air Disaster.

The match was staged primarily to provide funds for the Munich Memorial Fund but it also turned into an occasion of mutual appreciation for Cantona and the multitude of fans who idolised him during his five and half years at the club.

The evening ended with United 8-4 winners, but the score didn't really matter. United's faithful had seen their hero in a red shirt again, (he played one half for the European XI and the other for United), and they all went home at the end of the night with a whole new store of memories to cherish.

United fulfilled just one other friendly fixture during the season and that was one which manager Alex Ferguson enjoyed immensely. It gave him the chance to return to Pittodrie and pay tribute to Teddy Scott, one of Aberdeen's greatest servants.

United's manager had long promised his old friend that he would take a full strength team to play the Dons in his testimonial. Alex Ferguson, as ever, was true to his word.

The game concluded with each side having scored once, but Aberdeen took the honours by winning the subsequent penalty shoot-out.

However, this was another evening when the result mattered little. Ferguson had kept his promise and everyone, particularly Teddy Scott had a night to remember.

First Team Friendlies

names in bold indicate goalscorers

Saturday 25 July 1998 **v BIRMINGHAM CITY (away) • Attendance 20,708 • Lost 3-4**

Culkin • Curtis • Neville P. • Wallwork • May • Irwin
Mulryne 3 (1 pen) • Butt • Cole • Cruyff • Giggs
Substitutes: Twiss (for Irwin) • Wilson (for Cruyff) • Ford (for Mulryne) • Notman (for Cole)

PRE-SEASON TOUR – SCANDINAVIA

Monday 27 July 1998 **v VALERENGA IF (Norway) • Attendance 19,700 • Drawn: 2-2**

Schmeichel • Neville G. • Neville P. • Berg • Johnsen • Keane
Beckham • Butt • **Solskjaer** • **Scholes** • Giggs
*Substitutes: Irwin (for Butt) • Culkin • May • Sheringham (for Scholes) • Cole (for Keane)
Cruyff (for Giggs) • Stam • Curtis (for Beckham)*

Friday 31 July 1998 **v BRONDBY IF (Denmark) • Attendance 27,022 • Won: 6-0**

Schmeichel • Neville G. • Irwin • Keane • Johnsen • Stam
Beckham • **Scholes** • Solskjaer • **Sheringham 2** • Giggs
Substitutes: Neville P. • Culkin • Berg (for Stam) • Butt (for Beckham)
Cole 2 *(for Solskjaer) •* ***Cruyff*** *(for Sheringham) • Curtis (for Johnsen)*

Tuesday 4 August 1998 **v SK BRANN (Norway) • Attendance 16,100 • Won: 4-0**

Schmeichel • Curtis • **Irwin 3 (2 pens)** • Keane • Berg • Stam
Neville P. • Butt • **Cole** • Scholes • Solskjaer
*Substitutes: Johnsen • Culkin (for Schmeichel) • May (for Berg) • Sheringham
(for Scholes) • Beckham (for Solskjaer) • Neville G. • Cruyff (for Keane) • Giggs*

FA CHARITY SHIELD

v ARSENAL (Wembley) • Attendance: 67,342 • Lost: 0-3

Sunday 9 August 1998

Schmeichel • Neville G. • Irwin • Keane • Johnsen • Stam
Beckham • Butt • Cole • Scholes • Giggs
Substitutes: May • Sheringham (for Cole) • Neville P. (for Scholes) • Cruyff (for Giggs)
Solskjaer (for Butt) • Berg (for Keane) • Culkin

MUNICH MEMORIAL MATCH

v ERIC CANTONA EUROPEAN XI (home) • Attendance: 55,210 • Won: 8-4

Tuesday 18 August 1998

Culkin • Neville G. • **Neville P.** • May • Brown • Keane
Beckham • **Butt** • Sheringham • **Scholes** • **Giggs**
*Substitutes: **Cantona** (for Scholes) • Gibson (for Culkin) • Casper (for May)*
Cruyff *(for Giggs) •* ***Notman 2*** *(for Sheringham) • Greening (for Beckham)*
Higginbotham (for Keane) • Clegg (for Neville G.)

TEDDY SCOTT TESTIMONIAL

v ABERDEEN (away) • Drawn 1-1*

Monday 18 January 1999

Schmeichel • Neville P. • Irwin • May • **Johnsen** • Butt
Beckham • Scholes • Cole • Solskjaer • Giggs
Substitutes: Yorke (for Cole) • van der Gouw • Greening (for Beckham)
Blomqvist (for Giggs) • Mulryne • Berg • Curtis (for Irwin) • Brown (for May)
*** Lost 7-6 on penalties**
Penalty scorers: **Neville P. • Butt • Scholes • Solskjaer • Yorke • Greening**

DAVID BECKHAM

Position: midfielder
Born: Leytonstone, 2 May 1975
Height: 6ft **Weight:** 11st 9lb
Signed trainee: 8 July 1991
Signed professional: 23 January 1993
Other club: Preston North End (loan)
Senior United debut: 23 September 1992 v Brighton at the Goldstone Ground (League Cup, substitute for Andrei Kanchelskis)
United record: League: 128 (16) games, 30 goals; FA Cup: 16 (2) games, 5 goals; League Cup: 5 (2) games, 0 goals; Europe: 33 games, 5 goals
Total: 182 (20) games, 40 goals
Full international: England
In 1998-99: confronted by constant moronic abuse in the wake of his World Cup dismissal, David coped admirably, demonstrating remarkable strength of character and single-mindedness. As the season wore on he displayed some of the most devastating form of his career, with his crossing, in particular, attaining new heights of excellence.

HENNING BERG

Position: defender
Born: Eidsvoll, Norway, 1 September 1969
Height: 6ft **Weight:** 12st 1lb
Transferred: from Blackburn Rovers, 11 August 1997
Other clubs: Valerengen IF, Lillestrom, Blackburn Rovers
Senior United debut: 13 August 1997 v Southampton at Old Trafford (League, substitute for Ronny Johnsen)
United record: League: 33 (10) games, 1 goal; FA Cup: 7 games, 0 goals; League Cup: 3 games, 0 goals; Europe: 8 (3) games, 1 goal
Total: 51 (13) games, 2 goals
Full international: Norway
In 1998-99: probably for the first time, and for a frustratingly short period, United fans saw the best of the Norwegian central defender. Finally free from fitness problems, Henning compiled an impressive sequence of performances in the New Year, establishing a splendid partnership with Jaap Stam, only to fall prey to injury once again.

JESPER BLOMQVIST

Position: forward
Born: Tavelsjo, Sweden, 5 February 1974
Height: 5ft 9in **Weight**: 11st 3lb
Transferred: from Parma, 21 July 1998
Other clubs: Tavelsjo IK, Umea, IFK Gothenburg, AC Milan, Parma
Senior United debut: 9 September 1998 v Charlton Athletic at Old Trafford (League)
United record: League: 20 (5) games, 1 goal; FA Cup: 3 (2) games, 0 goals; League Cup: 0 (1) game, 0 goals; Europe: 6 (1) games, 0 goals
Total: 29 (9) games, 1 goal
Full international: Sweden
In 1998-99: Jesper is brimming with ability and he can be satisfied with his first term at Old Trafford, though he has not yet revealed his full potential. The left-sided Swede has been hampered by a niggling foot injury and his opportunities have been limited by Ryan Giggs, but he has offered much-needed balance when the Welshman has been absent.

WESLEY BROWN

Position: defender
Born: Manchester, 13 October 1979
Height: 6ft 1in **Weight**: 11st 11lb
Signed trainee: 8 July 1996
Signed professional: 4 November 1996
Senior United debut: 4 May 1998 v Leeds United at Old Trafford (League, substitute for David May)
United record: League: 12 (4) games, 0 goals; FA Cup: 2 games, 0 goals; League Cup: 0 (1) game, 0 goals; Europe: 3 (1) games, 0 goals
Total: 17 (6) games, 0 goals
Full international: England
In 1998-99: emerged as the find of the season, his meteoric rise being marked by full England recognition. Wesley is stylish, pacy and remarkably composed for a player of his tender years and there appears no limit to his horizons. Played most of his games at right-back, but is a natural centre-half who seems an ideal long-term partner for Jaap Stam.

NICKY BUTT

Position: midfielder
Born: Manchester, 21 January 1975
Height: 5ft 10 in **Weight:** 11st 5lb
Signed trainee: 8 July 1991
Signed professional: 23 January 1993
Senior United debut: 21 November 1992 v Oldham Athletic at Old Trafford (League, substitute for Paul Ince)
United record: League: 119 (27) games, 13 goals; FA Cup: 16 (2) games, 1 goal; League Cup: 5 games, 0 goals; Europe: 26 (6) games, 0 goals
Total: 166 (35) games, 14 goals
Full international: England
In 1998-99: his characteristic enthusiasm, industry and burning desire to win have been bolstered by improved range of passing and more mature reading of the game. Sometimes excluded from the side in favour of Paul Scholes, nevertheless he has been a crucially important contributor, especially when Roy Keane has been absent.

MICHAEL CLEGG

Position: defender
Born: Ashton-under-Lyne, 3 July 1977
Height: 5ft 8in **Weight:** 11st 10lb
Signed trainee: 5 July 1993
Signed professional: 1 July 1995
Senior United debut: 23 November 1996 v Middlesbrough at Riverside Stadium (League)
United record: League: 4 (3) games, 0 goals; FA Cup: 3 (1) games, 0 goals; League Cup: 4 games, 0 goals; Europe: 0 (1) games, 0 goals
Total: 11 (5) games, 0 goals
In 1998-99: a fiercely committed competitor, Michael passed a season of consolidation in the reserve ranks, from which he stepped up only for League Cup outings.

ANDY COLE

Position: forward
Born: Nottingham, 15 October 1971
Height: 5ft 10in **Weight:** 12st 4lb
Transferred: from Newcastle United, 12 January 1995.
Other clubs: Arsenal, Fulham (loan), Bristol City, Newcastle United
Senior United debut: 22 January 1995 v Blackburn Rovers at Old Trafford (League)
United record: League: 116 (21) games, 61 goals; FA Cup: 18 (2) games, 9 goals; League Cup: 2 games, 0 goals; Europe: 19 (4) games, 11 goals
Total: 155 (27) games, 81 goals
Full international: England
In 1998-99: Andy fully justified the continuing faith of his manager and revelled in his new partnership with Dwight Yorke. Few defences could successfully counter his movement and his strike rate continued to be outstanding. His glorious title-winner against Tottenham Hotspur finally laid to rest the memory of his Upton Park misses in 1995.

JORDI CRUYFF

Position: forward
Born: Amsterdam, 9 February 1974
Height: 6ft 1in **Weight:** 10st 12lb
Transferred: from Barcelona, 8 August 1996
Other clubs: Ajax, Barcelona, Celta Vigo (loan).
Senior United debut: 17 August 1996 v Wimbledon at Selhurst Park (League).
United record: League: 14 (12) games, 5 goals; FA Cup: 0 (1) games, 0 goals; League Cup: 4 games, 0 goals; Europe: 3 (4) games, 0 goals
Total: 21 (17) games, 5 goals
Full international: Holland
In 1998-99: when fully fit Jordi proved himself a valuable member of the squad, contributing fine goals at Southampton and Derby. But so hot was the competition for places at Old Trafford that he accepted a loan spell with the high-riding Spanish club, Celta Vigo, thus missing out on United's treble bid.

JOHN CURTIS

Position: defender
Born: Nuneaton, 3 September 1978
Height: 5ft 10in **Weight:** 11st 7lb
Signed trainee: 10 July 1995
Signed professional: 23 September 1995
Senior United debut: 14 October 1997 v Ipswich Town at Portman Road (League Cup)
United record: League: 4 (8) games, 0 goals; FA Cup: 0 games, 0 goals; League Cup: 4 games, 0 goals; Europe: 0 games, 0 goals
Total: 8 (8) games, 0 goals
In 1998-99: provided defensive strength in depth though not often called upon for senior duty. But John is young and hugely talented, and his future remains immensely promising.

RYAN GIGGS

Position: forward
Born: Cardiff, 29 November 1973
Height: 5ft 11in **Weight:** 10st 10lb
Signed trainee: 9 July 1990
Signed professional: 29 November 1990
Senior United debut: 2 March 1991 v Everton at Old Trafford (League, substitute for Denis Irwin)
United record: League: 237 (23) games, 53 goals; FA Cup: 34 (3) games, 7 goals; League Cup: 17 (4) games, 6 goals; Europe: 31 (1) games, 10 goals
Total: 319 (31) games, 76 goals
Full international: Wales
In 1998-99: Ryan touched peaks of incandescent brilliance, notably with his unforgettable FA Cup semi-final replay goal against Arsenal. He is a magnificent team performer, too, harnessing the work ethic to breathtaking skills and the versatility to play in any midfield or forward position.

JONATHAN GREENING

Position: forward or midfielder

Born: Scarborough, 2 January 1979

Height: 6ft **Weight:** 11st 3lb

Transferred: from York City, 24 March 1998

Senior United debut: 28 October 1998 v Bury at Old Trafford (League Cup)

United record: League: 0 (3) games, 0 goals; FA Cup: 0 (1) game, 0 goals; League Cup: 3 games, 0 goals; Europe: 0 games, 0 goals

Total: 3 (4) games, 0 goals

In 1998-99: showed why United were so keen to sign him after he had made only a handful of starts for York City. Jonathan has pace and skill, verve and confidence, and it would be a surprise if he did not make the grade as a Red Devil.

DANNY HIGGINBOTHAM

Position: defender

Born: Manchester, 29 December 1978

Height: 6ft 1in **Weight:** 12st 3lb

Signed trainee: 10 July 1995

Signed professional: 1 July 1997

Other club: Royal Antwerp (loan)

Senior United debut: 10 May 1998 v Barnsley at Oakwell (League, substitute for Michael Clegg)

United record: League: 0 (1) game, 0 goals; FA Cup: 0 (0) games, 0 goals; League Cup: 0 games, 0 goals; Europe: 0 games, 0 goals

Total: 0 (1) game, 0 goals

In 1998-99: played all his senior football for Royal Antwerp in Belgium, honing his abilities in a highly competitive league.

DENIS IRWIN

Position: defender

Born: Cork, 31 October 1965

Height: 5ft 8in **Weight:** 10st 10lb

Transferred: from Oldham Athletic, 8 June 1990

Other clubs: Leeds United, Oldham Athletic

Senior United debut: 25 August 1990 v Coventry City at Old Trafford (League)

United record: League: 301 (9) games, 19 goals; FA Cup: 41 (1) games, 7 goals; League Cup: 28 (3) games, 0 goals; Europe: 45 (0) games, 2 goals

Total: 415 (13) games, 28 goals

Full international: Republic of Ireland

In 1998-99: though he passed his 33rd birthday during the campaign, Denis showed no sign of declining standards, keeping a bevy of young would-be replacements at bay. Both his defensive work and his attacking overlaps were as telling as ever and the Irishman remains a model professional in every respect.

RONNY JOHNSEN

Position: defender or midfielder

Born: Sandefjord, Norway, 10 June 1969

Height: 6ft 3in **Weight:** 13st 2lb

Transferred: from Besiktas, 10 July 1996

Other clubs: Stokke, EIK-Tonsberg, Lyn Oslo, Lillestrom, Besiktas

Senior United debut: 17 August 1996 v Wimbledon at Selhurst Park (League, substitute for Nicky Butt)

United record: League: 63 (12) games, 5 goals; FA Cup: 8 (2) games, 1 goals; League Cup: 2 (0) games, 0 goals; Europe: 20 (2) games, 0 goals

Total: 93 (16) games, 6 goals

Full international: Norway

In 1998-99: since his signing the athletic Norwegian has established an enviable reputation as a high-quality central defender, quick, alert and decisive. In addition, he can double as a midfielder. Stymied by injuries early in season but came back well.

ROY KEANE

Position: midfielder
Born: Cork, 10 August 1971
Height: 5ft 11in **Weight:** 12st 1lb
Transferred: from Nottingham Forest, 19 July 1993
Other clubs: Cobh Ramblers, Nottingham Forest
Senior United debut: 15 August 1993 v Norwich City at Carrow Road (League)
United record: League: 149 (7) games, 19 goals; FA Cup: 29 (1) games, 1 goal; League Cup: 9 (2) games, 0 goals; Europe: 28 (0) games, 6 goals
Total: 215 (10) games, 26 goals
Full international: Republic of Ireland
In 1998-99: no superlative is adequate to convey the scale of Roy's input. The skipper cut an inspirational figure, frequently lifting his side as if by sheer force of will, never more memorably than in Turin when the odds were stacked against United. He takes his place as one of the finest footballers in Old Trafford history.

DAVID MAY

Position: defender
Born: Oldham, 24 June 1970
Height: 6ft **Weight:** 13st 5lb
Transferred: from Blackburn Rovers, 1 July 1994
Other club: Blackburn Rovers
Senior United debut: 20 August 1994 v Queen's Park Rangers at Old Trafford (League)
United record: League: 65 (14) games, 6 goals; FA Cup: 6 (0) games, 0 goals; League Cup: 7 (0) games, 1 goal; Europe: 11 (1) games, 1 goal
Total: 89 (15) games, 8 goals
In 1998-99: sidelined by a combination of injuries and the superb form of colleagues for most of the campaign, David bounced back when he was needed in the spring, performing purposefully and reliably during the title run-in. Combative in the air and a formidable tackler, the blond Lancastrian remains an important asset.

GARY NEVILLE

Position: defender
Born: Bury, 18 February 1975
Height: 5ft 11in **Weight:** 12st 7lb
Signed trainee: 8 July 1991
Signed professional: 23 January 1993
Senior United debut: 16 September 1992 v Torpedo Moscow at Old Trafford (UEFA Cup, substitute for Lee Martin)
United record: League: 145 (4) games, 2 goals; FA Cup: 21 (2) games, 0 goals; League Cup: 4 (1) games, 0 goals; Europe: 32 (3) games, 0 goals
Total: 202 (10) games, 2 goals
Full international: England
In 1998-99: though his customary metronomic consistency was marred by the occasional uncharacteristic error, Gary consolidated his stature as an international-class defender. Spent most of the season at right-back but also excelled in central defence at times, notably when marking Liverpool's Michael Owen at Old Trafford in September.

PHIL NEVILLE

Position: defender or midfielder
Born: Bury, 21 January 1977
Height: 5ft 11in **Weight:** 11st 11lb
Signed trainee: 5 July 1993
Signed professional: 1 June 1994
Senior United debut: 28 January 1995 v Wrexham at Old Trafford (FA Cup)
United record: League: 80 (22) games, 1 goal; FA Cup: 14 (4) games, 0 goals; League Cup: 5 (1) games, 0 goals; Europe: 12 (6) games, 1 goal
Total: 111 (33) games, 2 goals
Full international: England
In 1998-99: his confidence seemed visibly jolted by his omission from England's final party for the World Cup Finals in France, and thereafter his game took several months to pick up. But come the spring Phil was close to his best again, whether operating at left-back or in midfield, though frequently he was used as a substitute.

ERIK NEVLAND

Position: forward

Born: Stavanger, Norway, 10 November 1977

Height: 5ft 10in **Weight:** 11st 12lb

Transferred: from Viking Stavanger, 2 July 1997

Other clubs: Viking Stavanger, IFK Gothenburg (loan)

Senior United debut: 14 October 1997 v Ipswich Town at Portman Road (League Cup, substitute for Philip Mulryne)

United record: League: 0 (1) game, 0 goals; FA Cup: 2 (1) games, 0 goals; League Cup: 0 (2) games, 1 goal; Europe: 0 (0) games, 0 goals

Total: 2 (4) games, 1 goal

In 1998-99: with so many strikers ahead of him in the Old Trafford pecking order, Erik received few senior opportunities and will have benefited from his extended loan stint with Swedish club, IFK Gothenburg.

ALEX NOTMAN

Position: forward

Born: Edinburgh, 10 December 1979

Height: 5ft 7in **Weight:** 10st 11lb

Signed trainee: 10 December 1995

Signed professional: 17 December 1996

Other clubs: Aberdeen (loan)

Senior United debut: 2 December 1998 v Tottenham Hotspur at White Hart Lane (League Cup, substitute for Nicky Butt)

United record: League: 0 (0) games, 0 goals; FA Cup: 0 (0) games, 0 goals; League Cup: 0 (1) games, 0 goals; Europe: 0 (0) games, 0 goals

Total: 0 (1) games, 0 goals

In 1998-99: made a favourable impression in his only senior outing, showing enterprise and courage in difficult circumstances at White Hart Lane, before completing the season on loan at Aberdeen.

PAUL SCHOLES

Position: midfielder or forward
Born: Salford, 16 November 1974
Height: 5ft 7in **Weight:** 11st 8lb
Signed trainee: 8 July 1991
Signed professional: 23 January 1993
Senior United debut: 21 September 1994 v Port Vale (away, League Cup)
United record: League: 90 (39) games, 32 goals; FA Cup: 8 (7) games, 4 goals; League Cup: 6 (2) games, 5 goals; Europe: 17 (10) games, 7 goals
Total: 121 (58) games, 48 goals
Full international: England
In 1998-99: after shining in the World Cup Finals, Paul enjoyed another highly influential domestic campaign, even if it seemed easier, at times, for him to claim a regular berth with England than with United. He has matured into a compelling all-rounder who combines heart with inspiration and continues to chip in with priceless goals.

TEDDY SHERINGHAM

Position: forward
Born: Highams Park, 2 April 1966
Height: 6ft **Weight:** 13st
Transferred: from Tottenham Hotspur, 27 June 1997
Other clubs: Millwall, Aldershot (loan), Djurgaarden (loan), Nottingham Forest, Tottenham Hotspur
Senior United debut: 10 August 1997 v Tottenham Hotspur at White Hart Lane (League)
United record: League: 35 (13) games, 11 goals; FA Cup: 3 (4) games, 4 goals; League Cup: 1 (0) game, 1 goal; Europe: 9 (2) games, 3 goals
Total: 48 (19) games, 19 goals
Full international: England
In 1998-99: suffered a good deal of frustration while waiting in the wings, and injuries did not help the Londoner's cause. But he did make a significant contribution to the campaign, particularly during the breathtaking finale, bringing intelligence, creativity and height to the attack. And no one looked more joyous when the title medals were presented!

OLE GUNNAR SOLSKJAER

Position: forward
Born: Kristiansund, Norway, 26 February 1973
Height: 5ft 10in **Weight**: 11st 6lb
Transferred: from Molde, 29 July 1996
Other clubs: Clausenengen FK, Molde
Senior United debut: 25 August 1996 v Blackburn Rovers at Old Trafford (League, substitute for David May)
United record: League: 49 (25) games, 36 goals; FA Cup: 5 (8) games, 3 goals; League Cup: 3 (0) games, 3 goals; Europe: 12 (10) games, 4 goals
Total: 69 (43) games, 46 goals
Full international: Norway
In 1998-99: showed his commitment to the Old Trafford cause by turning down a move to Tottenham, then paraded his talents to the tune of 17 goals despite making only 16 starts. Ole remains one of the deadliest marksmen in the land and would be a first-team regular at practically any other club. A massive asset and an enduringly popular figure.

JAAP STAM

Position: defender
Born: Kampen, Holland, 17 July 1972
Height: 6ft 3in **Weight**: 13st 9lb
Transferred: from PSV Eindhoven, 1 July 1998
Other clubs: Dos Kampen, FC Zwolle, Cambuur Leeuwarden, Willem II, PSV Eindhoven
Senior United debut: 12 August 1998 v LKS Lodz at Old Trafford (Champions League)
United record: League: 30 (0) games, 1 goal; FA Cup: 6 (1) games, 0 goals; League Cup: 0 (0) games, 0 goals; Europe: 13 (0) games, 0 goals
Total: 49 (1) games, 1 goal
Full international: Holland
In 1998-99: after his arrival as the world's most expensive defender, Jaap needed a little time to adjust to the frenetic pace of the English game, and was pilloried in some quarters. Soon, though, he emerged as a veritable colossus, his speed and strength matched by his skill and composure, and his dominance was crucial to United's success.

MICHAEL TWISS

Position: midfielder

Born: Salford, 26 December 1977

Height: 5ft 11in **Weight:** 12st 8lb

Signed trainee: 11 July 1994

Signed professional: 1 July 1996

Other club: Sheffield United (loan)

Senior United debut: 25 February 1998 v Barnsley at Oakwell (FA Cup, substitute for Michael Clegg)

United record: League: 0 (0) games, 0 goals; FA Cup: 0 (1) games, 0 goals; League Cup: 0 (0) games, 0 goals; Europe: 0 (0) games, 0 goals

Total: 0 (1) game, 0 goals

In 1998-99: widened his experience with a loan spell under the tutelage of Steve Bruce at Sheffield United. The benefits should become evident in 1999-2000.

RAIMOND VAN DER GOUW

Position: goalkeeper

Born: Oldenzaal, Holland, 24 March 1963

Height: 6ft 3in **Weight:** 13st 7lb

Transferred: from Vitesse Arnhem, 1 July 1996

Other clubs: Go Ahead Eagles, Vitesse Arnhem

Senior United debut: 21 September 1996 v Aston Villa at Villa Park (League)

United record: League: 10 (2) games, 0 goals ; FA Cup: 0 (0) games, 0 goals; League Cup: 6 (0) games, 0 goals; Europe: 2 (0) games, 0 goals

Total: 18 (2) games, 0 goals

In 1998-99: successfully combined his dual roles as goalkeeping coach and understudy to Peter Schmeichel. Cool, classy and safe, Raimond was rated so highly by Alex Ferguson that the Dane was dispatched for a mid-term holiday and the team did not suffer.

RONNIE WALLWORK

Position: defender
Born: Manchester, 10 September 1977
Height: 5ft 10in **Weight:** 12st 12lb
Signed trainee: 11 July 1994
Signed professional: 17 March 1995
Other clubs: Carlisle United (loan), Stockport County (loan), Royal Antwerp (loan)
Senior United debut: 25 October 1997 v Barnsley at Old Trafford (League, substitute for Gary Pallister)
United record: League: 0 (1) games, 0 goals ; FA Cup: 0 (0) games, 0 goals; League Cup: 0 (1) games, 0 goals; Europe: 0 (0) games, 0 goals
Total: 0 (2) games, 0 goals
In 1998-99: found himself in a lengthy queue of central defenders, and joined Danny Higginbotham on loan to Royal Antwerp.

MARK WILSON

Position: midfielder
Born: Scunthorpe, 9 February 1979
Height: 6ft **Weight:** 13st 2lb
Signed trainee: 10 July 1995
Signed professional: 9 February 1996
Other club: Wrexham (loan)
Senior United debut: 21 October 1998 v Brondby at the Parken Stadium (Champions League, substitute for Dwight Yorke)
United record: League: 0 (0) games, 0 goals ; FA Cup: 0 (0) games, 0 goals; League Cup: 2 (0) games, 0 goals; Europe: 0 (1) games, 0 goals
Total: 2 (1) games, 0 goals
In 1998-99: emerged as a hugely promising prospect, both industrious and imaginative, and he slotted seamlessly into United's flowing style.

DWIGHT YORKE

Position: forward
Born: Canaan, Tobago, 3 November 1971
Height: 5ft 10in **Weight:** 12st 4lb
Transferred: from Aston Villa, 28 August 1998
Senior United debut: 22 August 1998 v West Ham United at Upton Park (League)
United record: League: 32 (0) games, 18 goals ; FA Cup: 5 (3) games, 3 goals; League Cup: 0 (0) games, 0 goals; Europe: 11 (0) games, 8 goals
Total: 48 (3) games, 29 goals
Full international: Trinidad and Tobago
In 1998-99: countless pundits wrote him off as over-priced, but Dwight answered them in the most eloquent manner imaginable. He scored freely, offered a perceptive link between midfield and attack and established a bountiful partnership with Andy Cole. Gave the team a new dimension and, through his ebullient personality, promoted a much-needed feelgood factor, too.

YOUNG PROFESSIONALS

LUKE CHADWICK

Position: forward
Birthdate: 18 November 1980
Birthplace: Cambridge
Height: 5ft 1in
Weight: 10st 9lb
Signed trainee: 30 June 1997
Signed professional: 5 February 1999

GEORGE CLEGG

Position: forward
Birthdate: 16 November 1980
Birthplace: Manchester
Height: 5ft 10in
Weight: 11st 2lb
Signed trainee: 30 June 1997
Signed professional: 1 July 1999

STEPHEN COSGROVE

Position: midfield
Birthdate: 29 December 1980
Birthplace: Glasgow
Height: 5ft 9in
Weight: 10st 5lb
Signed trainee: 30 June 1997
Signed professional: 1 July 1998

NICK CULKIN

Position: goalkeeper
Birthdate: 6 July 1978
Birthplace: York
Height: 6ft 2in
Weight: 13st 5lb
Transferred: from York City 25 September 1995

BOJAN DJORDIC

Position: midfield
Birthdate: 6 February 1982
Birthplace: Belgrade, Yugoslavia
Height: not known
Weight: not known
Signed professional: 17 February 1999

WAYNE EVANS

Position: midfield
Birthdate: 23 October 1980
Birthplace: Carmarthen
Height: 5ft 9in
Weight: 9st 12lb
Signed trainee: 30 June 1997

RYAN FORD

Position: midfield
Birthdate: 3 September 1978
Birthplace: Worksop
Height: 5ft 9in
Weight: 10st 4lb
Signed trainee: 10 July 1995
Signed professional: 1 July 1997

IAN FITZPATRICK

Position: forward
Birthdate: 22 September 1980
Birthplace: Manchester
Height: 5ft 9in
Weight: 10st
Signed trainee: 30 June 1997
Signed professional: 1 July 1998

DAVID HEALY

Position: forward
Birthdate: 5 August 1979
Birthplace: Downpatrick
Height: 5ft 8in
Weight: 10st 9lb
Signed trainee: 8 July 1996
Signed professional: 24 November 1997

KIRK HILTON

Position: defender
Birthdate: 2 April 1981
Birthplace: Flixton
Height: 5ft 6in
Weight: 9st 12lb
Signed trainee: 30 June 1997
Signed professional: 1 July 1999

JOSHUA HOWARD

Position: midfield
Birthdate: 15 November 1980
Birthplace: Ashton-under-Lyne
Height: 5ft 8in
Weight: 9st 10lb
Signed trainee: 30 June 1997
Signed professional: 1 July 1999

ALAN McDERMOTT

Position: defender
Birthdate: 22 January 1982
Birthplace: Dublin
Height: 6ft 1in
Weight: 11st 13lb
Signed trainee: 6 July 1998
Signed professional: 22 January 1999

ALLAN MARSH

Position: goalkeeper
Birthdate: 10 September 1980
Birthplace: Wigan
Height: 6ft 0in
Weight: 11st
Signed trainee: 30 June 1997
Signed professional: 1 July 1999

JOHN O'SHEA

Position: defender
Birthdate: 30 April 1981
Birthplace: Waterford
Height: 6ft 3in
Weight: 11st 12lb
Signed professional: 3 August 1998

PAUL RACHUBKA

Position: goalkeeper
Birthdate: 21 May 1981
Birthplace: San Luis Obispo, California
Height: 6ft 1in
Weight: 13st 5lb
Signed trainee: 30 June 1997
Signed professional: 1 July 1999

LEE ROCHE

Position: defender
Birthdate: 28 October 1980
Birthplace: Bolton
Height: 5ft 10in
Weight: 10st 11lb
Signed trainee: 30 June 1997
Signed professional: 5 February 1999

STEPHEN ROSE

Position: defender
Birthdate: 23 November 1980
Birthplace: Salford
Height: 5ft 11in
Weight: 10st 10lb
Signed trainee: 30 June 1997
Signed professional: 1 July 1999

MICHAEL STEWART

Position: midfield
Birthdate: 26 February 1981
Birthplace: Edinburgh
Height: 5ft 11in
Weight: 11st 6lb
Signed trainee: 30 June 1997
Signed professional: 13 March 1998

GARETH STRANGE

Position: midfield
Birthdate: 3 October 1981
Birthplace: Bolton
Height: 5ft 9in
Weight: 10st 9lb
Signed trainee: 6 July 1998
Signed professional: 3 October 1998

DOMINIC STUDLEY

Position: defender
Birthdate: 9 October 1980
Birthplace: Manchester
Height: 5ft 5in
Weight: 9st 8lb
Signed trainee: 30 June 1997
Signed professional: 1 July 1999

PAUL TEATHER

Position: defender
Birthdate: 28 December 1977
Birthplace: Rotherham
Height: 6ft
Weight: 11st 8lb
Signed trainee: 11 July 1994
Signed professional: 29 December 1994

JOHN THORRINGTON

Position: forward
Birthdate: 17 October 1979
Birthplace: Johannesburg, South Africa
Height: 5ft 7in
Weight: 10st 5lb
Signed professional: 15 September 1997

DANNY WEBBER

Position: forward
Birthdate: 28 December 1981
Birthplace: Manchester
Height: 5ft 9in
Weight: 10st 3lb
Signed trainee: 6 July 1998
Signed professional: 28 December 1998

RICHARD WELLENS

Position: midfield
Birthdate: 26 March 1980
Birthplace: Manchester
Height: 5ft 9in
Weight: 11st 5lb
Signed trainee: 8 July 1996
Signed professional: 12 May 1997

PAUL WHEATCROFT

Position: forward
Birthdate: 22 November 1980
Birthplace: Manchester
Height: 5ft 8in
Weight: 9st 9lb
Signed trainee: 30 June 1997
Signed professional: 1 July 1998

JAMIE WOOD

Position: forward
Birthdate: 21 September 1978
Birthplace: Salford
Height: 5ft 10in
Weight: 12st 11lb
Signed trainee: 10 July 1995
Signed professional: 1 July 1997

TRAINEE PROFESSIONALS 1999-2000

SECOND YEAR

Name	Position	Birthdate	Birthplace	Date Signed
James DAVIS	forward	6 February 1982	Bromsgrove	6 July 1998
Ashley DODD	midfield	7 January 1982	Stafford	6 July 1998
Kevin GROGAN	midfield	15 November 1981	Dublin	6 July 1998
Rhodri JONES	defender	19 January 1982	Cardiff	6 July 1998
Mark LYNCH	defender	2 September 1981	Manchester	6 July 1998
Eric MOLLOY	forward	21 December 1981	Galway	2 March 1998
Michael ROSE	defender	28 July 1982	Salford	6 July 1998
Mark STUDLEY	defender	27 December 1981	Manchester	6 July 1998
Marek SZMID	defender	2 March 1982	Nuneaton	6 July 1998
Joshua WALKER	midfield	20 December 1981	Birmingham	6 July 1998

FIRST YEAR

Name	Position	Birthdate	Birthplace	Date Signed
Ben CLARK	defender	24 January 1983	Shotley Bridge	5 July 1999
Steven CLEGG	defender	16 April 1982	Ashton-under-Lyne	5 July 1999
Craig COATES	forward	26 October 1982	Dryburn	5 July 1999
David MORAN	goalkeeper	21 January 1983	Ballinasloe	5 July 1999
Ben MUIRHEAD	forward	5 January 1983	Doncaster	5 July 1999
Daniel NARDIELLO	forward	22 October 1982	Coventry	5 July 1999
Daniel PUGH	midfield	19 October 1982	Manchester	5 July 1999
John RANKIN	midfield	27 June 1983	Bellshill	5 July 1999
Gary SAMPSON	midfield	13 September 1982	Manchester	5 July 1999
Alan TATE	defender	2 September 1982	Easington	5 July 1999
Andrew TAYLOR	midfield	17 September 1982	Exeter	5 July 1999
Paul TIERNEY	midfield	15 September 1982	Salford	5 July 1999
Marc WHITEMAN	forward	1 October 1982	St Hellier	5 July 1999
Matthew WILLIAMS	forward	5 November 1982	St Asaph	5 July 1999
Neil WOOD	forward	4 January 1983	Manchester	5 July 1999

DEPARTURES 1998-99

Russell BEST*	released	8 October 1998
Grant BREBNER	to Reading	12 June 1998
Chris CASPER	to Reading	4 November 1998
Terry COOKE	to Manchester City	16 April 1999
Gerard GAFF	released	30 June 1999
Paul GIBSON	to Notts County	25 March 1999
Jason HICKSON	released	30 June 1999
Philip MULRYNE	to Norwich City	25 March 1999
Gary PALLISTER	to Middlesbrough	17 July 1998
Michael RYAN	free transfer	24 March 1999
Peter SCHMEICHEL		
Ben THORNLEY	to Huddersfield Town	1 July 1998
Lee WHITELEY	released	30 June 1999

** Signed professional 8th July 1998*

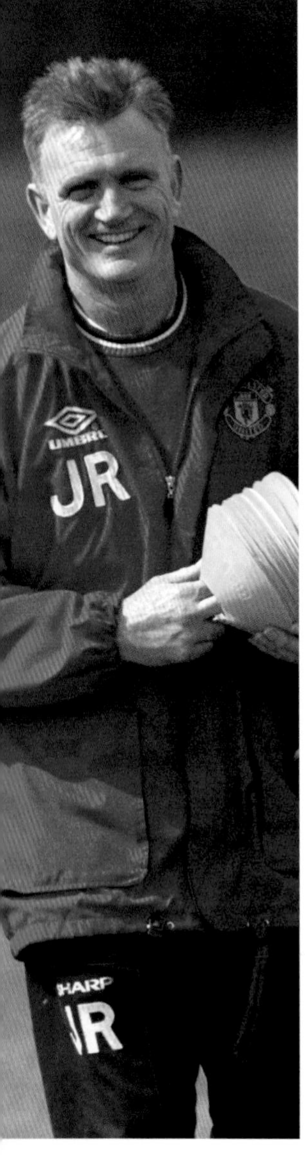

PONTIN'S LEAGUE PREMIER DIVISION

United had high hopes of lifting the Pontin's League Premier Division title for most of the season.

Early results suggested that the race could be over by Christmas with Jimmy Ryan's lads stacking up points at a furious rate in first three months of the campaign.

They started the season with a home draw against Sunderland, but then a run of eight consecutive victories placed United proudly at the top of the table.

They then came back to earth with a bump in the last week of November when they were beaten 5-1 by Leeds United at Elland Road. A 2-0 defeat at Sunderland, before a 20,583 crowd, was next and suddenly United's unhindered charge to the championship had been checked.

Another unbeaten sequence stretched well into the New Year and they once again looked on course for the title. Sunderland, in the meanwhile, had also strung a series of good results together and had emerged as United's biggest challengers.

Nevertheless, despite a couple of defeats in mid-March, at Stoke and Blackburn, United still remained in a strong position.

As the campaign approached its finale, United found themselves in command of their own destiny. The bare facts were simple. Four home matches to play, win all of them and the title was in the bag. Unfortunately, it wasn't quite as simple as that and of the four home fixtures only one, against Leeds United, produced a win. The others, against Leicester, Liverpool and Preston, all ended in defeat and as a result the Reds' challenge fizzled out.

Michael Clegg completed the season with 21 starts, while Mark Wilson made 22 appearances, two of which were as substitute. Wilson also shared the top goalscoring slot with Jonathan Greening, both players netting on nine occasions. Experienced senior players, Cruyff and Sheringham were joined by Alex Notman with three goals each.

Match Details • 1998-99

names in bold indicate goalscorers

v SUNDERLAND (home) • Drawn: 0-0 — Thursday 20 August 1998

Gibson • Clegg M. • Curtis • Casper • Wallwork • Wilson • Cooke • Wellens • Greening • Notman • Higginbotham
Substitutes: Teather • Wood (for Greening) • Nevland (for Cooke)

v ASTON VILLA (home) • Won: 4-0 — Wednesday 2 September 1998

van der Gouw • Clegg M. • Higginbotham • May • Wallwork • Teather • Cooke • **Wilson 2** • **Greening** • Cruyff • Blomqvist (**Jaszczun o.g.**)
Substitutes: Wood • Healy (for Blomqvist) • Best (for Wallwork)

v EVERTON (away) • Won: 2-0 — Saturday 5 September 1998

van der Gouw • Clegg M. • Higginbotham • May • Casper • Teather • Cooke • Wilson • **Greening** • **Cruyff** • Blomqvist
Substitutes: Wallwork (for Teather) • Wood (for Greening) • Healy

v BIRMINGHAM CITY (home) • Won: 3-2 — Thursday 17 September 1998

van der Gouw • Clegg M. • Curtis • May • Brown • Mulryne • **Cruyff (pen)** • Butt • Cole • **Sheringham 2** • Blomqvist
Substitutes: Wallwork • Culkin • Nevland (for Cole) • Cooke (for Sheringham) • Wilson (for Mulryne)

v LIVERPOOL (away) • Won: 2-0 — Friday 25 September 1998

van der Gouw • Clegg M. • Curtis • May • Berg • Wilson • Cooke • **Cruyff** • Nevland • **Notman** • Mulryne
Substitutes: Wallwork • Culkin • Teather (for Wilson) • Greening (for Nevland) • Wood

v NOTTINGHAM FOREST (home, at LFA County Ground) • Won: 1-0 — Thursday 1 October 1998

Culkin • Clegg M. • Curtis • Brown • Wallwork • Wilson • **Cooke** • Wellens • Greening • Notman • Mulryne
Substitutes: Ford • Gibson • Best • Healy (for Notman) • Roche (for Brown)

v BLACKBURN ROVERS (home, at Gigg Lane, Bury) Won: 3-2 — Wednesday 14 October 1998

Gibson • Clegg M. • Studley D. • Wallwork • O'Shea • **Wilson** • Cooke • Mulryne • **Greening 2** • Cruyff • Ford
Substitutes: Wellens (for Studley D.) • Rachubka • Wood • Healy • Thorrington

v STOKE CITY (home, at Gigg Lane, Bury) Won: 4-1 — Tuesday 3 November 1998

Gibson • Clegg M. • Curtis • May • Johnsen • Wallwork • **Wilson** • Butt • Nevland • **Notman** • **Greening**
*Substitutes: **Wood** (for Notman) • Culkin • Ford (for Butt) • Healy • Teather (for Curtis)*

Reserves

Monday 16 November 1998 — **v LEICESTER CITY (away) Won: 6-2**

van der Gouw • **Clegg M.** • Roche • O'Shea • Wallwork • Teather • **Wellens** • **Wilson (pen)** • Nevland • **Greening 3** • Ford
Substitutes: Wood • Culkin • Ryan • Thorrington • Chadwick (for Teather)

Tuesday 24 November 1998 — **v LEEDS UNITED (away) Lost: 1-5**

Culkin • Stewart • Roche • O'Shea • Wallwork • Teather • Wellens • Mulryne • Nevland • **Sheringham** • Greening
Substitutes: Wood • Notman • Healy • Ford • Chadwick

Thursday 17 December 1998 — **v SUNDERLAND (away) Lost: 0-2**

van der Gouw • Clegg M. • Curtis • Berg • Teather • Ford • Thorrington • Mulryne • Notman • Cruyff • Greening
Substitutes: Healy (for Notman) • Culkin • Ryan • McDermott • Rose M

Wednesday 6 January 1999 — **v ASTON VILLA (away) Won: 5-1**

Culkin • Clegg M. • Neville P. • May • Curtis • Teather • **Cruyff** • **Mulryne** • Bakircioglu • **Solskjaer 2** • **Greening**
Substitutes: Wilson (for Teather) • Gibson • Nevland • Notman (for Bakircioglu) • Healy

Tuesday 19 January 1999 — **v DERBY COUNTY (away) • Drawn: 2-2**

van der Gouw • Ryan • Curtis • May • O'Shea • Ford • Mulryne • **Wilson** • **Nevland** • Notman • Greening
Substitutes: Healy (for Notman) • Culkin • Rose S.(for Ryan) • Clegg G. • Wellens

Wednesday 27 January 1999 — **v DERBY COUNTY (home, at Gigg Lane, Bury) • Won: 4-0**

van der Gouw • Clegg M. • Curtis • May • Brown • Neville P. • Mulryne • **Wilson** • **Nevland** • **Notman** • Greening
*Substitutes: Healy • Culkin • Wellens • **Chadwick** (for Notman) • Ford*

Wednesday 3 February 1999 — **v BIRMINGHAM CITY (away, at Keys Park, Hednesford) • Drawn: 1-1**

Culkin • Clegg M.` • Curtis • Rose S. • Brown • Wilson • Chadwick • Mulryne • Nevland • **Healy** • Greening
Substitutes: Ford • Gibson • Hilton • Wellens • Ryan

Monday 8 February 1999 — **v PRESTON NORTH END (away) • Won: 1-0**

van der Gouw • Rose S. • Clegg M. • May • O'Shea • Ford • Wellens • Wilson • Notman • Fitzpatrick • **Mulryne**
Substitutes: Thorrington • Gibson • Clegg G. • Stewart • Ryan (for Fitzpatrick)

NOTTINGHAM FOREST (away, at Field Mill, Mansfield) • Drawn: 1-1 — Wednesday 24 February 1999

van der Gouw • **Clegg M.** • Curtis • May • Brown • O'Shea • Mulryne • Wilson • Healy • Greening • Stewart
Substitutes: Thorrington (for May) • Culkin • Ryan • Clegg • Cosgrove

v BLACKBURN ROVERS (away) Lost: 0-1 — Monday 15 March 1999

Culkin • Clegg M. • Curtis • May • Brown • Ford • Mulryne • Wilson • Healy • Chadwick • Greening
Substitutes: Ryan • O'Shea (for Brown) • Wellens (for Ford) • Stewart • Roche

v STOKE CITY (away) • Lost: 1-3 — Monday 22 March 1999

Culkin • Clegg M. • Roche • **May** • O'Shea • Ford • Mulryne • Wilson • Healy • Sheringham • Chadwick
Substitutes: Rose S. • Stewart • Cosgrove • Wellens (for Ford)

v EVERTON (home) • Won: 3-0 — Saturday 27 March 1999

Culkin • Clegg M. • Curtis • May • **O'Shea** • Ford • Wellens • Wilson • **Fitzpatrick 2** • Stewart • Greening
Substitutes: Hilton • Cosgrove • Evans

v LEICESTER CITY (home) • Lost: 0-2 — Tuesday 13 April 1999

Culkin • Ford • Curtis • May • O'Shea • Stewart • Wellens • Wilson • Fitzpatrick • Healy • Chadwick
Substitutes: Cosgrove • Marsh • Wheatcroft (for Fitzpatrick) • Howard • Lynch

v LIVERPOOL (home) • Lost: 0-1 — Thursday 22 April 1999

Hoie • Clegg M. • Curtis • May • Brown • Ford • Wellens • Wilson • Healy • Neville P. • Greening
Substitutes: O'Shea (for Brown) • Culkin • Fitzpatrick • Howard (for Neville P.) • Clegg G. (for Ford)

v LEEDS UNITED (home) • Won: 4-1 — Wednesday 28 April 1999

van der Gouw • Rose S. • Clegg G. • Clegg M. • O'Shea • Ford • Wellens • **Wilson 2** • **Healy** • Thorrington • **Chadwick**
Substitutes: Fitzpatrick • Culkin • Wheatcroft • Cosgrove • Howard

v PRESTON NORTH END (home, at Gigg Lane, Bury) • Lost: 0-1 — Monday 3 May 1999

Culkin • Rose S. • Curtis • Clegg M. • O'Shea • Ford • Wellens • Wilson • Healy • Chadwick • Greening
Substitutes: Fitzpatrick (for Healy) • Rachubka • Thorrington (for Greening) • Hilton • Howard

RESERVES

APPEARANCES

Name	Appearances (as sub)	Name	Appearances (as sub)
CLEGG • Michael	21	ROCHE • Lee	3 (1)
WILSON • Mark	20 (2)	BLOMQVIST • Jesper	3
GREENING • Jonathan	18 (1)	GIBSON • Paul	3
CURTIS • John	16	HIGGINBOTHAM • Danny	3
MAY • David	15	NEVILLE • Phil	3
MULRYNE • Philip	14	SHERINGHAM • Teddy	3
FORD • Ryan	12 (1)	THORRINGTON • John	2 (2)
O'SHEA • John	11 (2)	BERG • Henning	2
VAN DER GOUW • Raimond	11	BUTT • Nicky	2
WELLENS • Richard	10 (3)	CASPER • Chris	2
HEALY • David	8 (4)	CLEGG • George	1 (1)
NOTMAN • Alex	8 (1)	RYAN • Michael	1 (1)
CULKIN • Nick	9	BAKIRCIOGLU • Kennedy	1
NEVLAND • Erik	7 (2)	COLE • Andy	1
BROWN • Wesley	7	HOIE • Kenneth	1
CRUYFF • Jordi	7	JOHNSEN • Ronny	1
WALLWORK • Ronnie	7 (1)	SOLSKJAER • Ole Gunnar	1
CHADWICK • Luke	6 (2)	STUDLEY • Dominic	1
TEATHER • Paul	6 (2)	WOOD • Jamie	0 (3)
COOKE • Terry	6 (1)	BEST • Russell	0 (1)
ROSE • Stephen	4 (1)	HOWARD • Joshua	0 (1)
STEWART • Michael	4	WHEATCROFT • Paul	0 (1)
FITZPATRICK • Ian	3 (1)		

GOALSCORERS

Name	Goals (penalties)
GREENING • Jonathan	9
WILSON • Mark	9 (1)
CRUYFF • Jordi	4 (1)
NOTMAN • Alex	3
SHERINGHAM • Teddy	3
CHADWICK • Luke	2
CLEGG • Michael	2
FITZPATRICK • Ian	2
HEALY • David	2
MULRYNE • Philip	2
NEVLAND • Erik	2
SOLSKJAER • Ole Gunnar	2
COOKE • Terry	1
MAY • David	1
O'SHEA • John	1
WELLENS • Richard	1
WOOD • Jamie	1

Own Goals

JASZCZUN • Tommy (Aston Villa) 1

PONTIN'S LEAGUE PREMIER DIVISION

FINAL TABLE 1998-99

	P	W	D	L	F	A	Pts
Sunderland	24	14	7	3	46	18	49
Liverpool	24	13	7	4	28	16	46
MANCHESTER UNITED	**24**	**13**	**4**	**7**	**48**	**28**	**43**
Nottingham Forest	24	11	6	7	35	26	39
Everton	24	11	5	8	34	28	38
Blackburn Rovers	24	8	7	9	31	26	31
Leeds United	24	9	3	12	40	43	30
Leicester City	24	8	6	10	30	41	30
Aston Villa	24	8	5	11	36	37	29
Stoke City	24	7	7	10	24	32	28
Preston North End	24	7	5	12	20	42	26
Birmingham City	24	5	9	10	24	33	24
Derby County	24	3	7	14	26	52	16

names in bold indicate goalscorers

MANCHESTER SENIOR CUP

v OLDHAM ATHLETIC (away) • Won: 3-2 — Wednesday 10 March 1999

Gibson • **Clegg M.** • Curtis • Rose S. • O'Shea • Ford • Stewart • Wilson • Healy • **Sheringham** • **Greening**
Substitutes: Ryan • Culkin • Hilton • Howard • Cosgrove

v BURY (away) • Won: 4-1 — Wednesday 31 March 1999

van der Gouw • Clegg M. • Curtis • **May** • Brown • Ford • Wellens • **Wilson** • **Fitzpatrick** • Stewart • Greening
*Substitutes: **O'Shea** (for Brown) • Culkin • Hilton • Cosgrove • Howard*

v MANCHESTER CITY (away, at Ewen Fields, Hyde) • Won: 5-1 — Tuesday 6 April 1999

Culkin • **Clegg M.** • Curtis • May • O'Shea • **Ford** • Wellens • **Wilson** • **Healy** • Stewart • **Greening**
Substitutes: Fitzpatrick • Evans • Wheatcroft • Hilton • Howard

v BURY (home, at Gigg Lane) • Lost: 2-4 — Friday 16 April 1999

Marsh • Strange • Studley M. • Gaff • Jones • Ford • Wellens • Rose M. • **Healy** • Stewart • **Wood**
Substitutes: Hickson • Whiteley (for Jones) • Walker

v MANCHESTER CITY (home, at Gigg Lane) • Drawn: 2-2* — Monday 19 April 1999

Culkin • Clegg M. • Studley M. • May • Curtis • Ford • Wellens • Wilson • **Healy** • Stewart • **Greening**
Substitutes: Chadwick (for Greening) • Rachubka • Whiteley (for May) • Hickson • Strange (for Stewart)
* **Lost 1-4 on penalties** Penalty scorer: **Healy**

v OLDHAM ATHLETIC (home, at The Cliff) • Lost: 0-1 — Wednesday 5 May 1999

Culkin • Clegg M. • Clegg G. • Rose S. • O'Shea • Ford • Wellens • Thorrington • Wheatcroft • Fitzpatrick • Chadwick
Substitutes: Howard (for Wheatcroft) • Marsh • Stewart • Evans • Cosgrove

	P	W	D	L	F	A	Pts
MANCHESTER UNITED	6	3	0	3	16	11	9
Oldham Athletic	6	3	0	3	9	9	9
Bury	6	3	0	3	10	11	9
Manchester City	6	3	0	3	8	12	9

v OLDHAM ATHLETIC – FINAL (away, at Boundary Park) Won: 3-0 — Thursday 13 May 1999

Culkin • Clegg M. • Curtis • O'Shea • Brown • Ford • Wellens • **Wilson** • **Healy** • **Chadwick** • Greening
Substitutes: Rose S. • Thorrington • Hilton • Fitzpatrick • Clegg G

FRIENDLIES

names in bold indicate goalscorers

Saturday 25 July 1998 — **v MACCLESFIELD TOWN (away) • Won: 2-1**

Gibson • Ryan • Roche • Teather • Higginbotham • Thorrington • Cooke • Greening • **Nevland** • Wellens • Wood
Substitutes: ***Healy*** *(for Cooke) • Stewart (for Thorrington) • Brown (for Teather)*

Wednesday 29 July 1998 — **v GAINSBOROUGH TRINITY – 125th Anniversary (away) • Won: 10-0**

Gibson • Ryan • Higginbotham • Wallwork • Brown • Ford • **Cooke** • **Wilson** • **Nevland 4** • **Notman 3** • Twiss
Substitutes: Wood (for Nevland) • Thorrington (for Twiss) • Wellens (for Ryan) • Greening (for Wilson) Healy (for Notman) • ***Mulryne (pen)*** *(for Cooke) • Teather*

Tuesday 4 August 1998 — **v BAMBER BRIDGE (away) • Drawn: 2-2**

Gibson • Clegg M. • Twiss • Brown • Wallwork • Teather • Cooke • Wellens • **Greening 2** • Notman • Mulryne
Substitutes: Wilson (for Wellens) • Nevland (for Notman) • Higginbotham (for Brown) • Wood (for Wallwork) Ford (for Cooke)

Saturday 8 August 1998 — **v BROMSGROVE ROVERS (away) Won: 4-1**

Gibson • Ryan • Higginbotham • Teather • Brown • Wellens • Cooke • **Wilson** • **Nevland 2** • **Notman** • Healy
Substitutes: Wheatcroft (for Nevland) • Rose S. (for Ryan) • Stewart

Wednesday 12 August 1998 — **v STOCKPORT COUNTY XI (away) Won: 2-1**

Gibson • Clegg M. • Higginbotham • Brown • Casper • **Wilson** • Cooke • **Greening** • Nevland • Wellens • Ford
Substitutes: Notman (for Cooke) • Evans • Studley D

Thursday 14 August 1998 — **v DROYLSDEN (away) • Drawn: 1-1**

Gibson • Ryan • Hilton • Curtis • Teather • Stewart • Cooke • Thorrington • Notman • Wood • **Healy**
Substitutes: Roach (for Ryan) • Evans (for Cooke) • Cosgrove • Fitzpatrick

Monday 24 August 1998 — **v NEWRY TOWN (away) • Lost: 3-4**

Gibson • Clegg M. • Higginbotham • **Casper** • Wallwork • **Teather** • Cooke • **Mulryne (pen)** • Nevland • Healy • Wood
Substitutes: Notman (for Cooke) • Wellens (for Mulryne) • Wilson (for Wood) • Greening (for Healy)

Wednesday 26 August 1998 — **v BOLTON WANDERERS – Friendly/Training Match (home) • Drawn: 4-4**

Gibson • Clegg M. • Higginbotham • Casper • Wallwork • Wellens • **Cooke** • Wilson • Wood • **Notman (pen)** • Blomqvist
Substitutes: ***Greening*** *(for Wood) •* ***Healy*** *(for Notman) • Thorrington (for Cooke) • Best (for Casper) Teather (for Wellens)*

v ROYAL ANTWERP (BELGIUM) (away) • Lost: 1-3 — **Monday 28 September 1998**

Gibson • Clegg M. • Curtis • Brown • Wallwork • Wilson • Thorrington • Wellens • **Wood** • Notman • Greening
Substitutes: Healy (for Thorrington) • Culkin (for Gibson) • Fitzpatrick

v SHEFFIELD UNITED – Friendly/Training Match (home, at The Cliff) • Won: 3-1 — **Tuesday 6 October 1998**

Gibson • Roche • Studley D. • Best • O'Shea • Wilson • Cooke • Wellens • Wood • **Healy 3** • Ford
Substitutes: Thorrington (for Cooke) • Chadwick (for Ford) • Rose S.

v NOTTINGHAM FOREST – Friendly/Training Match (home) • Drawn: 1-1 — **Wednesday 21 October 1998**

Gibson • Ryan • Hilton • May • Wallwork • Teather • Cooke • Wellens • Wood • **Notman** • Ford
Substitutes: Thorrington (for Cooke) • Greening • Healy

v LIVINGSTON (away) • Lost: 2-3 — **Tuesday 27 October 1998**

Culkin • Roche • Studley D. • Teather • Wallwork • Ford • Cooke • Wellens • **Nevland** • Notman • Chadwick
Substitutes: Wood (for Nevland) • ***Healy*** *(for Notman) • Thorrington (for Cooke) • Stewart (for Ford) • Cosgrove (for Wellens)*

v MAJOR SOCCER LEAGUE – UNDER 21 (USA) (home, at The Cliff) Lost: 0-3 — **Saturday 5 December 1998**

Culkin • Roche • Hilton • Ford • Teather • Mulryne • Ryan • Wilson • Healy • Notman • Jacob
Substitutes: Wellens (for Jacob) • Rachubka • O'Shea (for Teather) • Webber (for Ryan) • Szmid (for Roche)

v MACCLESFIELD TOWN – Friendly/Training Match (home, at Littleton Road) Lost: 0-1 — **Saturday 23 January 1999**

Culkin • Clegg M. • Hilton • May • Rose S. • Ryan • Mulryne • Wilson • Greening • Healy • Wellens
Substitutes: Notman (for Greening) • Gibson (for Culkin) • Nevland (for Healy) • Ford (for Ryan)

FA PREMIER ACADEMY LEAGUE

United ended their association with the Lancashire League, which stretched back almost 50 years, at the end of end of the 1997-98 season and began the new campaign as members of the FA Premier Academy League. This new competition which had began twelve months earlier, had been expanded to include clubs from all regions of the country.

United were represented in both age groups, the under 19s & under 17s and they gave a good account of themselves in both sections.

David Williams' under-19s looked set to finish the season at the head of their table, but they foundered towards the end of the season and had to be content with runners-up spot on goal difference behind Everton.

The end of season play-offs saw them eliminate Millwall, 4-1, before going out, 2-1, to Chelsea in round two. Both games being played at The Cliff.

The under-17s, coached by Neil Bailey, lost just one match all season and, not surprisingly, finished at the top of their group.

Their participation in the play-offs saw them reach the semi-final after receiving a bye in the first round and then despatching Leicester City 5-4, (after extra time), and Sunderland 3-0. They then faced Blackburn Rovers in the last-four in an amazing match. The teams were level without a goal being scored in the allotted 90 minutes, but then Rovers swamped United to take the tie 5-1 in extra-time.

It was a disappointing end to the season for the youngsters, particularly after winning their group in such fine style.

names in bold indicate goalscorers

UNDER 19s

v WEST HAM UNITED (away) • Lost: 0-3 — Saturday 5th September 1998

Rachubka • Ryan • Studley D. • Roche, • Rose S. • Cosgrove • Thorrington • Stewart • Clegg G. • Wheatcroft • Chadwick
Substitutes: O'Shea (for Wheatcroft) • Evans (for Stewart) • Hickson (for Clegg G.)

v DERBY COUNTY (home) • Drawn: 1-1 — Saturday 12th September 1998

Rachubka • Ryan • Rose S. • O'Shea • Roche • Cosgrove • Chadwick • Evans • **Healy (pen)** • Wheatcroft • Studley D
Substitutes: Clegg G. (for Ryan) • Marsh • Fitzpatrick (for Wheatcroft) • Whiteley • Hickson

v WATFORD (home) • Lost: 2-4 — Saturday 19th September 1998

Rachubka • Rose S. • Studley D. • Roche • **O'Shea** • Stewart • Thorrington • Evans • Clegg G. • Fitzpatrick • **Chadwick**
Substitutes: Marsh • Hilton (for Thorrington) • Whiteley (for Evans) • Hickson (for Stewart)

v WIMBLEDON (home) • Won: 4-0 — Saturday 26th September 1998

Rachubka • Rose S. • Studley D. • Roche • O'Shea • Stewart • Wellens • Thorrington • **Healy 3 (2 pens)** • Fitzpatrick • **Chadwick**
Substitutes: Clegg G. • Cosgrove • Hilton • Evans

v FULHAM (home) • Won: 4-0 — Saturday 3rd October 1998

Rachubka • Rose S. • Hilton • Roche • O'Shea • Clegg G. • **Evans** • Stewart • **Healy 3 (1 pen)** • Fitzpatrick • Chadwick
Substitutes: Studley D. (for Chadwick) • Wheatcroft (for Healy) • Cosgrove

v MANCHESTER CITY (away) • Won: 4-1 — Saturday 19th October 1998

Rachubka • Rose S. • Studley D. • Roche • O'Shea • Stewart • **Evans** • **Clegg G.** • **Healy** • Fitzpatrick • Chadwick
(**Daly o.g.**)
Substitutes: Wheatcroft (for Fitzpatrick) • Marsh • Hilton (for Evans) • Howard (for Roche)

v EVERTON (away) • Won: 1-0 — Saturday 24th October 1998

Rachubka • Ryan • Hilton • Roche • O'Shea • Clegg G. • Thorrington • Stewart • Wheatcroft • Fitzpatrick • Chadwick
(**Knowles o.g.**)
Substitutes: Studley D. • Marsh • Rose S. • Evans (for Fitzpatrick) • Howard

v LIVERPOOL (home) • Drawn: 1-1 — Saturday 31st October 1998

Rachubka • Ryan • Hilton • Roche • Rose S. • Clegg G. • Wellens • Stewart • **Healy** • Wheatcroft • Thorrington
Substitutes: Studley D. (for Wellens) • Howard • Evans (for Wheatcroft) • Cosgrove • Chadwick (for Thorrington)

Saturday 7th November 1998

v BOLTON WANDERERS (away) • Won: 2-1

Rachubka • **Ryan** • Studley D. • Roche • O'Shea • Howard • Evans • Stewart • **Wheatcroft** • Fitzpatrick • Chadwick
Substitutes: Hilton • Cosgrove • Clegg G. (for Howard)

Saturday 14th November 1998

v BLACKBURN ROVERS (away) • Lost: 1-5

Rachubka • Ryan • Hilton • Stewart • Clegg G. • Cosgrove • Thorrington • Howard • Healy • **Fitzpatrick** • Chadwick
Substitutes: Evans • Marsh • Gaff • Wheatcroft (for Fitzpatrick) • Whiteley

Saturday 21st November 1998

v ASTON VILLA (home) • Won: 4-0

Rachubka • Roche • Hilton • Cosgrove • O'Shea • Clegg G. • Thorrington • Stewart • **Notman 3** • Wheatcroft • **Chadwick**
Substitutes: Howard • Marsh • Healy (for Thorrington) • Gaff • Whiteley

Saturday 28th November 1998

v CREWE ALEXANDRA (home) • Won: 2-1

Rachubka • Lynch • Hilton • Roche • O'Shea • Clegg G. • Evans • **Howard** • Wheatcroft • **Fitzpatrick** • Chadwick
Substitutes: Cosgrove • Marsh (for Rachubka) • Stewart (for Evans) • Hickson

Saturday 12th December 1998

v MANCHESTER CITY (home) • Won: 1-0

Rachubka • Lynch • Hilton • Roche • Clegg G. • Cosgrove • Evans • Stewart • Wheatcroft • **Fitzpatrick** • Chadwick
Substitutes: Whiteley (for Evans) • Marsh • Studley D. (for Stewart) • Gaff, Hickson

Saturday 16th January 1999

v LIVERPOOL (away) • Drawn: 1-1

Marsh • Ryan • Studley D. • **Rose S.** • O'Shea • Cosgrove • Whiteley • Howard • Healy • Wheatcroft • Clegg G.
Substitutes: Stewart (for Whiteley) Rachubka Fitzpatrick Gaff Hickson

Saturday 30th January 1999

v BOLTON WANDERERS (home) • Won: 5-0

Rachubka • Ryan • Hilton • Rose S. • McDermott • Cosgrove • Wellens • **Howard** • **Healy** • **Fitzpatrick** • **Chadwick 2**
Substitutes: Stewart Marsh Whiteley (for Cosgrove) Clegg G. Wheatcroft

Saturday 6th February 1999

v EVERTON (home) • Won: 1-0

Marsh • Ryan • Hilton • Rose S. • O'Shea • Whiteley • Wellens • Stewart • Wheatcroft • **Fitzpatrick** • Clegg G.
Substitutes: Evans (for Wheatcroft) Rachubka Chadwick (for Whiteley) Cosgrove (for Wellens) Gaff

v BLACKBURN ROVERS (home) • Lost: 0-4 Saturday 13th February 1999

Rachubka • Roche • Hilton • Rose S. • O'Shea • Clegg G. • Evans • Stewart • Wheatcroft • Fitzpatrick • Chadwick
Substitutes: Studley D. (for Evans) • Cosgrove (for Wheatcroft) • Marsh • Howard • Whiteley

v ASTON VILLA (away) • Won: 2-0 Saturday 20th February 1999

Marsh • **Ryan** • Hilton • Roche • O'Shea • Cosgrove • Evans • Howard • **Healy** • Wheatcroft • Chadwick
Substitutes: Rose S. • Rachubka • Stewart • Clegg G. • Fitzpatrick

v CREWE ALEXANDRA (away) • Lost: 0-1 Saturday 27th February 1999

Rachubka • Ryan • Hilton • Roche • Rose S. • Cosgrove • Evans • Howard • Wheatcroft • Fitzpatrick • Clegg G.
Substitutes: O'Shea • Marsh • Stewart • Chadwick (for Evans) • Studley D.

v CRYSTAL PALACE (away) • Won: 1-0 Saturday 6th March 1999

Marsh • Cosgrove • Hilton • Rose S. • O'Shea • Howard • Thorrington • Stewart • Healy • **Fitzpatrick** • Studley D.
Substitutes: Evans (for Fitzpatrick) • Rachubka • Whiteley (for Studley D.)

v BRISTOL CITY (home) • Lost: 1-2 Saturday 20th March 1999

Rachubka • Lynch • Hilton • Stewart • Rose S. • Cosgrove • Wellens • Evans • **Wheatcroft** • Fitzpatrick • Whiteley
Substitutes: Howard • Marsh • Hickson (for Fitzpatrick) • Gaff

v SHEFFIELD WEDNESDAY (away) • Drawn: 0-0 Saturday 27th March 1999

Marsh • Lynch • Studley M. • Gaff • McDermott • Whiteley • Szmid • Howard • Davis • Wood • Studley D.
Substitutes: Hickson (for Studley D.) • Dodd • Clegg S. • Taylor • Williams M.

v MILLWALL – Play-Off First Round (home) • Won: 4-1 Saturday 17th April 1999

Rachubka • Lynch • Studley D. • McDermott • O'Shea • Cosgrove • **Evans** • Howard • Wheatcroft • **Fitzpatrick** • **Chadwick 2**
Substitutes: Whiteley (for McDermott) • Marsh • Hickson • Walker (for Evans)

v CHELSEA – Play-Off Second Round (home) • Lost: 1-2 Wednesday 21st April 1999

Rachubka • Lynch • Clegg G. • Rose S. • O'Shea • Whiteley • Evans • Howard • **Wheatcroft** • Fitzpatrick • Chadwick
Substitutes: Disang (for Wheatcroft) • Marsh • Gaff • Hickson • Molloy (for Chadwick)

JUNIORS

UNDER 19s APPEARANCES

Name	Appearances (as sub)	Name	Appearances (as sub)
RACHUBKA • Paul	19	THORRINGTON • John	8
CHADWICK • Luke	17 (3)	LYNCH • Mark	6
FITZPATRICK • Ian	17 (1)	WHITELEY • Lee	5 (5)
WHEATCROFT • Paul	16 (3)	MARSH • Allan	5 (1)
O'SHEA • John	16 (1)	WELLENS • Richard	5
CLEGG • George	15 (2)	McDERMOTT • Alan	3
STEWART • Michael	15 (2)	DAVIS • Jimmy	1
ROCHE • Lee	15	GAFF • Gerard	1
ROSE • Stephen	15	NOTMAN • Alex	1
HILTON • Kirk	14 (2)	SZMID • Marek	1
EVANS • Wayne	13 (5)	STUDLEY • Mark	1
COSGROVE • Stephen	12 (2)	WOOD • Neil	1
HOWARD • Joshua	11 (1)	HICKSON • Jason	0 (4)
RYAN • Michael	11	DISANG • Edwin	0 (1)
STUDLEY • Dominic	10 (4)	MOLLOY • Eric	0 (1)
HEALY • David	10 (1)	WALKER • Joshua	0 (1)

GOALSCORERS

Name	Goals (penalties)
HEALY • David	11 (3)
CHADWICK • Luke	7
FITZPATRICK • Ian	7
EVANS • Wayne	3
NOTMAN • Alex	3
WHEATCROFT • Paul	3
HOWARD • Joshua	2
RYAN • Michael	2
CLEGG • George	1
O'SHEA • John	1
ROSE • Stephen	1
Own goals	
DALY • Lee (Man. City)	1
KNOWLES • David (Everton)	1

FA PREMIER ACADEMY LEAGUE UNDER 19

GROUP A FINAL TABLE 1998-99

	P	W	D	L	F	A	Pts
Everton	22	12	4	6	39	25	40
MANCHESTER UNITED	**22**	**12**	**4**	**6**	**38**	**25**	**40**
Crewe Alexandra	22	11	6	5	30	19	39
Blackburn Rovers	22	11	3	8	46	29	36
Liverpool	22	9	9	4	33	17	36
Aston Villa	22	7	4	11	34	44	25
Manchester City	22	4	3	15	20	50	15
Bolton Wanderers	22	3	3	16	28	63	12

Dr. Martens
UMBRO
SHARP
VIEWCAM

JUNIORS

Saturday 5th September 1998 — **v WEST HAM UNITED (away) • Won: 2-1**

Moran • Lynch • Studley M. • Strange • Rose M. • Szmid • **Walker** • Dodd • **Webber** • Wood • Molloy
Substitutes: Whiteman (for Molloy) • Clegg S. • Taylor • Williams

Saturday 12th September 1998 — **v DERBY COUNTY (home) • Won: 4-0**

Moran • Lynch • Studley M. • Strange • **McDermott** • **Szmid** • Walker • **Rose M.** • Whiteman • Wood • **Muirhead**
Substitutes: Grogan (for Walker) • Williams M. (for Whiteman) • Pugh • Mortimer

Saturday 19th September 1998 — **v WATFORD (home) • Won: 2-1**

Moran • Lynch • Studley M. • Strange • McDermott • Szmid • Walker • Rose M. • Whiteman • **Wood** • **Muirhead**
Substitutes: Grogan (for Walker) • Molloy (for Whiteman) • Williams M • Taylor

Saturday 26th September 1998 — **v WIMBLEDON (home) • Won: 5-0**

Marsh • **Lynch** • Studley M. • Strange • McDermott • Szmid • **Grogan** • Rose M. • **Webber** • **Wood** • Muirhead
Substitutes: Walker • Molloy (for Wood) • Taylor • Whiteman • ***Davis*** *(for Webber)*

Saturday 3rd October 1998 — **v FULHAM (home) • Won: 9-0**

Moran • **Lynch** • Studley M. • Strange • **McDermott** • Szmid • Grogan • Rose M. • **Webber 5** • **Davis** • Muirhead
Substitutes: Walker (for Grogan) • ***Whiteman*** *(for Davis) • Williams M. (for Muirhead) • Sampson*

Saturday 17th October 1998 — **v MANCHESTER CITY • (away) Won: 2-0**

Moran • Lynch • Studley M. • Strange • McDermott • Szmid • Grogan • Rose M. • **Webber** • **Davis** • Muirhead
Substitutes: Walker • Molloy • Whiteman • Sampson

Saturday 24th October 1998 — **v EVERTON (home) • Won: 3-2**

Moran • Lynch • Studley M. • Molloy • **McDermott** • Szmid • Walker • Rose M. • **Webber** • **Davis** • Muirhead
Substitutes: Grogan • Dodd • Whiteman • Taylor

Saturday 31st October 1998 — **v LIVERPOOL (home) • Drawn: 2-2**

Moran • **Lynch** • Studley M. • Strange • McDermott • Szmid • Walker • Rose M. • Webber • Davis • **Molloy**
Substitutes: Grogan • Dodd • Muirhead • Clark

v WIMBLEDON (away) • **Drawn: 1-1** — Saturday 7th November 1998

Moran • Lynch • Studley M. • Strange • McDermott • Szmid • Muirhead • Rose M. • **Webber** • Davis • Molloy
Substitutes: Grogan • Walker • Dodd • Wood (for Molloy) • Whiteman

v BLACKBURN ROVERS (away) • **Won: 2-0** — Saturday 14th November 1998

Moran • Lynch • Wood • Strange • Clark • Szmid • Muirhead • Rose M. • **Webber** • **Davis** • Molloy
Substitutes: Walker • Whiteman • Taylor • Tierney • McDermott

v ASTON VILLA (home) • **Won: 5-0** — Saturday 21st November 1998

Moran • Lynch • Studley M. • Strange • **McDermott** • Szmid • Muirhead • Rose M. • **Webber 2** • **Davis** • Walker
(**Samuels o.g.**)
Substitutes: Whiteman (for Szmid) • Sampson (for Rose M.) • Tierney • Pugh

v CREWE ALEXANDRA (home) • **Drawn: 1-1** — Saturday 28th November 1998

Moran • Szmid • Studley M. • Strange • Rose M. • Whiteley • Muirhead • Whiteman • **Webber** • Davis • Walker
Substitutes: Sampson (for Strange) • Taylor • Tierney

v MANCHESTER CITY (home) • **Won: 4-0** — Saturday 12th December 1998

Moran • Szmid • Studley M. • Clark • McDermott • Walker • Muirhead • Rose M. • **Webber 2** • **Davis** • **Molloy**
Substitutes: Wood (for Davis) • Sampson (for Rose M.) • Whiteman • Tierney

v LIVERPOOL (away) • **Drawn: 3-3** — Saturday 16th January 1999

Moran • Lynch • Studley M. • Clark • McDermott • Szmid • Walker • Rose M. • **Webber** • **Davis 2** • Molloy
Substitutes: Strange (for Walker) • Jones • Muirhead • Wood (for Molloy)

v EVERTON (away) • **Won: 5-1** — Saturday 6th February 1999

Moore • Lynch • Studley M. • Strange • McDermott • Szmid • **Walker** • **Rose M.** • Webber • **Davis** • Molloy
*Substitutes: Jones (for Strange) • **Wood 2** (for Webber) • Pugh (for Molloy) • Whiteman*

v BLACKBURN ROVERS (home) • **Drawn: 1-1** — Saturday 13th February 1999

Moore • Lynch • Studley M. • Strange • Jones • Szmid • Walker • **Rose M.** • Muirhead • Davis • Wood
Substitutes: Molloy • Whiteman • Tierney • Clegg S.

JUNIORS

Saturday 20th February 1999 — **v ASTON VILLA (away) • Won: 5-1**

Moran • Lynch • Studley M. • Strange • Jones • **Clark** • Muirhead • Whiteley • **Nardiello 2 (1 pen)** • **Wood** • **Molloy**
Substitutes: Taylor (for Muirhead) • Moore • Pugh • Tierney (for Studley M.) • Tate

Saturday 27th February 1999 — **v CREWE ALEXANDRA (away) • Drawn: 1-1**

Moran • Lynch • Studley M. • **Strange** • McDermott • Jones • Muirhead • Whiteley • Nardiello • Wood • Molloy
Substitutes: Clark (for Nardiello) • Tierney • Taylor • Williams M.

Saturday 6th March 1999 — **v CRYSTAL PALACE (home) • Won: 3-0**

Moran • Lynch • Studley M. • Strange • McDermott • Clark • Szmid • Rose M. • **Wood 2** • **Davis** • Molloy
Substitutes: Walker • Muirhead (for Molloy) • Whiteman • Taylor • Tate

Saturday 13th March 1999 — **v TOTTENHAM HOTSPUR (away) • Drawn: 2-2**

Moran • Lynch • Studley M. • Strange • McDermott • Szmid • Walker • Rose M. • Whiteman • **Davis 2** • Molloy
Substitutes: Dodd • Taylor (for Rose M.) • Williams M. (for Whiteman) • Tate • Pugh (for Molloy)

Saturday 20th March 1999 — **v BRISTOL CITY (home) • Won: 3-1**

Ford • Strange • Studley M. • Jones • McDermott • **Szmid** • Walker • Rose M. • **Muirhead** • **Davis** • Wood
Substitutes: Dodd (for Szmid) • Whiteman • Sampson • Clegg S.

Saturday 27th March 1999 — **v SHEFFIELD WEDNESDAY (away) • Lost: 1-2**

Price • Strange • Pugh • Clark • Tate • Sampson • Walker • Rose M. • **Whiteman** • Muirhead • Molloy
Substitutes: Mooniaruck • Dodd • Clegg S. • Taylor (for Sampson)

Saturday 25th April 1999 — **v LEICESTER CITY Play-Off Second Round (home) • Won: 5-4 after extra time (full time: 3-3)**

Williams B. • **Lynch** • Studley M. • Strange • Jones • Grogan • Walker • **Rose M.** • **Muirhead** • **Williams M. 2** • Wood
Substitutes: Dodd • Molloy • Sampson (for Grogan) • Clegg S. • Whiteman (for Williams M.)

Saturday 1st May 1999 — **v SUNDERLAND Play-Off Third Round (home) • Won: 3-0**

Williams B. • Lynch • Studley M. • Strange • McDermott • **Jones** • Walker • **Rose M. (pen.)** • Muirhead • Williams M. • Wood
Substitutes: ***Grogan*** *(for Walker) • Dodd • Molloy • Pugh • Whiteman (for Williams M.)*

v BLACKBURN ROVERS Play-Off Semi-Final (home), Lost: 1-5 after extra time (full time: 0-0) Saturday 8th May 1999

Williams B. • Lynch • Studley M. • Strange • McDermott • Jones • Szmid • Rose M. • Muirhead • **Davis** • Wood
Substitutes: Walker (for Szmid) • Grogan (for Lynch) • Molloy • Pugh • Williams M.

UNDER 17s APPEARANCES

Name	Appearances (as sub)	Name	Appearances (as sub)
ROSE • Michael	23	GROGAN • Kevin	4 (4)
STUDLEY • Mark	23	WHITELEY • Lee	3
STRANGE • Gareth	22 (1)	WILLIAMS • Ben	3
LYNCH • Mark	21	WILLIAMS • Matthew	2 (3)
SZMID • Marek	20	MOORE • David	2
MUIRHEAD • Ben	19 (1)	NARDIELLO • Daniel	2
McDEMOTT • Alan	18	PUGH • Daniel	1 (3)
MORAN • David	17	SAMPSON • Gary	1 (3)
WALKER • Joshua	16 (2)	DODD • Jason	1 (1)
DAVIS • Jimmy	16 (1)	FORD • Mark	1
WOOD • Neil	13 (4)	MARSH • Allan	1
MOLLOY • Eric	13 (2)	PRICE • Michael	1
WEBBER • Danny	13	TATE • Alan	1
JONES • Rhodri	7 (1)	TAYLOR • Andrew	0 (3)
CLARK • Ben	6 (1)	TIERNEY • Paul	0 (1)
WHITEMAN • Marc	5 (5)		

GOALSCORERS

Name	Goals (penalties)
WEBBER • Danny	17
DAVIS • Jimmy	15
WOOD • Neil	7
ROSE • Michael	5 (1)
LYNCH • Mark	4
McDEMOTT • Alan	4
MUIRHEAD • Ben	4
MOLLOY • Eric	3
GROGAN • Kevin	2
NARDIELLO • Daniel	2 (1)
SZMID • Marek	2
WALKER • Joshua	2
WHITEMAN • Marc	2
WILLIAMS • Matthew	2
STRANGE • Gareth	1
JONES • Rhodri	1
CLARK • Ben	1
Own goals	
SAMUELS • Jlloyd (Aston Villa)	1

FA PREMIER ACADEMY LEAGUE UNDER 17

GROUP A FINAL TABLE 1998-99

	P	W	D	L	F	A	Pts
MANCHESTER UNITED	22	**14**	**7**	**1**	**66**	**20**	**49**
Blackburn Rovers	22	14	5	3	56	23	47
Liverpool	22	9	10	3	47	36	37
Everton	22	10	5	7	44	33	35
Manchester City	22	9	6	7	49	42	33
Crewe Alexandra	22	6	8	8	30	32	26
Aston Villa	22	7	4	11	34	44	25

THE TIMES FA YOUTH CUP 1998-99

Saturday 19th December 1998

v EVERTON Third Round (home, at Gigg Lane, Bury) • Drawn: 2-2

Rachubka • Lynch • Hilton • Roche • O'Shea • Clegg G. • Evans • Stewart • Wheatcroft • Fitzpatrick • **Chadwick 2**
Substitutes: Studley D. • Marsh • Cosgrove (for Clegg) • Webber • Davis

Wednesday 6th January 1999

v EVERTON Third Round Replay (away) • Lost: 0-4

Rachubka • Lynch • Hilton • Roche • O'Shea • Clegg G. • Evans • Stewart • Wheatcroft • Fitzpatrick • Chadwick
Substitutes: Rose S. (for Lynch) • Marsh • Studley D. (for Evans) • Cosgrove • Webber (for Fitzpatrick)

OTHER EVENTS AT OLD TRAFFORD

Saturday 24th October 1998

JJS Super League Grand Final

WIGAN WARRIORS 10	**LEEDS RHINOS 4**
Try: Robinson	Try: Blackmore
Goals: Farrell 3	

Attendance: 43,533

Sunday 11th April 1999

FA CUP (Sponsored by AXA) Semi-Final

NEWCASTLE UNITED 2	**TOTTENHAM HOTSPUR 0**
Shearer 2 (1 pen)	

Attendance: 53,609

FRIENDLIES

v IFK GOTHENBURG (Sweden) (home) • Lost: 1-2 — Thursday 9th April 1998

Culkin • Ryan • Higginbotham • Millard • Brown • Ford • Wellens • Wood • Healy • Notman • **Greening**
Substitutes: Thorrington • Rowland (for Culkin) • Rose S. (for Ryan) • Roche • Fitzpatrick (for Greening)
*This match was omitted in error from Manchester United Official Yearbook 1998

v BRISTOL CITY (away) • Lost: 1-2 — Friday 17th July 1998

Rachubka • Ryan • Hilton • Rose S. • Roche • Evans • Thorrington • Stewart • **Wheatcroft** • Healy • Chadwick
Substitutes: Gaff (for Ryan) • Marsh • Fitzpatrick (for Healy) • Clegg G. (for Wheatcroft) Studley D. (for Thorrington) Cosgrove (for Stewart) • Hickson (for Chadwick)

v FOREST GREEN ROVERS (away) • Lost: 1-4 — Sunday 19th July 1998

Rachubka • Ryan • Studley D. • Rose S. • Roche • Cosgrove • Thorrington • Stewart • **Healy** • Clegg G. • Fitzpatrick
Substitutes: Gaff (for Rose S.) • Marsh (for Rachubka) • Wheatcroft (for Clegg G.) • Hickson (for Thorrington) Hilton (for Studley D.) • Chadwick (for Fitzpatrick)

v DARWEN (away) • Won: 6-1 — Tuesday 21st July 1998

Rachubka • Ryan • Hilton • Cosgrove • Gaff • Clegg G. • Hickson • Thorrington • **Healy** • **Wheatcroft 4** • **Chadwick**
Substitutes: Rose S. (for Healy) • Marsh (for Rachubka) • Roche • Studley D. (for Ryan) • Stewart (for Thorrington)

v ASHTON UNITED (away) • Won: 6-3 — Saturday 25th July 1998

Rachubka • Lynch • Hilton • Rose S. • Gaff • Cosgrove • **Hickson 3 (1 pen)** • **Studley D.** • **Wheatcroft** • **Clegg G.** • Chadwick
Substitutes: Webber (for Wheatcroft) • Marsh • Jones (for Lynch) • Grogan (for Clegg G.)

v FULWOOD AMATEURS (away) • Won: 5-2 — Saturday 1st August 1998

Baker • Lynch • Studley M. • Rose M. • Jones • **Stewart** • Davis • Dodd • **Webber 2** • **Fitzpatrick** • **Molloy**
Substitutes: Gaff • Marsh (for Baker) • Hickson (for Davis) • Walker (for Dodd)

v UPTON ATHLETIC ASSOCIATION (away) • Won: 2-0 — Tuesday 4th August 1998

Rachubka • Rose S. • Studley D. • Cosgrove • Best • Gaff • Hickson • Evans • Clegg G. • **Wheatcroft 2** • Chadwick
Substitutes: Roche (for Gaff) • Marsh (for Rachubka) • Stewart (for Chadwick) • Hilton (for Evans) • Fitzpatrick (for Clegg G.)

v SAN DIEGO NOMADS (home, at Littleton Road) • Won: 2-0 — Friday 7th August 1998

Marsh • Lynch • Studley M. • Strange • Jones • Rose M. • Szmid • **Whiteley** • **Webber** • Wood N. • Molloy
Substitutes: Walker (for Molloy) • Baker • Dodd (for Wood N.) • Clegg S. • Muirhead (for Szmid)

Saturday 8th August 1998 — **v USA Under-23 (home • at The Cliff) • Lost: 1-4**

Rachubka • **Clegg M.** • Roche • Casper • Wallwork • Ford • Thorrington • Evans • Greening • Wood J. • Chadwick
Substitutes: Clegg G. (for Greening) • Studley D. (for Roche) • Fitzpatrick (for Chadwick) • Cosgrove

Wednesday 12th August 1998 — **v SAN DIEGO NOMADS (home • at Littleton Road) • Drawn: 2-2**

Moran • Lynch • Studley M. • McDermott • O'Shea • Rose M. • Smith • Walker • **Webber** • **Muirhead** • Whiteley
Substitute: Clegg S.

Wednesday 19th August 1998 — **v WIMBLEDON (home • at The Cliff) • Won: 1-0**

Marsh • Ryan • Hilton • Rose S. • Gaff • Cosgrove • Thorrington • Healy • Hakansson • Wheatcroft • Studley D.
Substitutes: ***Fitzpatrick*** *(for Studley) • O'Shea (for Gaff) • Hickson (for Thorrington) • Stewart (for Healy)*

Wednesday 19th August 1998 — **v WIMBLEDON (home • at Littleton Road) • Drawn: 1-1**

Moran • Lynch • Studley M. • McDermott • Rose M. • Walker • Szmid • Dodd • **Webber** • Muirhead • Whiteley
Substitutes: Wood N. (for Muirhead) • Whiteman • Sampson • Clegg S. • Tierney • Mortimer

Wednesday 26th August 1998 — **v WREXHAM (home • at Littleton Road) • Won: 6-0**

Rachubka • Ryan • Studley D. • Roche • Rose S. • Cosgrove • Hickson • Stewart • **Wheatcroft 2** • **Fitzpatrick 3 (1 pen)** • Chadwick
(**Mazzarella o.g.**)
Substitutes: Hilton • Marsh • Clegg G. (for Cosgrove) • Gaff • Whiteley

Tuesday 1st September 1998 — **v HUDDERSFIELD TOWN (home) • Won: 4-0**

Marsh • Ryan • Hilton • Rose S. • Gaff • **Whiteley** • Thorrington • Stewart • Clegg G. • **Fitzpatrick 2 (1 pen)** • Studley D.
Substitutes: Cosgrove (for Ryan) • ***Hickson*** *(for Thorrington) • Evans (for Stewart) • Healy (for Hickson)*

LIAM WHELAN MEMORIAL CHALLENGE MATCH

Tuesday 22nd September 1998 — **v HOME FARM (Republic of Ireland) (away) • Won: 4-1**

Marsh • Rose S. • Hilton • Roche • O'Shea • Cosgrove • Hickson • Whiteley • **Healy** • **Notman 3** • Chadwick
Substitutes: Studley D. (for Hickson) • Rachubka (for Marsh) • Stewart (for Whiteley) • Clegg G. (for Cosgrove)
Wheatcroft (for Chadwick)

Tuesday 13th October 1998 — **v JERSEY Under-21 (away) • Won: 10-0**

Rachubka • Cosgrove • Hilton • Stewart • Rose S. • Clegg G. • Hickson • **Evans 3** • **Healy 5** • Fitzpatrick • **Thorrington**
Substitutes: Gaff (for Cosgrove) • ***Howard*** *(for Evans) • Cosgrove (for Clegg G.) • Evans (for Fitzpatrick)*

Match Details • 1998-99

v DUBLIN SCHOOLBOYS' LEAGUE (home, at Littleton Road) • Won: 7-1 — Monday 26th October 1998

Marsh • Grogan • Molloy • **Whiteley** • O'Shea • Gaff • Hickson • **Evans (pen)** • **Wheatcroft 3** • Howard • **Fitzpatrick**
Substitutes: ***McDermott*** *(for O'Shea) • Moran • Lynch (for Fitzpatrick)*

v BRISTOL CITY (away) • Lost: 2-3 — Tuesday 16th February 1999

Culkin • Ryan • Hilton • Roche • O'Shea • Ford • **Mulryne** • **Stewart** • Healy • Chadwick • Clegg G.
Substitutes: Lynch (for Ryan) • Rachubka • Fitzpatrick (for Clegg G.)

v NIRASAKI HIGH SCHOOL (Japan) • Won: 7-0 — Wednesday 17th March 1999

Marsh • Strange • Rose M. • Gaff • Jones • **Szmid** • Evans • Walker • **Hickson 2** • **Davis 3** • **Whiteley**
Substitutes: Lynch (for Strange) • Dodd (for Walker) • McDermott (for Jones) • Studley M. (for Szmid)

v IFK START (Norway) (home, at Littleton Road) • Lost: 1-3 — Tuesday 30th March 1999

Marsh • Lynch • Hilton • Gaff • O'Shea • Cosgrove • Evans • Whiteley • **Wheatcroft** • Hickson • Studley D.
Substitutes: Strange (for O'Shea) • Williams B. (for Marsh) • Walker (for Whiteley) • Grogan (for Wheatcroft) Studley M. (for Hilton)

v IFK GOTHENBURG (Sweden) (home, at The Cliff) • Lost: 1-3 — Saturday 3rd April 1999

Culkin • Hickson • Studley M. • Cosgrove • Gaff • Hilton • Evans • Howard • Healy • **Wheatcroft** • Whiteley
Substitutes: Studley D. (for Studley M.) • Murphy (for Culkin) • Grogan (for Whiteley) • Walker (for Wheatcroft)

NIVEA 19th JUNIOR (UNDER 17s) FOOTBALL TOURNAMENT – BLUDENZ, AUSTRIA

Saturday 3 April 1999 — **Group B v TURKEY • Won:1-0**

Williams B. • Clegg • Pugh • Tate • McDermott • Szmid • Davis • Rose • Whiteman • **Williams M.** • Taylor
Substitutes Nardiello (for Whiteman) • Coates (for Williams M.)

Sunday 4 April 1999 — **Group B v AUSTRIA • Drawn: 1-1**

Williams B. • Sampson • Pugh • Tate • McDermott • Szmid • Davis • Rose • Coates • **Nardiello** • Dodd

Sunday 4 April 1999 — **Group B v VfB STUTTGART (Germany) • Lost: 0-1**

Williams B. • Clegg • Pugh • Tate • McDermott • Szmid • Davis • Rose • Whiteman • Williams M. • Taylor
Substitute Coates (for Williams M.)

Monday 5 April 1999 — **Semi-final v BAYERN MUNICH • Won: 1-0**

Williams B. • Clegg • Pugh • Tate • McDermott • Szmid • Davis • Rose • **Williams M.** • Nardiello • Taylor
Substitutes Coates (for Williams M.) • Sampson (for Taylor)

Monday 5 April 1999 — **Final v AUSTRIA • Drawn: 1-1***

Williams B. • Clegg • Pugh • **Tate** • McDermott • Szmid • Davis • Rose • Williams M. • Nardiello • Taylor
Substitutes Whiteman (for Nardiello) • Sampson (for Taylor) • Coates (for Williams M.)
***Lost 4-3 on penalties**
Penalty scorers: **Whiteman • Davis • Rose**

TOURNAMENT SQUAD

1. Ben WILLIAMS
2. Steven CLEGG
3. Danny PUGH
4. Alan TATE
5. Alan McDERMOTT
6. Marek SZMID
7. Jimmy DAVIS
8. Michael ROSE
9. Marc WHITEMAN
10. Daniel NARDIELLO
11. Ashley DODD
12. Andrew TAYLOR
13. Michael PRICE
14. Gary SAMPSON
15. Matthew WILLIAMS
16. Chris COATES

MANCHESTER UNITED ACADEMY

UNDER 16s SQUAD 1998-99

Ryan ALBISTON	Ben MUIRHEAD
Sean CAME	Daniel NARDIELLO
Benjamin CLARKE	Michael PRICE
Steven CLEGG	Daniel PUGH
Craig COATES	Gary SAMPSON
Stephen COOKE	Alan TATE
Neil FAIRHURST	Andrew TAYLOR
Paul HOLLAND	Paul TIERNEY
Chris HUGHES	Michael TONGE
Andy MOORE	Marc WHITEMAN
David MORAN	Matthew WILLIAMS
Alex MORTIMER	Neil WOOD

Due to unforeseen circumstances we regret that the Under 16 Academy match details were unavailable at the time of going to press

NORTHERN IRELAND MILK CUP INTERNATIONAL YOUTH TOURNAMENT 1998 (UNDER 16s)

Monday 20 July 1998 — **v COUNTY DOWN Group B • Won: 4-0**

Moran • Lynch • Rose • Szmid • Jones • Strange • **Davis** • Studley • **Webber 3** • Whiteley • Molloy
Substitutes: Taylor (for Strange) • Walker (for Lynch) • Muirhead (for Webber) • Wood (for Molloy)

Tuesday 21 July 1998 — **v CHILE Group B • Lost: 0-3**

Moran • Lynch • Rose • Szmid • Jones • Strange • Davis • Studley • Webber • Whiteley • Molloy
Substitutes: Clegg (for Rose) • Muirhead (for Strange) • Wood (for Molloy)

Wednesday 22 July 1998 — **v FRAM Group B (Iceland) • Won: 6-0**

Moran • Lynch • Rose • Szmid • Jones • **Davis 2** • **Whiteley** • Studley • **Webber** • **Muirhead** • **Wood**
Substitutes: Strange (for Jones) • Taylor (for Szmid) • Walker (for Whiteley)

Wednesday 22 July 1998 — **v SUNDERLAND Quarter-final • Drawn: 2-2***

Moran • Lynch • Rose • Szmid • Jones • **Davis** • Whiteley • Studley • **Webber** • Muirhead • Wood
*** Won 5-3 on penalties**
Penalty scorers: **Davis • Whiteley • Wood • Webber • Rose**

Thursday 23 July 1998 — **v WEST HAM UNITED Semi-final • Lost: 2-3**

Moran • Lynch • Rose • Szmid • Jones • Davis • Whiteley • Studley • **Webber** • Muirhead • **Wood**
Substitute: Strange (for Szmid)

Friday 24 July 1998 — **v CREWE ALEXANDRA Third/Fourth Place Playoff • Lost: 1-2**

Baker • Walker • Clegg • Muirhead • Studley • Strange • Davis • Taylor • Webber • Dodd • Molloy
Substitutes: Lynch (for Dodd) • ***Wood*** *(for Davis)*

TOURNAMENT SQUAD

1. David MORAN
2. Mark LYNCH
3. Michael ROSE
4. Marek SZMID
5. Rhodri JONES
6. Gareth STRANGE
7. Jimmy DAVIS
8. Andrew TAYLOR
9. Danny WEBBER
10. Ashley DODD
11. Eric MOLLOY
12. Joshua WALKER
13. Christian BAKER
14. Mark STUDLEY
15. Lee WHITELEY
16. Ben MUIRHEAD
17. Neil WOOD
18. Steven CLEGG

NORTH TYNESIDE INTERNATIONAL YOUTH TOURNAMENT (UNDER 16s)

names in bold indicate goalscorers

Group Stage v MIDDLESBROUGH • Won: 4-1 — Wednesday 29 July 1998

Moran • Tonge • Tierney • Taylor • Clegg • Mortimer • Muirhead • Sampson • **Pugh** • **Williams** • **Wood 2 (1 pen)**
Substitutes: Tate • Whiteman • Fairhurst • Came • Cogger

Group Stage v HARTLEPOOL UNITED • Won: 5-1 — Wednesday 29 July 1998

Moran • Tate • Tierney • Taylor • Clegg • Came • Fairhurst • Sampson • **Whiteman 3** • **Pugh** • Wood
*Substitutes: Mortimer • Muirhead (for Pugh) • **Williams** (for Taylor) • Tonge (for Wood) • Cogger*

Group Stage v WASHINGTON WEST (USA) • Won: 9-0 — Thursday 30 July 1998

Moran • Tate • Came • Taylor • Clegg • Mortimer • Fairhurst • Sampson • **Whiteman 3** • **Williams 3** • **Pugh 2**
*Substitutes: Tierney (for Pugh) • Muirhead • Wood • **Tonge** • Cogger (for Clegg)*

Group Stage v NOTTS COUNTY • Won: 4-0 — Friday 31 July 1998

Moran • Tate • Tierney • Cogger • Came • Mortimer • Muirhead • **Sampson** • Whiteman • Tonge • **Wood 2**
*Substitutes: Taylor • Clegg (for Cogger) • **Williams** (for Whiteman) • Fairhurst • Pugh (for Mortimer)*

Semi-final v NEWCASTLE UNITED • Won: 5-1 — Saturday 1 August 1998

Moran • Tonge • Tierney • Taylor • Clegg • Came • Muirhead • Sampson • **Pugh** • **Williams** • **Wood 3**
Substitutes: Mortimer (for Tonge) • Whiteman (for Muirhead) • Waud (for Tierney) • Cogger

Final v HEART OF MIDLOTHIAN • Won: 4-2 — Sunday 2 August 1998

Moran • Came • Tierney • Taylor • Clegg • Mortimer • **Muirhead** • Sampson • **Pugh** • Williams • **Wood 2**
Substitutes: Tonge (for Sampson) • Whiteman (for Williams) • Waud (for Mortimer) • Cogger

TOURNAMENT SQUAD

1. David MORAN
2. Alan TATE
3. Paul TIERNEY
4. Andrew TAYLOR
5. Steven CLEGG
6. Alex MORTIMER
7. Ben MUIRHEAD
8. Gary SAMPSON
9. Marc WHITEMAN
10. Matthew WILLIAMS
11. Neil WOOD
12. Neil FAIRHURST
14. Daniel PUGH
15. Michael TONGE
16. Shaun CAME
17. John COGGER
18. Ben WAUD

MANCHESTER UNITED ACADEMY (UNDER 15s)

Sunday 6 September, 1998 — **v LIVERPOOL (away) • Lost: 2-3**

Thewlis • Thompson • Price • Waud • Cogger • Taylor • Eckersley • Humphreys • McTaggart • **Mooniaruck** • **Hutchinson**
Substitutes: Woodcock • Rea • Ahmed • Heath • Bancroft

Sunday 13 September 1998 — **v SUNDERLAND (away) • Won: 2-1**

Thewlis • Thompson • Taylor • Eckersley • Cogger • Waud • Ahmed • Humphreys • **Heath** • McTaggart • **Hutchinson (pen)**
Substitutes: Price • Rea • Bancroft

Monday 15 September 1998 — **v NORTH WALES SELECT (away) • Drawn: 0-0**

Thewlis • Fairhurst • Thompson • Ahmed • Came • Mortimer • Eckersley • Humphreys • Holland • McDonagh • Hutchinson
Substitutes: Rea • Bancroft • Price

Sunday 20 September 1998 — **v PRESTON NORTH END (home) • Drawn: 3-3**

Thewlis • Eckersley • Thompson • Rea • Cogger • Waud • Mooniaruck • Humphreys • **Heath 3** • McTaggart • Hutchinson
Substitutes: Ahmed • Bancroft • Price

Sunday 27 September 1998 — **v OLDHAM ATHLETIC (home) • Won: 4-0**

Thewlis • Eckersley • Taylor • Thompson • Waud • Rea • **Mooniaruck** • Ahmed • **Heath 2** • Bancroft • **Hutchinson**
Substitutes: Humphreys • Price

Sunday 4 October 1998 — **v COVENTRY CITY (away) • Drawn: 2-2**

Woodcock • **Eckersley** • Rea • Thompson • Taylor • Ahmed • Bancroft • Humphreys • Heath • Mooniaruck • **Hutchinson**
Substitute: Collett

Sunday 18 October 1998 — **v MANCHESTER CITY (away) • Lost: 1-2**

Thewlis • Ahmed • Taylor • Eckersley • Waud • Mortimer • Mooniaruck • Humphreys • **McTaggart** • Hutchinson • Rea • Bancroft • Price
Substitutes: Bancroft • Price

Sunday 1 November 1998 — **v LIVERPOOL (home) Lost: 1-2**

Thewlis • Thompson • Taylor • Dootson • Came • Waud • Eckersley • Humphreys • McTaggart • **Mooniaruck** • Hutchinson
Substitutes: Rea • Bancroft • Ahmed • Price

v BOLTON WANDERERS (home) • Lost: 3-4 Sunday 8 November 1998

Woodcock • Thompson • Taylor • **Eckersley** • Waud • Came • Bancroft • Rea • **McTaggart** • Humphreys • **Mooniaruck**
Substitutes: Hutchinson • Ahmed • Price

v ASTON VILLA (away) • Drawn: 2-2 Sunday 22 November 1998

Thewlis • Cogger • Thompson • Humphreys • Came • Waud • Ahmed • Taylor • McTaggart • **Mooniaruck • Hutchinson**
Substitutes: Rea • Bancroft • Eckersley

v MANCHESTER CITY (home) • Lost: 0-3 Sunday 13 December

Woodcock • Eckersley • Thompson • Humphreys • Came • Waud • Ahmed • Holland • McTaggart • Taylor • Rea
Substitutes: Price • Bancroft

v EVERTON (away) • Won: 1-0 Sunday 20 December 1998

Thewlis • Ahmed • Thompson • Came • Waud • Taylor • **Bancroft** • Humphreys • McTaggart • Eckersley • Rea
Substitute: Johnson

v LIVERPOOL (away) • Lost: 1-4 Sunday 17 January 1999

Woodcock • Eckersley • Price • Came • Waud • Humphreys • Ahmed • Rea • **McTaggart** • Mooniaruck • Hutchinson
Substitutes: Bancroft • Thewlis

v MIDDLESBROUGH (home) • Drawn: 1-1 Sunday 24 January 1999

Woodcock • Eckersley • Rea • Cogger • Waud • Humphreys • Mooniaruck • Ahmed • **Heath** • Poole • Hutchinson
Substitute: Bancroft

v BOLTON WANDERERS (away) • Won: 6-1 Sunday 31 January 1999

Woodcock • Eckersley • Rea • **Fotheringham** • Cogger • Taylor • McTaggart • Fletcher • **Heath • Humphreys 2** • Mooniaruck
*Substitutes:: **Hutchinson 2** • Bancroft • Ahmed • Price*

v BLACKBURN ROVERS (home) • Lost: 1-3 Sunday 14 February 1999

Cushon • Cogger • Tierney • Tate • Clegg • Taylor • Humphreys • Holland • **Heath** • Whiteman • Hutchinson
Substitutes: Eckersley • Rea • McTaggart

Sunday 28 February 1999 **v CREWE ALEXANDRA (home) • Lost: 2-5**

Thewlis • Eckersley • Rea • Waud • Taylor • Fiachra • Ahmed • Humphreys • **Mooniaruck** • **McTaggart** • Grant
Substitutes: Hutchinson • Bancroft • Thompson • Woodcock

Sunday 21 March 1999 **v EVERTON (home) • Drawn: 0-0**

Woodcock • Eckersley • Thompson • Humphreys • Cogger • Waud • Ahmed • Taylor • Heath • Mooniaruck • Hutchinson
Substitutes: McTaggart • Bancroft • Thewlis

Sunday 11 April 1999 **v BARNSLEY (home) • Won: 2-1**

Thewlis • Eckersley • Thompson • Humphreys • Cogger • Waud • **Mooniaruck** • Taylor • Heath • **McTaggart** • Hutchinson
Substitutes: Bancroft • Woodcock

Sunday 18 April 1999 **v DERBY COUNTY (away) • Won: 4-2**

Woodcock • Sparrow • Thompson • Cogger • Waud • Taylor • Ahmed • Trialist • **Heath** • **Humphreys** • **Mooniaruck 2**
Substitutes: Hutchison • Eckersley • McTaggart • Rea • Bancroft

Sunday 25 April 1999 **v MANCHESTER CITY (home) • Won: 3-0**

Trialist • Ahmed • Taylor • Thompson • Waud • Fletcher • McArdle • Fox • Heath • **Humphreys 3** • Mooniaruck
Substitutes: Eckersley • Hutchinson • Rea • Bancroft

UNDER 14s

Sunday 6 September 1998 **v LIVERPOOL (home) • Lost: 0-5**

Carnell • Adamson • Lawrence • Bruce • Rodgers • Jones • Mattison • Eames • Poole • Johnson • Collett
Substitutes: Quinlan • Bennett • Stamford • Baguley • Bardsley • Ney

Sunday 13 September 1998 **v SUNDERLAND (home) • Won: 3-0**

Woodcock • Bardsley • Lawrence • Bruce • Bell • Jones • O'Conner • Poole • **Johnson 2** • **Shields** • Collett
Substitutes: Bennett • Rodgers

Match Details • 1998-99

v PRESTON NORTH END (away) • Won 5-2 — Sunday 20 September 1998

Woodcock • Bardsley • Lawrence • **Rodgers** • Howard • **Jones** • Bennett • O'Conner • **Poole 2** • Mattison • **Collett**
Substitutes: Ney • Baguley

v OLDHAM ATHLETIC (away) • Drawn: 2-2 — Sunday 27 September 1998

Woodcock • Bruce • Lawrence • Howard • Bell • Baguley • Bennett • O'Conner • **Poole** • **Shields** • Collett
Substitutes: Quinlan • Ney • Eames

v BURNLEY (home) • Won: 3-0 — 4 October 1998

Higginbottom • Bardsley • Lawrence • Bruce • Rodgers • Jones • Ney • Fraser • **Johnson 2** • Quinlan • **Baguley**
Substitute Eames

v MANCHESTER CITY (home) • Won: 3-2 — Sunday 18 October 1998

Woodcock • Bardsley • Lawrence • Rodgers • Bell • Jones • Quinlan • **Bruce** • **Poole 2** • Johnson • Collett
Substitutes: Eames • Baguley • Bennett • Ney

v LIVERPOOL (away) • Drawn: 3-3 — Sunday 1 November 1998

Woodcock • Bruce • Lawrence • Rodgers • Ashley • **Jones** • Eames • Bouskie • Poole • **Johnson** • **Collett**
Substitutes: Bardsley • Baguley • Quinlan • Ney

v BOLTON WANDERERS (home) • Won: 5-3 — Sunday 8 November 1998

Higginbottom • Bardsley • Lawrence • Bruce • Conner • **Jones 2** • Eames • Bouskie • **Johnson** • **Poole** • **Collett**
Substitutes: Quinlan • Ney • Mattison

v BLACKBURN ROVERS (away) • Won: 3-2 — Sunday 15 November 1998

Nelson • Bruce • Lawrence • Conner • Bell • Jones • Shields • Beaumont • **Poole** • **Brown** • **Collett**
Substitutes: Baguley • Mattison • Johnson

v ASTON VILLA (home) Lost: 0-2 — Sunday 22 November 1998

Woodcock • Bardsley • Lawrence • Bruce • Rodgers • Jones • Mattison • Baguley • Brown • Quinlan • Ney
Substitutes: Eames • Poole • Johnson

Sunday 29 November 1998 **v CREWE ALEXANDRA (home) • Lost: 1-2**

Nelson • Bardsley • Lawrence • Bruce • Bell • Jones • Shields • Baguley • Brown • **Johnson** • Collett.
Substitutes: Poole • Rodgers • Byrne

Sunday 13 December 1998 **v MANCHESTER CITY (away) • Lost: 0-7**

Higginbottom • Ney • Lawrence • Rodgers • Bruce • Jones • Mattison • Baguley • Johnson • Poole • Collett
Substitute Connor

Sunday 20 December 1998 **v EVERTON (away) • Lost: 0-2**

Woodcock • Bardsley • Lawrence • Bruce • Conner • Beaumont • Eames • Poole • Johnson • Brown • Jones
Substitutes: Mattison • Bouksie • Ney • Rodgers • Baguley • Higginbottom

Sunday 17 January 1999 **v LIVERPOOL (home) • Won: 3-1**

Nelson • Bardsley • Lawrence • Kelly • Conner • Jones • Shields • **Brown** • **Johnson 2** • Poole • Collett
Substitutes: Eames • Baguley • Rodgers

Sunday 24 January 1999 **v MIDDLESBROUGH (home) • Drawn: 1-1**

Higginbottom • Bruce • Lawrence • Hengler • Connor • Jones • Eames • Beaumont • Johnson • **Brown** • Collett
Substitutes: Baguley • Bardsley

Sunday 31 January 1999 **v BOLTON WANDERERS (home) • Won: 3-0**

Nelson • Kelly • Jones • Hengler • Conner • **Poole** • **Shields** • Bruce • **Johnson** • Brown • Collett
Substitutes: Baguley • Bardsley • Eames • Lawrence • Higginbottom

Sunday 7 February 1999 **v COVENTRY CITY (away) • Won: 4-1**

Nelson • Bardsley • Lawrence • Hengler • Conner • **Jones** • Shields • Bruce • Quinlan • **Poole 3** • Collett
Substitutes: Eames • Baguley • Higginbottom

Sunday 14 February 1999 **v BLACKBURN ROVERS (home) • Drawn: 3-3**

Higginbottom • Bardsley • Lawrence • Kelly • Conner • Jones • Quinlan • Bruce • **Johnson** • **Poole 3** • Collett
Substitutes: Eames • Hengler • Baguley • Woodcock

v ASTON VILLA (away) • Lost: 2-4 — Sunday 21 February 1999

Higginbottom • Bardsley • Jones • Kelly • Conner • **Watt** • Quinlan • Bruce • **Johnson** • Poole • Collett
Substitutes: Baguley • Hengler

v CREWE ALEXANDRA (away) • Lost: 1-2 — Sunday 28 February 1999

Nelson • Bardsley • Baguley • Hengler • Conner • Jones • Eames • Bruce • Johnson • **Watt** • Collett
Substitute Quinlan

v BARNSLEY (away) • Won: 6-3 — Sunday 11 April 1999

Higginbottom • Kelly • Lawrence • Hengler • Conner • Jones • Beaumont • **Watt** • **Johnson 2** • **Poole 2** • **Collett**
Substitutes: Bruce • Baguley • Quinlan • Eames

v DERBY COUNTY (home) • Won: 3-2 — Sunday 18 April 1999

Higginbottom • Bruce • Lawrence • **Watt** • Conner • Hengler • McKay • Jones • **Johnson** • **Poole** • Collett
Substitutes: Howard • Quinlan • Baguley • Bardsley

v MANCHESTER CITY (away) • Lost: 2-3 — Sunday 25 April 1999

Higginbottom • Bruce • Lawrence • Hengler • Connor • Jones • Quinlan • Bradley • **Johnson** • Poole • **Collett**
Substitutes: Shields • Howard • Bardsley • Baguley • Eames

NORTHERN IRELAND MILK CUP INTERNATIONAL YOUTH TOURNAMENT 1998 (UNDER 14s)

Group 4 **v MID-ULSTER YL** (Northern Ireland) • Lost: 0-5 — Monday 20 July 1998

Cole • Patterson • Taylor • Eckersley • Cogger • Humphreys • Waud • Bancroft • Heath • McTaggart • Hutchinson
Substitutes: Burke (for Patterson) • Hamilton (for McTaggart)

Group 4 **v SUNDERLAND** • Lost: 1-2 — Tuesday 21 July 1998

Cole • Waud • Taylor • Eckersley • Cogger • Humphreys • **Burke** • Bancroft • Heath • Hamilton • Hutchinson
Substitute McTaggart (for Bancroft)

Wednesday 22 July 1998 — **Group 4 v BALLYMENA & DISTRICT YL (Northern Ireland) • Won: 4-0**

Woodcock • Patterson • Taylor • Eckersley • Cogger • Humphreys • Burke • Waud • **Heath** • **Hamilton 2** • Hutchinson **(1 o.g.)**
Substitutes: McTaggart (for Hutchinson) • Thompson (for Taylor) • Bancroft (for Heath) • Ahmed (for Burke)

Thursday 23 July 1998 — **Quarter-final v CHARLTON ATHLETIC • Won: 2-0**

Woodcock • Patterson • Taylor • **Eckersley** • Cogger • Humphreys • Burke • Waud • **Heath** • Hamilton • Hutchinson
Substitutes: Rea (for Hutchinson) • McTaggart (for Hamilton)

Thursday 23 July 1998 — **Semi-final v MIDDLESBROUGH) • Lost: 0-2**

Woodcock • Patterson • Taylor • Eckersley • Cogger • Humphreys • Burke • Waud • Heath • McTaggart • Hutchinson
Substitutes: Hamilton (for Heath) • Rea (for Humphreys) • Thompson (for Taylor) • Ahmed (for Burke)

Friday 24 July 1998 — **Third/Fourth Place Play-Off v DUNDALK SBL • Drawn 0-0***

Cole • Waud • Taylor • Eckersley • Cogger • Rea • Ahmed • Bancroft • McTaggart • Hamilton • Thompson
Substitutes: Patterson (for Bancroft) • Burke (for McTaggart) • Hutchinson (for Rae)
***Lost 3-4 on penalties**

TOURNAMENT SQUAD

1. Simon COLE
2. Andrew PATTERSON
3. Kris TAYLOR
4. Michael ECKERSLEY
5. John COGGER
6. Christopher HUMPHREYS
7. Christopher BURKE
8. Darren FLETCHER
9. Colin HEATH
10. Mark HAMILTON
11. Ryan HUTCHINSON
12. Matthew REA
13. Gary WOODCOCK
14. Benjamin WAUD
15. Daniel McTAGGART
16. James THOMPSON
17. James BANCROFT
18. Adnan AHMED

MANCHESTER UNITED ACADEMY (UNDER-13s)

Sunday 6 September 1998 — **v LIVERPOOL (away) • Drawn: 1-1**

Yeomans • Picken • Howard • Hogg • Eckersley • Brennan • **Hartley** • Kelliher • Corvins • Dyke • Redshaw
Substitutes: Heaton • Walker • Coffey • Allen

v SUNDERLAND (home) • Won: 3-0 Sunday 13 September 1998

Yeomans • Picken • Howard • Hogg • Eckersley • Kingsbury • Green • Corvins • Coffey • **Walker 2** • Redshaw
Substitutes: ***Hartley*** *• Allen*

v PRESTON NORTH END (away) • Won: 7-2 Sunday 20 September 1998

Heaton • Picken • Green • **Hogg** • Eckersley • **Brennan** • Hartley • Corvins • **Walker 2** • **Redshaw 3** • Coffey
Substitutes: Allen • Dyke • Kelliher

v CELTIC (home) • Lost: 1-3 Sunday 27 September 1998

Yeomans • Picken • Green • Hogg • Eckersley • Kingsbury • Hartley • Corvins • Kelliher • Dyke • **Flanaghan**
Substitutes: Allen • Coffey

v BRADFORD CITY (home) • Won: 7-0 Sunday 4 October

Heaton • Picken • Howard • Green • Kelliher • **Brennan** • Allen • Corvins • Coffey • **Flanaghan 5** • Walker
Substitute ***Dyke***

v MANCHESTER CITY (away) • Won: 1-0 Sunday 18 October 1998

Yeomans • Picken • Howard • Green • Kelliher • Brennan • Allen • Corvins • Coffey • **Flanaghan** • Redshaw
Substitutes: Hartley • Walker • Dyke

v LIVERPOOL (home) • Won: 4-1 Sunday 1 November 1998

Yeomans • Picken • Howard • **Hogg** • Kelliher • Brennan • Allen • **Corvins** • Coffey • Flanaghan • **Redshaw 2**
Substitutes: Eckersley • Walker • Dyke • Hartley

v BOLTON WANDERERS (home) • Won: 5-0 Sunday 8 November 1998

Yeomans • Picken • Howard • Hogg • Eckersley • **Dyke** • **Brennan 2** • Hartley • Coffey • **Flanaghan** • **Walker**
Substitutes: Corvins • Redshaw

v BLACKBURN ROVERS (home) • Won: 3-2 Sunday 15 November 1998

Yeomans • Picken • Howard • Hogg • **Eckersley** • Kingsbury • Brennan • Corvins • Kelliher • Flanaghan • **Redshaw 2**
Substitutes: Coffey • Walker

Sunday 22 November 1998 — **v ASTON VILLA (away) • Lost: 1-3**

Heaton • Picken • Howard • Hogg • Eckersley • Brennan • Allen • Corvins • Kelliher • Flanaghan • **Redshaw**
Substitutes: Coffey • Walker

Sunday 13 December 1998 — **v MANCHESTER CITY (home) • Lost: 0-1**

Yeomans • Picken • Howard • Hogg • Kelliher • Kingsbury • Brennan • Corvins • Coffey • Flanaghan • Redshaw
Substitute: Walker

Sunday 20 December 1998 — **v EVERTON (home) • Won: 5-0**

Heaton • Picken • Howard • Hogg • Eckersley • **Dyke** • Kelliher • Corvins • Coffey • **Flanaghan** • **Redshaw 3**
Substitutes: Brennan • Walker • Yeomans • Allen

Sunday 17 Janaury 1999 — **v LIVERPOOL (away) • Drawn: 2-2**

Yeomans • Picken • Howard • Hogg • Eckersley • Dyke • Jones • Corvins • Kelliher • Flanaghan • **Redshaw**
*Substitutes: Coffey • **Walker** • Brennan • Allen*

Sunday 31 January 1999 — **v BOLTON WANDERERS (away) • Won: 4-1**

Heaton • Picken • Howard • Hogg • Eckersley • Dyke • Jones • **Corvins** • Coffey • **Flanaghan** • Walker
*Substitutes: Adams • **Redshaw 2***

Sunday 7 February 1999 — **v COVENTRY CITY (away) • Drawn: 1-1**

Yeomans • Picken • Howard • Hogg • Eckersley • Dyke • Jones • **Corvins** • Coffey • Flanaghan • Walker
Substitute: Kelliher

Sunday 14 February 1999 — **v BLACKBURN ROVERS (home) • Won: 2-0**

Heaton • Simpson • **Eckersley** • Howard • Hogg • Dyke • Jones • **Corvins** • Coffey • Calliste • Walker
Substitute: McMahon

Sunday 28 February 1999 — **v CREWE ALEXANDRA (away) • Won: 2-0**

Heaton • Picken • Howard • Hogg • Eckersley • Dyke • **Jones** • Kelliher • Coffey • **Flanaghan 2** • Walker
Substitute: Jones K.

v SHEFFIELD UNITED (home) • Won: 3-1 — Sunday 7 March 1999

Yeomans • Simpson • Howard • Picken • Harkness • Dyke • Jones S.• Hogg • Coffey • **Wanlass 2 • Fox**
Substitutes: McMahon • Flanaghan

v EVERTON (away) • Drawn: 1-1 — Sunday 21 March 1999

Heaton • Eckersley • Howard • Picken • Kelliher • Dyke • Jones • Hogg • Coffey • **Flanaghan** • Walker
Substitute: Corvins

v BARNSLEY (away) • Drawn: 2-2 — Sunday 11 April 1999

Yeomans • Picken • Howard • Hogg • Eckersley • Kingsbury • Corvins • Kelliher • Coffey • **Flanaghan 2** • Walker
Substitute: Dyke

v DERBY COUNTY (home) • Won: 2-1 — Sunday 18 April 1999

Heaton • Eckersley • Howard • Picken • Kelliher • Dyke • Jones • Corvins • Coffey • Flanaghan • **Walker** • **(1 o.g.)**
Substitute: Holt

v MANCHESTER CITY (home) • Lost: 2-3 — Sunday 25 April 1999

Yeomans • Picken • Howard • Jones • Eckersley • Kingsbury • McGready • Corvins • Kelliher • **Wanlass • Fox**
Substitutes: Heaton • Coffey • Flanaghan • Walker • Hogg • Dyke

v PROVENCE SELECT (France) – Cultural Exchange Visit* (home) • Won: 2-1 — Saturday 1 May 1999

Heaton • Picken • Howard • Hogg • **Eckersley** • Kingsbury • Jones • **Corvins** • Coffey • Flanaghan • Walker
Substitutes: Yeomans • Gennions • Dyke • Kelliher
***Manchester United FC & Ashton-on-Mersey School**

v LIVERPOOL (home) • Won: 2-1 — Thursday 6 May 1999

Yeomans • Picken • Howard • Hogg • Eckersley • Dyke • Jones • Corvins • Kelliher • **Flanaghan • Walker**
Substitutes: Heaton • Coffey • Gennions

3rd INTERNATIONAL CHAMPIONSHIP OF FOOTBALL 7 (UNDER 13s) – MARBELLA, SPAIN

Sunday 27 December 1998
Group B v ATLETICO MADRID (Spain) • Lost: 0-1
Heaton • Howard • Knights • Guthrie • Jones • McMahon
Grimes *Substitute: Wilcox-Crooks (for Grimes)*

Sunday 27 December 1998
Group B v ATHLETIC BILBAO (Spain) • Lost: 0-4
Heaton • Howard • Knights • Guthrie • Jones • McMahon
Wilcox-Crooks *Substitutes: Adams (for Knights) • Evans (for McMahon) • Allen (for Howard)*

Sunday 27 December 1998
Group B v PSV EINDHOVEN (Holland) • Lost: 0-1
Heaton • Howard • Knights • Wilcox-Crooks • Jones
McMahon • Grimes *Substitutes: Allen (for Jones) Guthrie (for McMahon)*

Monday 28 December 1998
Group B v OLYMPIQUE MARSEILLE (France) • Drawn: 1-1
Heaton • Howard • Knights • Guthrie • Jones • McMahon
Wilcox-Crooks *Substitutes: Allen (for Howard) • Grimes (for Guthrie) • Marsh-Evans (for McMahon)*

TOURNAMENT SQUAD

Nicholas ADAMS
Damien ALLEN
Ashley GRIMES
Danny GUTHRIE
Tom HEATON
Mark HOWARD
Richie JONES
Chris McMAHON
Robert MARSH-EVANS
Mark KNIGHTS
Aaron RATCHFORD
Chris WILCOX-CROOKS

UNDER 12s

Nicolas ADAMS • Joe BROOKS • Bradley DEMPSEY
Robert MARSH-EVANS • Ashley GRIMES • Danny GUTHRIE
James HOLDEN • Joe HOLT • Richie JONES • Chris KEATING
Mark KNIGHTS • Sean McALLISTER • Nick McLOUGHLIN
Chris McMAHON • Kieron SALMON • Jon SARCEVIC
Daniel SIMPSON • Robert WALKER • Chris WAUGH
Chris WILCOX-CROOKS

UNDER 11s

Chris BAGULEY • Richard BAKER
Lee BARNES • Tom BLACK • Aaron BURNS
Jack BUTTERWORTH • Fraizer CAMPBELL
Leigh CRAVEN • Luke DANIELS • Gareth EVANS
Gary HILLMAN • Iain HOWARD
Jonathan HUNT • Michael LEA
Anthony PILKINGTON • Daniel PRINCE
Aaron RATCHFORD • Ryan SHAWCROSS
Luke SYLVESTER

UNDER 10s

Febian BRANDY • James CHESTER
Theo COLEMAN • Christopher COOKE
Alex DRINKWATER • Richard ECKERSLEY
Lee HANSON • Gianluca HAVERN
Sam HEWSON • Adam INGRAM-HUGHES
Lee JOHNSON • Zaj JONES • Luke MORGAN
David OWENS • Sean QUINLAN
Thomas ROWE • Daniel TOWNSEND
Joseph THOMPSON

UNDER 9s

Nick BLACKMAN • Jacob BUTTERFIELD
Jamie BYRNE • Michael CONNOR
Jon CROMPTON • James DERBYSHIRE
Daniel DRINKWATER • Michael EATON
Chris EVENS • Daniel GORMAN
Dominic HUGHES • Paul JACKSON
Craig McCOLL • Michael McFALONE
Matthew MAINWARING • Tom MELLOR
Matthew ROBERTS • Alex SKIDMORE
James WAGETT • Liam YATES

DALLAS CUP XX 1999 (UNDER 12s)

Sunday 28 March 1999
Group A v SOLAR (USA) • Lost: 0-1
Tuffey • Simpson • Adams • Holt • Knights • Jones • Salmon
Guthrie • Wilcox-Crooks • Grimes • McMahon
Substitute: Campbell (for Salmon)

Monday 29 March 1999
v SCOTT GALLAGHER (USA) • Won: 5-0
Tuffey • Simpson • Adams • Holt • Knights • Jones • Salmon
Guthrie • **Wilcox-Crooks** • **Grimes** • McMahon
*Substitutes: Daniels (for Tuffey) • Best (for Simpson)
Evans J. (for Adams)* • **Evans G.** *(for Knights)
Campbell (for Salmon)* • **Burns** *(for Wilcox-Crooks)
Brooks (for McMahon)*

Wednesday 31 March 1999
v HOUSTONIANS (USA) • Lost: 1-3
Adams • Holt • Knights • Jones • Salmon • Guthrie
Wilcox-Crooks • **Grimes (pen)** • McMahon
*Substitutes: Evans G. (for Adams) • Evans J. (for Knights)
Campbell (for Salmon) • Brooks (for McMahon)*

v FC DELCO RASS (USA) – Friendly Match • Drawn: 3-3
Thursday 1 April 1999
Tuffey • Simpson • Adams • Holt • Evans J. • Campbell
Evans G. • Jones • **Wilcox-Crooks** • Burns • Brooks
*Substitutes: Daniels (for Tuffey) • Best (for Holt)
Salmon (for Campbell) • Guthrie (for Jones)*
Grimes *(for Wilcox-Crooks) McMahon (for Brooks)*

Friday 2 April 1999
v PATEADORES (USA) – Friendly Match • Won: 2-1
Daniels • Simpson • Adams • Holt • Evans J. • Salmon
Jones • **Evans G.** • Grimes • Wilcox-Crooks • McMahon
Substitutes: Campbell (for Salmon) • Best (for Evans G.)
Burns *(for Grimes) • Brooks (for McMahon)*

Saturday 3 April 1999
v ATALANTA (Mexico) – Friendly Match • Won: 9-1
Simpson • Best • Knights • Evans J. • **Salmon** • **Guthrie 2**
Jones • Brooks • **Burns 2** • Campbell
Substitutes: Daniels (for Tuffey) • Evans G. (for Simpson)
Grimes 3 *(for Brooks) •* ***Wilcox-Crooks*** *(for Burns)*

TOURNAMENT SQUAD

Nicholas ADAMS
Scott BEST
Joseph BROOKS
Aaron BURNS
Fraizer CAMPBELL
Luke DANIELS
Gareth EVANS
Jonathan EVANS
Ashley GRIMES
Danny GUTHRIE
Joseph HOLT
Richard JONES
Mark KNIGHTS
Christopher McMAHON
Kieron SALMON
Daniel SIMPSON
Jonathan TUFFEY
Chris WILCOX-CROOKS

DANONE CUP (UNDER 12s) – PARC DES PRINCES, PARIS

Sunday 9 May 1999
Group A v DC UNITED • Lost: 0-1
Ratchford • Simpson • Evans J. • Campbell • Baker
Guthrie • McMahon • Burns • Wilcox-Crooks
Substitutes: Daniels • Hunt • Evans G.

Snnday 9 May 1999
Group A v JUVENTUS (Italy) • Won: 3-1
Ratchford • Simpson • Evans J. • **Campbell** • Baker
Guthrie • McMahon • **Evans G.** • Wilcox-Crooks
Substitutes: Daniels • Hunt • Burns

Sunday 9 May 1999
Group A v RC LENS (France) • Won: 2-1
Ratchford • Simpson • Evans J. • **Campbell** • Hunt • Guthrie
Evans G. • Burns • **Wilcox-Crooks** *Substitutes: Daniels*
Baker • McMahon

Sunday 9 May 1999
Semi-final v BAYERN MUNICH (Germany) • Drawn: 2-2*
Ratchford • Simpson • Evans J. • Campbell • Hunt • Guthrie
McMahon • Evans G. • **Wilcox-Crooks**
Substitutes: Daniels • Baker • Burns
*** Lost 3-4 on penalties** Penalty-scorers: **Wilcox-Crooks**
Evans G. • Guthrie

Sunday 9 May 1999
Third /Fourth Place Play-Off v OLYMPIQUE LYONNAIS (France) • Lost: 1-3
Daniels • Simpson • Evans J. • Campbell • Hunt • Guthrie
Evans G. • Burns • **Wilcox-Crooks**
Substitutes: Ratchford • McMahon • Baker

TOURNAMENT SQUAD

Richard BAKER
Aaron BURNS
Fraizer CAMPBELL
Luke DANIELS
Gareth EVANS
Jonathan EVANS
Danny GUTHRIE
Jonathan HUNT
Christopher McMAHON
Aaron RATCHFORD
Daniel SIMPSON
Chris WILCOX-CROOKS

Membership and Travel Information

GENERAL INFORMATION

During the football season the Members & Supporters' Club office hours are as follows:

Monday to Friday: 9.00am – 5.00pm
Home Match Days: 9.00am – kick-off
(and 20 minutes after the game)

The office will be open one hour prior to departure to our away venues.

MEMBERSHIP

Once we deem Full Membership has reached its capacity, our books will close for the season and no further applications will be accepted. In the main, sales of match tickets for home games are restricted to Full Members. It is therefore important to note that anyone wishing to attend a home game must become a Full Member. Application forms are available upon request.

MEMBERS' PERSONAL INSURANCE

Under our special insurance policy with Lloyds Underwriters, all members are covered by insurance whilst in attendance and travelling to and from League and Cup matches involving Manchester United, both home and away, within the United Kingdom.

The benefits are as follows:

1. Death £10,000 (limited to £1,000 for persons under 16 years of age)
2. Total and irrecoverable loss of sight of both eyes £10,000
3. Total and irrecoverable loss of sight in one eye £5,000
4. Loss of two limbs £10,000
5. Loss of one limb £5,000
6. Total and irrecoverable loss of sight in one eye and loss of one limb £10,000

All enquiries should be addressed to the Membership Secretary.

BRANCHES OF THE SUPPORTERS' CLUB

A full list of all our official branches of the supporters club can be found on pages 220 to 224.

Due to the present demand for match tickets we will not allow any new branches to be formed. All enquiries in this respect should be forwarded for the attention of the Membership Secretary.

AWAY TRAVEL

Domestic Games:
All Club Members, which include Private Box holders, Executive Suite & Club Class Members and Season Ticket holders, are automatically enrolled in our Away Travel Club and, as such, are entitled to book coach travel from Old Trafford to all Premiership venues. Full details can be found on the opposite page.

How to make a Booking:
You can book a place on a coach, subject to availability upon personal application at the Membership Office, in which case you must quote your MUFC customer number. Alternatively, you can make a postal application by submitting the relevant payment, a stamped addressed envelope and a covering letter

quoting your MUFC customer number. Telephone reservations are also acceptable if making payment by credit/debit card. Cancellations must be made in advance of the day of the game.

Car park attendants will be on duty should you wish to park your car on one of our car parks before travelling to an away game. This service is offered at no extra charge but we wish to point out that the Club will not be held responsible for any damage or theft from your vehicle.

Members are advised to check match ticket availability before booking a place on a coach. Details can be obtained by telephoning our Ticket & Match Information line on **0161 872 0199**.

EUROPEAN TRAVEL

The Membership Office is also responsible for organising members travel and distribution of match tickets for our European away games. Full details will be made known when available, via all usual channels.

MEMBERS' COACH TRAVEL FROM OLD TRAFFORD

Opponents	Executive Coach	Luxury Coach	*Departure Time	**Estimated Return Time to Old Trafford
Arsenal	£18.00	£14.00	8.30am	9.30pm
Aston Villa	£13.00	£9.00	11.30am	7.30pm
Bradford City	£10.00	£7.00	1.00pm	6.15pm
Chelsea	£18.00	£14.00	8.30am	9.30pm
Coventry City	£13.00	£9.00	11.30am	7.30pm
Derby County	£11.00	£8.00	11.00am	8.00pm
Everton	£10.00	£7.00	1.00pm	6.15pm
Leeds United	£10.00	£7.00	1.00pm	6.15pm
Leicester City	£11.00	£8.00	11.00am	8.00pm
Liverpool	£10.00	£7.00	1.00pm	6.15 pm
Middlesbrough	£14.00	£10.00	11.00am	8.00pm
Newcastle United	£16.00	£12.00	10.30am	8.30pm
Sheffield Wednesday	£10.00	£7.00	12.30pm	7.15pm
Southampton	£18.00	£14.00	8.30am	10.30pm
Sunderland	£16.00	£12.00	10.30am	8.30pm
Tottenham Hotspur	£18.00	£14.00	9.00am	9.30pm
Watford	£17.00	£13.00	10.00am	8.30pm
West Ham United	£18.00	£14.00	8.30am	9.30pm
Wimbledon	£17.00	£13.00	8.30am	9.30pm
Wembley	£20.00	£16.00	8.30am	10.00pm

All times based on games with a 3.00pm kick-off

** Departure times are subject to change and it is vital to check the actual time when making your booking*

*** Return times shown are only estimated and are subject to traffic congestion*

SUPPORTERS' CLUBS UK BRANCHES 1999–2000

ABERDEEN Branch Secretary Billy Potts, 8 Broadinch Road, Mastrick, Aberdeen **Tel 01224 663803** *Departure points* Guild Street, Aberdeen 6.00am; bypass, Stonehaven 6.15am; The Kingsway, Dundee 7.00am

ABERGELE AND COAST Branch Secretary Eddie Williams, 14 Maes-y-Dre, Abergele, Clwyd, North Wales LL22 7HW **Tel 01745 823694** *Departure points* Aber; Llanfairfechen; Penmaen Mawr; Conwy; Llandudno Junction; Colwyn Bay; Abergele; Rhyl; Rhuddlan; Dyserth; Prestatyn; Mostyn; Holywell; Flint; Deeside

ABERYSTWYTH AND DISTRICT Branch Secretary Alan Evans, 6 Tregerddan, Bow Street, Dyfed SY24 5AW **Tel 01970 828117** after 6.00pm *Departure points* Please contact branch secretary

ASHBOURNE Branch Secretary Diane O'Connell, 2 Stanton Road, Ashbourne, Derbyshire DE6 1SH **Tel 01335 346105** (evenings) *Departure points* Markeaton Roundabout, Derby 11.45am (4.45pm); Ashbourne Bus Station 12.00noon (5.00pm), times in brackets denote evening fixtures. Contact branch secretary for details of travel to away fixtures

BARNSLEY Branch Secretary Mick Mitchell, 12 Saxon Crescent, Worsbrough, Barnsley S70 5PY **Tel 01226 283 983** *Departure points* Locke Park Working Mens' Club, Park Road, Barnsley via A628 12.30pm (5.30pm), or 2 ½ hours before any other kick-off times

BARROW AND FURNESS Branch Secretary Robert Bayliff, 31 Ashworth Street, Dalton-in-Furness, Cumbria LA15 8SH **Tel 01229 465277 Mobile 07788 762936** *Departure points* Barrow, Ramsden Square 9.30am (4.00pm); Dalton 9.45am (4.15pm); Ulverston and A590 route to M6 10.00am (4.30pm), times in brackets denote evening fixtures

BEDFORDSHIRE Branch Secretary Nigel Denton, 4 Abbey Road, Bedford MK41 9LG **Tel 0410 964329** *Departure points* Bedford Bus Station, Milton Keynes 'Coachways', Junction 14, M1

BERWICK-UPON-TWEED Branch Secretary Margaret Walker, 17 Lords Mount, Berwick-Upon-Tweed, Northumberland TD15 1LY **Tel 01289 304427** Chairman Raymond Dixon, 92 Shielfield Terrace, Berwick-upon-Tweed **Tel 01289 308671** SAE please for all enquiries. All telephone calls before 9.00pm please *Departure points* Berwick, Belford, Alnwick, Stannington, Washington; Scotch Corner, Leeming Bar and anywhere on the main A1 – by arrangement

BIRMINGHAM Branch Secretary John McGurk, 13 Sundial Lane, Great Barr, Birmingham B43 6PA **Tel 0121 357 1661** (6.00-9.00pm) *Departure points* The Rotunda; New Street Station; Tennis Courts Pub, A34; Junction 7, M6; Tamworth; Coventry. Coach fare for home games from £5.00 adult and £3.50 child. Coaches operate to all home and away games. For times and prices please send SAE

BLACK COUNTRY The branch attend all home and away games. *Departure points* St Lawrence Tavern, Darlaston 11.00am (4.00pm); Woden Public House, Wednesbury 11.10am (4.10pm); Friendly Lodge Hotel, J10, M6 11.15am (4.15pm); Wheatsheaf Public House, off J11, M6 11.25am (4.25pm), times in brackets denote evening fixtures. For further information contact Branch Secretary Ade Steventon **Tel 0121 531 0826** (6.30-9.00pm) **Mobile 07931 714318** (6.00-9.30pm) or Ken Lawton **Tel 01902 636393** (6.30-9.00pm)

BLACKPOOL, PRESTON AND FYLDE Branch Chairman Martin Day, **Tel 01253 891301** For coach bookings contact Travel Secretary Mrs Jean Halliday **Tel 01772 635887** *Departure points* Cleveleys; Blackpool; St. Annes; Lytham; Freckleton; Preston United members on holiday are very welcome

BRADFORD AND LEEDS Branch Secretary Sally Hampshire, P.O. Box 87, Cleckheaton, West Yorkshire BD19 6YN For further details, please contact the Branch Secretary

BRIDGNORTH AND DISTRICT Branch Secretary Ann Saxby, 30 Pitchford Road, Albrighton, Near Wolverhampton **Tel 01902 373840** *Departure points* Ludlow; Bridgnorth; Albrighton; Wolverhampton

BRIDGWATER AND SOUTH WEST Branch Secretary Ray White, 4 Spencer Close, Bridgwater, Somerset TA6 5SP **Tel 01278 452186** *Departure points* Taunton; Bridgwater; Weston-Super-Mare; Clevedon

BRIGHTON Branch Secretary Colin Singers, 34 Meadowview Road, Sompting, Lancing, West Sussex **Tel 01903 761679** *Departure points* Worthing Central 6.30am, Shoreham (George Pub) 6.40am; Brighton Railway Station 7.00am; Gatwick Airport 7.45am

BRISTOL, BATH & DISTRICT Branch Secretary Jim Smith, 108 Coriander Drive, Bradley Stoke, Bristol BS32 0DL **Tel 0117 979 2459** (5.30-8.30pm) *Departure points* Bath Railway Station 08.05 (12.45); Keynsham Church 08.25 (13.05); Temple Meads 08.40 (13.20); Bradley Stoke South 08.55 (13.35); Bradley Stoke North 09.00 (13.40); M5 Junction 14 09.10 (13.50); M5 Junction 13 09.20 (14.00). Coach fares for home matches (all 19 league matches booked before 1st August), luxury coach adult £10, juniors/OAPs £7; executive coach adult £12.50, juniors/OAPs £9; For individual matches, luxury coach adult £11.50, juniors/OAPs £8; executive coach adult £14, juniors/OAPs £10; All coach seats and match tickets are booked and paid for in advance. Away match details vary according to ticket availability. Times in brackets denote evening fixtures

BURTON-ON-TRENT Branch Secretary Mrs Pat Wright, 45 Foston Avenue, Burton-on-Trent, Staffordshire DE13 0PL **Tel 01283 532534** *Departure points* Moira (garage); Swadlincote; Burton (B&Q Lichfield Street); Stoke area

CARLISLE AND DISTRICT Branch Secretary Arnold Heard, 28 Kentmere Grove, Morton Park, Carlisle, Cumbria CA2 6JD **Tel/Fax 01228 538262 Mobile 0860 782769** *Departure points* For departure times and details on the branch, please contact branch secretary

CENTRAL POWYS Branch Secretary Bryn Thomas, 10 Well Lane, Bungalows, Llanidloes, Powys SY18 6BA **Tel 01686 412391(H) 01686 413 3200(W)** *Departure points* Crossgates 10.30am; Rhayader 10.45am; Llanidloes 11.05am; Newtown 11.25am

CHEPSTOW AND DISTRICT Branch Secretary Anthony Parsons, 56 Treowen Road, Newbridge, Newport, Gwent NP1 4DN **Tel 01495 246253** *Departure points* Newbridge; Pontypool; Cwmbran Bus Station; Newport; Coldra Langstone; Magor; Caldicot; Chepstow. For departure times and further details contact Branch Secretary

CHESTER AND NORTH WALES Branch Chairman Eddie Mansell, 45 Overlea Drive, Hawarden, Deeside, Clwyd CH5 3HR **Tel 01244 520332** Ticket & Travel Secretary Des Wright **Tel 01244 851464** Branch Secretary Mrs Barbra Hammond, 93 Broughton Hall Road, Broughton, Chester **Tel 01244 535161** Membership Secretary Mrs Irene Keidel, 3 Springfield Drive, Buckley, Clwyd **Tel 01244 550943** *Departure points* Oswestry; Ellesmere; Wrexham; Chester; Rhyl; Greenfield; Flint; Connah's Quay; Deeside Leisure Centre; Queensferry; Strawberry Roundabout; Whitby; Ellesmere Port

CLEVELAND Branch Secretary John Higgins, 41 Ashford Avenue, Acklam, Middlesbrough TS5 4QL **Tel 01642 643112** Treasurer Brian Tose, 2 Cowbar Cottages, Staithes, Cleveland TS13 5DA **Tel 01947 841372** *Departure points* Please contact branch secretary for details

COLWYN BAY AND DISTRICT Branch Secretary Bill Griffiths, Whitefield, 60 Church Road, Rhos-on-Sea, Colwyn Bay, Clwyd, Wales LL28 4YS **Tel 01492 540240** *Departure points* Alpine Travel coach garage, Builder Street West, Llandudno 10.45am (3.45pm); Bus Stop, Mostyn Broadway (opposite Asda stores) 11.00am (4.00pm); Labour Club, Llandudno Junction 11.45am (4.15pm); Guy's Newsagents, Conway Road, Colwyn Bay 11.30am (4.30pm); Honda Centre, Old Colwyn 11.35am (4.35pm); Queen's Hotel, Old Colwyn 11.40am (4.40pm); Fair View Inn, Llandulas 11.45am (4.45pm); Slaters Showrooms, Abergele 11.50am (4.50pm); Talardy Inn on the Park Hotel, St. Asaph 12.00noon (5.00pm) Plough Hotel, Aston Hill, Queensferry 12.45pm (5.45pm), times in brackets denote evening fixtures

CORBY Branch Chairman Jeff Charles **Tel 01536 409714** Branch Meetings 7.15pm first Sunday of the month, Lodge Park Sports Centre, Corby

CRAWLEY Branch Secretary Steve Whiting, 5 Bolney Court, Bewbush, Crawley, West Sussex **Mobile 01293 424552** Ticket & Travel Secretary Gary Hillier, 18 Westway, Three Bridges, Crawley, West Sussex RH10 1JY **Mobile 0976 272725** *Departure points* Contact ticket and travel secretary

CREWE AND NANTWICH Branch Secretary Andy Ridgway, 38 Murrayfield Drive, Willaston, Nantwich, Cheshire **Tel 01270 68418** *Departure points* Nantwich Barony 12.30pm (5.30pm); Earl of Crewe 12.40pm (5.40pm); Cross Keys 12.50pm (5.50pm); (times in brackets denote evening fixtures). Away travel subject to demand

DONCASTER AND DISTRICT Branch Secretary Albert Thompson, 89 Anchorage Lane, Sprotboro, Doncaster, South Yorkshire DN5 8EB **Tel 01302 782964** Branch Treasurer Sue Moyles, 217 Warning Tongue Lane, Cantley **Tel 01302 530422 Fax 01482 591708** Branch Chairman Paul Kelly, 58 Oak Grove, Conisbrough DN12 2HN **Tel 01709 324058** *Departure points* Broadway Dunscroft 10.30am (4.30pm); Edenthorpe 10.40am (4.40pm); Waterdale (opposite main library) 10.50am (4.50pm) ; The Highwayman, Woodlands 11.00am (5.00pm), times in brackets denote 8.00pm kick-off) Meetings held first Sunday of every month (unless there is a home match) in the Wheatley Hotel at 7.00pm

DORSET Branch Secretary Mark Pattison, 89 Parkstone Road, Poole, Dorset BH15 2NZ **Tel 01202 744348** *Departure points* Poole Railway Station 6.15am (10.30am); Banksome (Courts) 6.20am (10.35am); Bournemouth, 6.30am (10.45am); Christchurch (Bargates) 6.45am (11.00am); Ringwood 7.00am (11.15am); Rownham Services 7.15am (11.30am); Chieveley Services 8.30am (12.30pm), times in brackets denote evening fixtures

DUKINFIELD AND HYDE Branch Secretary Marilyn Chadderton, 12 Brownville Grove, Dukinfield, Cheshire SK16 5AS **Tel 0161 338 4892** *Departure points* Coach departs Railway Inn, Commercial Brow, Newton, Hyde one hour before kick-off for every home match – to book please contact Ian Hargreaves on **0161 367 9398**

EAST ANGLIA Branch Secretary Mark Donovan, 4 College Heath Road, Mildenhall, Suffolk IP28 7PH **Tel 01638 717075** (9.00am-6.00pm) **Fax 01638 717076** (24 hours)
Details of your local representative can also be obtained by telephoning this number.
Executive travel available to all home fixtures via the following services:
Service No.1 Clacton; Colchester; Braintree; Great Dunmow; Bishop Stortford.
Service No.2 Felixstowe; Nacton; Ipswich; Stowmarket; Bury St. Edmonds.
Service No.3 Thetford; Mildenhall; Newmarket; Cambridge; Huntingdon.
Service No.4 Lowestoft; Great Yarmouth; Norwich; East Dereham; Kings Lynn.
Coaches also operate to all away games for which departure details are dependent on demand and ticket availability

EAST YORKSHIRE Branch Secretary Branch Chairman Ian Baxter, 18 Soberhill Drive, Holme Moor, York YO43 4BH **Mobile 0468 821 844** Information for tickets and travel from Hull on **0374 775 078** Departure points (2 coaches) Hull Marina 10.30am (3.30pm); Bay Horse, Mat Weighton 10.30am (3.30pm); Junction 37, Howden M62 11.00am (4.00pm); Junction 34, M62 11.15am (4.15pm), times in brackets denote evening fixtures

ECCLES Branch Secretary Gareth Morris, 3 Matlock Street, Peel Green, Eccles, Manchester M30 7HG **Tel 0161 788 7015** *Departure point* (away games only) Rock House Hotel, Peel Green Road, Peel Green, Eccles. For departure times please contact branch secretary

FEATHERSTONE & DISTRICT Branch Secretary Paul Kingsbury, 11 Hardwick Road, Featherstone, Nr Pontefract W Yorks WF7 5JA **Tel 01977 793910 Mobile 07971 778161** Treasurer Andrew Dyson, 46 Northfield Drive, Pontefract, W Yorks WF8 2DL **Tel 01977 709561 Mobile 07979 326183** *Departure points* Pontefract Sorting Office 11.30am (4.30pm); Corner Pocket, Featherstone 11.40am (4.40pm); Green Lane, Featherstone 11.45am (4.45pm); Castleford Bus Station 11.55am (4.55pm), times in brackets denote evening fixtures. Meetings held every fortnight (Mondays) at the Girnhill Lane WMC, Featherstone at 8.00pm

GLAMORGAN AND GWENT Branch Secretary Paul Richards, 50 Western Drive, Gabalfa, Cardiff, South Wales CF4 2SF Branch Chairman Cameron Erskine **Tel 01222 623705** (10.00am-1.00pm Monday-Friday. Answerphone at other times) **Mobile 0585 615546** *Departure points* Skewen; Port Talbot; Bridgend; Cardiff; Newport

GLASGOW Branch Secretary David Sharkey, 45 Lavender Drive, Greenhills, East Kilbride G75 9JH **Tel 01355 902592** (7.00-11.00pm) Coach run to all home games *Departure points* Queen Street Station, Glasgow 8.00am (1.00pm); The Angel, Uddingston 8.15am (1.15pm); any M74 Service Stations, times in brackets denote evening fixtures

GLOUCESTER AND CHELTENHAM Branch Secretary Mike Brown, 14 Swanswell Drive, Granleyfields, Cheltenham GL51 6NA **Tel 01242 232267** (7.30-9.00pm) Coach Bookings Paul Brown, 59 Katherine Close, Churchdown, Gloucester GL3 1PB **Tel/Fax 01452 859553 Mobile 0961 573404** Email muscglos@aol.com *Departure points* Station Road, Gloucester (outside British School of Motoring) 9.15am (2.15pm); Midland Hotel, Cheltenham 9.25am (2.25pm); Cheltenham Gas Works 9.30am (2.30pm), times in brackets denote evening fixtures

GRIMSBY AND DISTRICT Branch Secretary Bob England, 61 Shaw Drive, Scartho, Grimsby DN33 2JB **Tel 01472 752130** Travel Arrangements Craig Collins (Branch Chairman) **Tel 01472 354003**

GUERNSEY Branch Secretary Eddie Martel, Ayia Napa, Rue des Barras, Les Maresqets, Vale, Guernsey, Channel Isles **Tel 01481 46285**

GWYNEDD Branch Secretary Gwyn Hughes, Sibrwd y Don, Tan y Cefn, Llanwnda, Caernarfon, Gwynedd LL54 7YB **Tel 01286 830073** Ticket Secretary Stephen Jones, Gwynant, Carmel, Caernarfon, Gwynedd LL54 7AA **Tel 07050 380804** *Departure points* Pwllheli; Llanwnda; Caernarfon; Bangor. For departure times, please contact branch secretary

HAMPSHIRE Branch Secretary Roy Debenham, 11 Lindley Gardens, Alresford, Hampshire SO24 9PU **Tel 01962 734420** Ticket & Coach Secretary Pete Boyd, 22 Weavers Crofts, Melksham Wilts SN12 8BP **Tel 01225 700354** Chairman Paul Marsh, Oaktree Cottage, Commonhill Road, Braisfield, Hants SO51 0QF **Tel 01794 368951** *Departure points* (1). St George's Playing Field, Cosham (Near IBM); (2) Fareham Railway Station; (3) Parkway, Eastleigh Airport; (4) Bullington Cross Pub, Bullington Cross; Cheively Services, Newbury Times vary for weekend/evening matches – check with P Boyd

HARROGATE AND DISTRICT Branch Secretary Michael Heaton, **Tel & Fax 01423 780679 Mobile 07957 172002** *Departure points* Coaches leave from Northallerton, Thirsk, Ripon, and also cater for the Nidderdale and Wenslydale areas, Harrogate and Skipton districts. For further information regarding the above branch, including pick-up times, please contact the secretary. Transport is provided to all home and away fixtures, which includes European

HASTINGS Branch Secretary Tim Martin, 30 Silvan Road, St Leonards-on-Sea, East Sussex TN38 9RD (NO PERSONAL CALLERS) Tel **01424 853189** (6.00-8.00pm) **Mobile 0973 656716** (Daytime) **Fax 01424 854989** You can also contact Rod Beckingham **Tel 01424 443477** (6.00-7.00pm) *Departure points* Eastbourne, Tesco's Roundabout 5.40am (10.00am); Bexhill, Viking Chip Shop 6.00am (10.20am); Silverhill Traffic lights 6.15am (10.30am); Hurst Green, George Pub 6.40am (10.55 am); Pembury, Camden Arms Pub 7.00am (11.10am), times in brackets denote evening fixtures For details of travel to away games please contact branch secretary

HEREFORD Branch Secretary Norman Elliss, 40 Chichester Close, Abbeyfields, Belmont, Hereford HR2 7YU **Tel 01432 359923** *Departure points* Leominster 8.30am (2.00pm); Bulmers Car Park, Hereford 9.00am (2.30pm); Ledbury 9.30am (3.00pm); Malvern Link BP Garage 9.45am (3.15pm); Oak Apple Pub, Worcester10.00am (3.30pm), times in brackets denote midweek fixtures

HERTFORDSHIRE Organised travel to home and away games. Pick-up points at Hertford, Welwyn, Stevenage, Hitchin and Luton. Travel arrangements – contact Mick Prior **Tel 01438 361900** Membership – contact Mick Slack **Tel 01462 622451** Correspondence to Steve Bocking, 64 Westmill Road, Hitchin, Herts SG5 2SD **Tel 01462 622076**

HEYWOOD Branch Secretary Lee Swettenham, 30 Wilton Grove, Heywood, Lancs OL10 1AZ **Tel 01706 360625** Email leeswett@aol.com Chairman Dennis Hall, 2 Hartford Avenue, Summit, Heywood, Lancashire *Departure point* Grapes Hotel, Peel Lane, Heywood1.00pm (Saturday matches)

HIGHLANDS & ISLANDS Branch Secretary Ken Glass, The Millers Cottage, Milton, Invergordon, Ross-Shire IV18 0NQ **Tel 01862 842395** *Departure points* Coach departs 5.30am Farraline Park Bus Station, Inverness. For other departure points, contact branch secretary

HYNDBURN & PENDLE Branch Secretary Alan Haslam, 97 Crabtree Avenue, Edgeside, Waterfoot, Rossendale BB4 9TB **Tel 01706 831736** *Departure points* Barnoldswick 11.15am (4.45pm); Nelson 11.30am (5.00pm); Burnley 11.45am (5.15pm); Accrington 12.15pm (5.45pm); Haslingden 12.20pm (5.50pm); Rawtenstall 12.30pm (6.00pm), times in brackets denote evening fixtures

INVICTA REDS (KENT) Branch Secretary John Sayer, 'Pop-In' Newsagents, 97 Boundary Road, Ramsgate, Kent CT11 7NP **Tel 01843 592533 Mobile 0860 930064** *Departure points* 'Pop-In' Newsagents, Ramsgate; Longport Coach Park, Canterbury; M2 Service Area; Thanet Way; Junction 3, M2; Little Chef M2; Cobham; Dartford Tunnel; Junction 28, M25. For pick-up times and away game travel please contact branch secretary

ISLE OF MAN Chairman Graham Barlow, 21 Thirlmere Drive, Onchan, Isle of Man **Tel 01624 661270** Branch Secretary Gill Keown, 5 King Williams Way, Castletown, Isle of Man IM9 1DH **Tel 01624 823143** Email Reddevil@enterprise.net

JERSEY Branch Secretary Mark Jones, 5 Rosemount Cottages, James Road, St. Saviour, Jersey, Channel Islands **Tel 01534 34786 (home) 01534 885885 (work)** Should any members be in Jersey during the football season, the branch shows television games in private club. Free food provided – everybody welcome, including children. Contact branch secretary for details

KEIGHLEY Branch Secretary Kevin Granger, 3 Spring Terrace, Long Lee, Keighley, West Yorkshire BD21 4SZ **Tel 01535 661862 Mobile 0410 861668** *Departure points* Keighley Technical College 12.00noon (5.15pm) to Colne, then M65 & M66 to Manchester

KNUTSFORD Branch Secretary John Butler, 4 Hollingford Place, Knutsford WA16 9DP **Tel/Fax 01565 651360** Meetings most Tuesdays, The Angel Hotel, King Street, Knutsford

LANCASTER AND DISTRICT Branch Secretary Ed Currie, 30 Dorrington Road, Lancaster, LA1 4TG **Tel 01524 36797 Mobile 07880 550247** *Departure points* Carnforth Ex-Servicemens 11.45am (4.45pm); Morecambe Shrimp Roundabout 12.00pm (5.00pm); Lancaster Dalton Square 12.20pm (5.20pm) and A6 route to Broughton Roundabout for M6, times in brackets denote evening fixtures

LEAMINGTON SPA Branch Secretary Mrs Norma Worton, 23 Cornhill Grove, Kenilworth, Warwickshire CV8 2QP **Tel 01926 859476** *Departure points* Newbold Terrace, Leamington Spa; Leyes Lane, Kenilworth; London Road, Coventry

LINCOLN Branch Secretary Steve Stone, 154 Scorer Street, Lincoln, Lincolnshire LN5 7SX **Tel 01522 885671** *Departure points* Unity Square at 10.00am on Saturdays (3.00pm kick-off). Midweek matches, depart at 3.00pm from same place

LONDON Branch Secretary Ralph Mortimer, 55 Boyne Avenue, Hendon, London NW4 2JL **Tel 0181 203 1213** (after 6.30pm) *Departure points* Coach times (Saturdays) 8.00am Semley Place, Victoria; 8.30am Staples Corner; 9.00am Junction 11, M1. Coach times (midweek) 1.00pm Semley Place, Victoria, 1.30pm Staples Corner, 2.00pm Junction 11, M1

LONDON ASSOCIATION Branch Secretary Najib Armanazi, 22 Campden Hill Court, Campden Hill Road, London W8 7HS **Tel 0171 937 3934** Membership Secretary Alison Watt **Tel 01322 558333** (between 7.00-9.00pm)

LONDON FAN CLUB Branch Secretary Paul Molloy, 65 Corbylands Road, Sidcup, Kent DA15 8JQ **Tel 0181 302 5826** Travel Secretary Mike Dobbin Email info@mulfc65.freeserve.co.uk *Departure points* Euston Station by service train – meeting point at top of escalator from Tube. Cheap group travel to most home and away games

MACCLESFIELD Assistant Secretary Ian Evans, 25 Pickwick Road, Poynton, Cheshire, SK12 1LD **Tel 01625 877260** Treasurer Rick Holland, 97 Pierce Street, Macclesfield **Tel 01625 427762** *Departure points* home games, meet Macclesfield Railway Station 11.45am (4.45pm). For away games, please contact branch secretary

MANSFIELD Branch Secretary Peggy Conheeney, 48 West Bank Avenue, Mansfield, Nottinghamshire NG19 7BP **Tel/Fax 01623 625140** *Departure points* Kirkby Garage 10.00am (4.00pm); Northern Bridge, Sutton 10.10am (4.10pm); Mansfield Shoe Co. 10.30am (4.25pm); Glapwell 10.40am (4.40pm); Hipper Street School, Chesterfield 10.50am (4.55pm); Baslow 11.15am (5.35pm), times in brackets denote evening fixtures. Coach seats should be booked well in advance. Away games are dependent on ticket availability, for information please contact branch secretary.

MID-CHESHIRE Branch Secretary Leo Lastowecki, 5 Townfield Court, Barnton, Northwich, Cheshire CW8 4UT **Tel 01606 784790** *Departure points* Please contact branch secretary

MIDDLETON & DISTRICT Branch Secretary Kevin Booth, 70 Wagstaffe Street, Middleton, Manchester M24 6BB

MILLOM AND DISTRICT Branch Secretary/Chairman Clive Carter, 47 Settle Street, Millom, Cumbria LA18 5AR **Tel 01229 773565** Treasurer Malcom French, 4 Willowside Park, Haverigg, Cumbria LA18 4PT **Tel 01229 774850** Assistant Treasurer Paul Knott, 80 Market Street, Millom, Cumbria **Tel 01229 772826**

NORTH DEVON Branch Secretary Dave Rogan, Leys Cottage, Hilltop, Fremington, Nr Barnstaple EX31 3BL **Tel/Fax 01271 328280** *Departure points* Please contact branch secretary

NORTH EAST Branch Secretary John Burgess, 10 Streatlam Close, Stainton, Barnard Castle, Co Durham DL12 8RQ **Tel 01833 695200** *Departure points* Central Station, Newcastle 8.30am (1.00pm); A19/A690 Roundabout 8.50am (1.20pm); Peterlee Roundabout 9.00am (1.30pm); Hartlepool Baths 9.15am (1.45pm); Owton Lodge, Hartlepool 9.20am (1.50pm); The Swan, Billingham 9.30am (2.00pm); Sparks Bakery 9.40am (2.10pm); Darlington Bus Station 10.00am (2.30pm); Leeming Bar Services A1 10.20am (2.50pm)

NORTH MANCHESTER Branch Secretary Graham May, 25 Walker Road, Chadderton OL9 8DB **Tel 0161 681 6149 Mobile 0850 133418** Coaches to all home and away games. Fortnightly meetings at Leggatts Wine Bar, Oldham Road, Failsworth. For all details contact Graham May **0973 128809** (Secretary), Garry Chapman **0161 795 0581**, Dixie **0161 682 3331**

NORTH POWYS Branch Secretary Glyn T Davies, 7 Tan-y-Mur, Montgomery, Powys SY15 6PR **Tel 01686 668841** Treasurer Mrs B Elesbury, 1 Llys Maldwyn, Caerhowel, Montgomery, Powys **Tel 01686 668709** *Departure points* Bus Station, Back Lane, Newtown Saturdays 10.30am, Car Park (Spar Shop) Welshpool 11.00am. For all information on tickets and travel, contact branch secretary. For areas of branch, contact your reps or direct to secretary. Seven weeks notice must be given when ordering tickets. Bus for night games leaves at 4.00pm

NORTH STAFFORDSHIRE Branch Secretary Peter Hall, Cheddleton Heath House, Cheddleton Heath Road, Leek ST13 7DX **Tel 01538 360364** *Departure points* Leek Bus Station 12.30pm (5.15pm), time in brackets denote evening fixtures

NORTH YORKSHIRE Branch Secretary Miss Jacky Potter, c/o MUSC N Yorkshire, P.O. Box 480, York YO26 5YL **Tel 01904 787291** (10.00am-12.00noon or 6.00-8.00pm) **Mobile 0402 014819** *Departure points* Coaches and tickets for all home games. Away games subject to demand and availability. Please ring Jacky for further details and bookings

NOTTINGHAM Branch Secretary Wayne Roe, **Tel 01773 510784** (home travel) Email wainy@aol.com Martyn Meek **Tel 01773 768424** (away travel) *Departure points* Nottingham 10.00am (3.00pm); Ilkeston 10.30am (3.30pm); Eastwood 10.45am (3.45pm); Junction 28, M1 11.00am (4.00pm), times in brackets denote evening fixtures

OLDHAM Branch Secretary Dave Cone, 67 Nelson Way, Washbrook, Chadderton, Lancashire OL9 8NL **Tel 0161 626 9734** Meeting every Tuesday night at Old White Hart, Chadderton Way, Oldham *Departure points* All coaches depart 1½ hours before kick-off time (regardless of day) from the Old White Hart, Chadderton Way, Oldham

SUPPORTERS' CLUBS UK AND IRISH BRANCHES 1999–2000

OXFORD, BANBURY AND DISTRICT Branch Secretary Mick Thorne, 'The Paddock', 111 Eynsham Road, Botley, Oxford OX2 9BY **Tel 01865 864924** (6.00-8.00pm Monday-Friday only) **Fax 01865 864924** (Anytime) *Departure points* McLeans Coach Yard, Witney 8.00am (2.00pm); Botley Road Park-n-Ride, Oxford 8.30am (2.30pm); Plough Inn, Bicester 9.00am (3.00pm); Bus Station, Banbury 9.15am (3.15pm), times in brackets denote evening fixtures Coach fare for home games adults £10.50, juniors/OAPs £7.50. All coach seats must be booked in advance. Away travel, including European, subject to match tickets. New members welcome. Large SAE for copy of branch review

PEMBROKESHIRE Branch Secretary Steve Griffiths, 53 Edward Street, Milford Haven, Dyfed NG16 3RB **Tel 01646 695512** *Departure points* Pembroke Dock 5.45am; Pembroke; Milford Haven; Haverfordwest; Whitland; Carmarthen

PETERBOROUGH AND DISTRICT Branch Secretary Andrew Dobney, 3 Northgate, West Pinchbeck, Spalding, Lincs PE11 3TB **Tel 01775 640743** *Departure points* Spalding Bus Station 9.00am (1.30pm); Peterborough, Key Theatre 9.45am (2.15pm); Grantham, Foston Services 10.30am (3.00pm), times in brackets denote evening fixtures

PLYMOUTH Branch Secretary Dave Price, 34 Princess Avenue, Plymstock, Plymouth PL9 9EP **Tel 01752 482049** or Branch Information Line **01579 348497** *Departure points* Tamar Bridge 6.30am (11.00am); Bretonside 6.45am (11.15am); Plympton 7.00am (11.30am); Ivybridge 7.15am (11.45am); South Brent (London Inn) 7.30am (12.00noon); Exeter Services 7.50am (12.20pm), times in brackets denote evening fixtures. 'This is a branch that welcomes all families'

PONTYPRIDD Branch Secretary Lawrence Badman, 11 Laura Street, Treforest, Pontypridd, Mid Glamorgan, South Wales CF37 1NW **Tel 01443 406894** *Departure points* For coach departure and pick-up points please contact branch secretary

REDDITCH Branch Secretary Mark Richardson, 90 Alcester Road, Hollywood, Worcestershire B47 5NS **Tel/Fax 0121 246 0237** *Departure points* Redditch and Bromsgrove

ROCHDALE Branch Chairman Paul Mulligan, 54 Norden Road, Bamford, Rochdale, Lancashire, OL11 5PN **Tel 01706 368909** Regular coach service to home games

RUGBY AND NUNEATON Branch Secretary Greg Pugh, 63 Catesby Road, Rugby, Warwickshire CV22 5JL **Tel 01788 567900** Chairman Mick Moore, 143 Marston Lane, Attleborough, Nuneaton, Warwickshire **Tel 01203 343 868** *Departure points* St Thomas Cross Pub, Rugby; McDonalds Junction 2, M6, Coventry; Council House, Coton Road, Nuneaton. Departure times vary according to kick-off time

RUNCORN AND WIDNES Branch Secretary Elizabeth Scott, 39 Park Road, Runcorn, Cheshire WA7 4SS

SCUNTHORPE Branch Secretary Colin Markham, 161 Cemetery Road, Scunthorpe, N Lincs DN16 1NT **Tel 01724 876593** Chairperson G Davis **Tel 01724 851359**

SHEFFIELD & ROTHERHAM Branch Secretary Roger Everitt, 27 South Street, Kimberworth, Rotherham, South Yorkshire S61 1ER **Tel 01709 563613** Coach Travel available to all home games *Departure points* 3.00pm kick-off Rotherham (Nellie Deans) 11.00am; Sheffield (Midland Railway Station) 11.20am; Stockbridge (Friendship Inn) 11.50am. Sunday games 4pm kick-off – Same departure points – one hour later. Midweek games – Rotherham 4.40pm; Sheffield 4.50pm; Stockbridge 5.10pm For midweek games always contact Branch Secretary to confirm departure times

SHOEBURYNESS, SOUTHEND AND DISTRICT Branch Secretary Bob Lambert, 23 Royal Oak Drive, Wickford, Essex SS11 8NT **Tel 01268 560168** Chairmain Gary Black **Tel 01702 219072** *Departure points* Cambridge Hotel, Shoeburyness 7.00am; Bell Public House, A127 7.15am; Rayleigh Weir 7.20am; McDonalds Burger Bar, A127 7.30am; Fortune of War Public House, A127 7.40am; Brentwood High Street 8.00am; Little Chef, Brentwood bypass 8.05am. Additional pick-ups by arrangement with branch secretary. All coach seats should be booked in advance. Ring for details of midweek fixtures

SHREWSBURY Branch Secretary Martyn Hunt, 50 Whitehart, Reabrook, Shrewsbury SY3 7TE **Tel 01743 350397** Chirk Secretary Mike Davies **Tel 01691 778733** *Departure points* Reabrook Island; Abbey Church; Monkmoor Inn; Heathgates Island; Harlescott Inn; Harlton Black Park, A5 Layby, Chirk; (3.00 & 4.00pm kick-off – depart Reabrook 10.30am; 7.30 & 8.00pm kick-off – depart Reabrook 2.00pm)

SOUTH ELMSALL & DISTRICT Branch Secretary Bill Fieldsend, 72 Cambridge St, Moorthorpe, South Elmsall, Pontefract, West Yorkshire WF9 2AR **Tel 01977 648358 Mobile 0585 716255** Treasurer Mark Bossons **Tel 01977 650316** Meetings held every Tuesday at Pretoria WMC, South Elmsall *Departure points* Hemsworth Market 11.45am (4.30pm); Mill Lane 11.50am (4.40pm); Pretoria WMC 12.00noon (5.00pm), times in brackets denote evening fixtures

SOUTHPORT Branch Secretary Robert Stephenson, 143 Heysham Road, Southport, Merseyside PR9 7ED **Tel 01704 220685** Weekly meetings held Tuesday evening at The Mount Pleasant Hotel, Manchester Road
Departure point The Mount Pleasant Hotel, Manchester Road, Southport, picking-up en route

STALYBRIDGE Branch Secretary Walter Petrenko, 58 Melbourne Street, Stalybridge, Cheshire **Tel 0161 338 3006** Chairman Adrien Dearnaley **Tel 0161 338 6751** Travel Secretary Nigel Barrett **Tel 0161 339 7566** Branch Membership Secretary A Baxter **Tel 0161 303 9750** Treasurer R A Wild **Tel 0161 337 7277** *Departure points* Travellers Call, Wakefield Road, Stalybridge **Tel 0161 338 3087** Home game transport leaves 1½ hours before kick-off

STOKE-ON-TRENT Branch Secretary Geoff Boughey, 63 Shrewsbury Drive, Newcastle, Staffordshire ST5 7RQ **Tel/Fax 01782 561680** (home) **Mobile 0468 561680**
Email geoffboughey@cwcom.net *Departure points* Hanley Bus Station 12.00noon (5.00pm); School Street, Newcastle 12.10pm (5.10pm); Little Chef A34 12.15pm (5.15pm); The Millstone Pub, Butt Lane 12.30pm (5.30pm), times in brackets denote evening fixtures
Branch meetings every Monday night, contact branch secretary for details

STOURBRIDGE & KIDDERMINSTER Branch Secretary, Robert Banks, 7 Croftwood Road, Wollescot, Stourbridge, West Midlands DY9 7EU **Tel 01384 826636** Contact branch secretary for departure points and times

SURREY Branch Secretary Mrs Maureen Asker, 80 Cheam Road, Ewell, Surrey KT17 1QF **Tel 0181 393 4763** *Departure point* Coach leaves Epsom Railway Station 7.45am

SWANSEA Branch Secretary Dave Squibb, 156 Cecil Street, Mansleton, Swansea SA5 8QJ **Tel 01792 641981** *Departure points* Swansea (via Heads of Valleys Road); Neath; Hirwaun; Merthyr; Tredegar; Ebbw Vale; Brynmawr; Abergavenny; Monmouth

SWINDON Branch Secretary Martin Rendle, 19 Cornfield Road, Devizes, Wiltshire SN10 3BA *Departure points* Kingsdown Inn; Stratton St Margaret; Swindon

TELFORD Branch Secretary Sal Laher, 4 Hollyoak Grove, Lakeside, Priorslee, Telford TF2 9GE **Tel 01952 299224** Members' and committee meetings held on the first Thursday of every month at Champion Jockey, Donnington from 7.30pm *Departure points* Saturday (3.00pm kick-off) Cuckoo Oak, Madeley 10.30am; Heath Hill, Dawley 10.40am; Bucks Head, Wellington 10.50am; Dakengates 11.00am; Bridge, Donnington 11.10am; Newport 11.20am. Midweek (8.00pm kick-off) departure starts 4.30pm with ten minutes later for each of the above locations. Contact branch secretary for membership and further details

TORBAY Branch Secretary Vernon Savage, 5 Courtland Road, Shiphay, Torquay, Devon TQ2 6JU **Tel 01803 616139** *Departure points* Upper Cockington Lane, Torquay 7.00am; Newton Abbot Railway Station 7.20am; Kingsteignton Fountain 7.30am; Countess Wear Roundabout, Exeter 7.45am; Granada Services, Exeter 8.00am. Other departure times by arrangement with the branch secretary. Midweek coach departure times, add 5 hours to above times

UTTOXETER & DISTRICT Branch Secretary Peter Quirk, The Smithfield Hotel, 37 High Street, Uttoxeter, Staffs ST14 7HN **Tel/Fax 01889 562682** Chairman Ray Phillips **Tel 01889 567323**

WALSALL Branch Secretary Ian Robottom, 157 Somerfield Road, Bloxwich, Walsall WS3 2EN **Tel 01922 861746** *Departure points* Junction 9 (M6) 10.50am (4.15pm); Bell Pub, Bloxwich 11.15am (4.50pm); Roman Way Hotel, A5 Cannock 11.30am (5.15pm); Dovecote Pub, Stone Road, Stafford 11.50am (5.35pm)

WARRINGTON Branch Secretary Su Buckley, 4 Vaudrey Drive, Woolston, Warrington, Cheshire WA1 4HG **Tel 01925 816966**

WELLINGBOROUGH Branch Secretary Andy Daly, 260 Obelisk Rise, Kingsthorpe, Northampton **Tel 01604 844464 Fax 01604 514221** *Departure points* Rushden 8.30am (1.30pm); Irchester 8.35am (1.35pm); Woolaston 8.45am (1.45pm); Wellingborough 8.55am (1.55pm); Northampton 9.10am (2.10pm)

WEST CUMBRIA Branch Secretary Robert Wilson, 23 Calder Drive, Moorclose, Workington, Cumbria CA14 3NZ **Tel 01900 870211 Mobile 0370 837634** *Departure points* Coach 1 departs Egremont 9.45am (3.15pm) Cleator Moor 10.00am (3.30pm); Whitehaven 10.15am (3.45pm); Distington 10.20am (3.50pm); Cockermouth 10.35am (4.05pm). Coach 2 departs Salterbeck 9.45am (3.15pm); Harrington Road 9.50am (3.20pm); Workington 10.00am (3.30pm); Station Inn 10.10am (3.40pm); Netherhall Cr 10.12am (3.42pm); Netherton 10.15am (3.45pm); Dearham 10.20am (3.50pm), times in brackets denote 8.00pm kick-off. Contact branch secretary for other kick-off times)

WEST DEVON Branch Secretary Mrs R M Bolt, 16 Moorview, North Tawton, Devon EX20 2HW **Tel 01837 82682** (all enquiries) *Departure points* North Tawton; Crediton; Exeter

WESTMORLAND Branch Secretary Dennis Alderson, 71 Calder Drive, Kendal, Cumbria LA9 6LR **Tel 01539 728248 Mobile 0973 965373** *Departure points* Ambleside; Windermere; Staveley; Kendal and Forton Services. For departure times and further details, please contact branch secretary

WORKSOP Branch Secretary Mick Askew, 20 Park Street, Worksop, Nottinghamshire **Tel 01909 486194**

YEOVIL Branch Secretary Ken Higgins, 35 Wingate Avenue, Yeovil, Somerset BA21 4QH **Tel 01935 28754** *Departure points* Please contact Branch Secretary

MANCHESTER UNITED DISABLED SUPPORTERS' ASSOCIATION – (MUDSA)
Branch Secretary Phil Downes, 422 Parrswood Road, East Didsbury, Manchester M20 5GP **Tel 0161 434 1989**

IRISH BRANCHES

ANTRIM TOWN Branch Secretary Alex Mould, 14 Donegore Drive, Parkhall, Antrim, Northern Ireland BT41 1EB **Tel 01849 462954 Mobile 07899 818623** Chairman William Cameron, 92 Donegore Drive, Parkhall, Antrim, N Ireland **Tel 01849 461634** Club meetings held every other Thursday in the Top of the Town Bar, Antrim. All members must be registered with Manchester United's official membership scheme

ARKLOW Branch Secretary James Cullen, 52 South Green, Arklow, Co Wicklow, Eire **Tel 0402 39816** (home) **051 841829; 087 2327859** *Departure point* All trips arranged via 19 Arches, Lower Main Street, Arklow **Tel 0402 31976**

BALLYCASTLE Branch Secretary Sean Fleming, Glenshesk Bar, 76 Castle Street, Ballycastle, Co Antrim, Northern Ireland BT54 6AR **Tel 012657 62322** Branch Chairman Derek McKendry

BALLYMONEY Branch Secretary Malachy McAleese, 17 Eastburn Drive, Ballymoney, Co Antrim, Northern Ireland BT53 6PJ **Tel 012656 67623 Mobile 0802 541730**
Email MUSC@Eastburndrive.Freeserve.co.uk Chairman Gerry McAleese, 11 Greenville Avenue, Ballymoney, Co Antrim, Northern Ireland **Tel 012656 65446** *Departure points* Ballymoney United Social Club, Grove Road, Ballymena; Larne Harbour
Meetings Last Thursday of every month, Ballymoney United Social Club **Tel 012656 66504**

BANBRIDGE Branch Secretary James Loney, 83 McGreavy Park, Derrymacash, Lurgan, Northern Ireland **Tel 01762 322723 Mobile 0790 1833076** Chairman Kevin Nelson, 10 Ballynamoney Park, Derrymacash, Lurgan, N Ireland **Tel 01762 344232** *Departure points* Corner House, Derrymacash; Lurgan Town Centre; First & Last Bar, Banbridge

BANGOR Branch Secretary Gary Wilsden, 4 Bexley Road, Bangor, Co Down BT19 7TS **Tel 01247 458485** Branch Meetings Fortnightly in The Rose and Chandler Bar, High Street, Bangor

BELFAST REDS Branch Secretary John Bond, 53 Hillhead Crescent, Belfast, Northern Ireland BT11 9FS **Tel 01232 627861**

BUNDORAN Branch Secretary Danny Tighe, 'United Cottage', The Rock, Bundoran, Co Donegal, Eire **Tel & Fax 072 42080** Chairman Paul Hanbury **Tel 072 42080** *Departure point* The Chasing Bull Bar and additional pick-up points by arrangement with branch secretary. As travel arrangements have to be organised, bookings should be made well in advance

CARLINGFORD LOUTH Branch Secretary Harry Harold, Mountain Park, Carlingford, Co Louth, Ireland **Tel 042 73379**

CARLOW Branch Secretary Michael Lawlor, Trafford House, 20 New Oak Estate, Carlow, Ireland **Tel 0503 43759**

CARRICKFERGUS Branch Secretary Gary Callaghan, 3 Red Fort Park, Carrickfergus, Co Antrim, Northern Ireland BT38 9EW **Tel 01960 355362/364779 Fax 01960 360422**

CARRYDUFF Branch Secretary John White, 'Stretford End', 4 Baronscourt Glen, Carryduff, Co Down, Northern Ireland, BT8 8RF **Tel 01232 812377** E-Mail whitedevil@nireland.com Chairman John Dempsey **Tel/Fax 01232 814823** E-Mail john.dempsey@dnet.co.uk Vice-Chairman Wilson Steele **Tel 018494 64987** *Departure points* The branch organise coach trips to Old Trafford for every home game from The Royal Ascot, Carryduff and The Grand Opera House, Belfast. No alcohol and no other club colours are permitted on the coach. Branch meetings are held every week. Junior members particularly welcome as we are a family orientated branch. Branch Membership exceeds 300. ALL members must be registered with Manchester United's official membership scheme

CASTLEDAWSON Branch Secretary Niall Wright, 22 Park View, Castledawson, Co Londonderry, Northern Ireland

CASTLEPOLLARD Branch Secretary Anne Foley, Coole, Mullingar, Co Westmeath, Ireland **Tel/Fax 044 61613** *Departure points* The Square, Castlepollard. Additional pick-up points by arrangement with Branch Secretary. Branch meetings on third Monday of every month. Notification of additional meetings by newsletter

CASTLEWELLAN Branch Secretary Seamus Owens, 18 Mourne Gardens, Dublin Road, Castlewellan, Co Down, Northern Ireland BT31 9BY **Tel 013967 78137 Fax 013967 70762** Chairman Tony Corr **Tel 013967 22885** Treasurer Michael Burns **Tel 013967 78665**

CITY OF DERRY Branch Secretary Mark Thompson, 210 Hill Crest, Kilfennan, Londonderry, Northern Ireland, BT47 6GF **Tel 01504 346537 Fax 01504 311331** Meetings First Tuesday of every month at the Upstairs Downstairs Bar, Dungiven Road, Londonderry at 8.30pm

CLARA Branch Secretary Michael Kenny, River Street, Clara, Co Offaly, Ireland

COLERAINE Branch Secretary Noel Adair, 106 Lisnablaugh Road, Harper's Hill, Coleraine, Co Derry, Northern Ireland **Tel 01265 57744**

COOKSTOWN Branch Secretary Geoffrey Wilson, 10 Cookstown Road, Moneymore, Co Londonderry, Northern Ireland, BT45 7QF **Tel 016487 48625** Meeting First Tuesday of every month at Royal Hotel, Cookstown – 9.00pm. All trips – branch members only. New members always welcome

CORK AREA Branch Secretary Paul Kearney, Beech Road, Passage West, Co Cork, Republic of Ireland **Tel 021 841190**

COUNTY CAVAN Chairman Owen Farrelly, **Tel 046 42184**; Joint Secretaries Richard Leddy **Tel 046 42209** Jimmy Murray **Tel 046 42501** Meetings Third Monday of each month in Jimmy's Bar, Main St, Mullagh

COUNTY LONGFORD Branch Secretary Seamus Gill, 17 Springlawn, Longford, Republic of Ireland **Tel 043 47848 Fax 043 41655** Chairman; Harry Ryan, 58 Teffia Park, Longford, Co. Longford Treasurer Noel Daly, 18 Shannonvale, Longford, Co Longford

COUNTY MONAGHAN Branch Secretary Seamus Gallagher **Tel 047 57232** Chairman Gerard Treanor **Tel 087 57232** Meetings fortnightly Bellevue Tavern, Dublin Street, Monaghan **Tel 047 84311 Fax 047 83265**

COUNTY ROSCOMMON Branch Secretary Noel Scally, Carrickmore, Boyle, Co Roscommon, Ireland **Tel 079 62973** or **63382** Chairman Seamus Sweeney, Croghan, Coyle, Co. Roscommon **Tel 079 68061** President George Tiernan, 8 Termon Road, Boyle, Co Roscommon **Tel 079 62930**

COUNTY TIPPERARY Branch Secretary Mrs Kathleen Hogan, 45 Canon Hayes Park, Tipperary, Republic of Ireland **Tel 062 51042**

COUNTY WATERFORD Branch Secretary Mrs Helen Grant, 'Old Trafford', Ballinamuck, Dungarvan, Co Waterford, Ireland **Tel/Fax 058 44219** Chairman Oliver Drummy, 8 Cloneety Tce., Dungarvan, Co. Waterford **Tel 058 42365** Vice-Chairman Pat Grant, 'Old Trafford', Ballinamuck, Dungarvan, Co Waterford, Ireland **Tel/Fax 058 44219** Treasurer Judy Connors, 26 Hillview Drive, Dungarvan, Co Waterford Membership Secretary Ann Houlihan, Feddans Cross, Rathgormac

CRAIGAVON Branch Secretary Eamon Atkinson, 8 Rowan Park, Tullygally Road, Craigavon, Co Armagh, Northern Ireland, BT65 5AY **Tel 01762 343870** Chairperson James Nolan **Tel 01762 341434** Treasurer Susan Atkinson *Departure points* Lurgan Town Centre; Tullygally Road, Craigavon; Mayfair Centre, Portadown; Tandragee & Banbridge

DONEGAL Branch Secretary Liam Friel, Kiltoal, Convoy, Lifford, Co Donegal **Tel 087 6736967** Chairman Paddy Delap, West Hill, Letterkenny, Co Donegal **Tel/Fax 074 22240** Treasurer Paul Dolan, Knockbrack, Letterkenny, Co Donegal **Tel 087 2865504** Meetings held at Club Rooms, Rossbracken *Departure point* O'Boyces, Letterkenny. Pick-up points as arranged with travel organiser, Tony Murray, Gortlee, Letterkenny, Co Donegal **Tel 074 24111**

DOWNPATRICK Branch Secretary Terry Holland, 20 Racecourse Road, Downpatrick, Co Down, Northern Ireland **Tel/Fax 01396 616467 Mobile 07712 622242**

DUNDALK Chairman Michael McCourt Secretary Joan Kirk Assistant Secretary Arthur Carron Treasurer Mary Laverty Tickets & Travel Dickie O'Hanrahan Committee Members Ollie Kelly, Gery Dullaghan

DUNGANNON Branch Secretary Ian Hall, 'Silveridge', 229 Killyman Road, Dungannon, Co Tyrone, Northern Ireland, BT71 6RS **Tel 018687 23085** (home) **Tel/Fax 018687 53048** (work); **Mobile 0411 145048** Meetings every 2 weeks (all year). For details on trips or meeting dates, contact branch secretary or Keith Houston on **018687 22735** or Lawrence McKinley **018687 24188**

ENNIS Branch Secretary Seamus Hughes, 'Old Trafford', Quin, Ennis, Co Clare, Republic of Ireland **Tel 065 68 20282 Mobile 086 239 3975** Branch Chairman Eamon Murphy, Knockboy, Ballynacally, Co Clare, Ireland **Tel 065 68 28105** Meetings held at Roslevan Arms, Tulla Road, Ennis

FERMANAGH Branch Secretary Gabriel Maguire, 80 Glenwood Gardens, Enniskillen, BT74 5LT **Tel 01365 325 950 Mobile 07788 421739** Chairman Eric Brown, 166 Main Street, Lisnaskea Treasurer Raymond McBrien, Ardlougher Road, Irvinestown Meetings held in Charlie's Lounge, Enniskillen

FIRST BALLYCLARE Branch Secretary Alan Munce, 7 Merion Park, Ballyclare, Co Antrim, Northern Ireland BT39 9XD

FIRST NORTH DOWN Branch Secretary Robert Quee, 'Stretford Ender', 67 Springhill Road, Bangor West, Co Down, Northern Ireland BT20 3PD **Tel 01247 453094** Branch hold their meetings on the first Tuesday of the month at the Sports Complex, situated on the Old Belfast Road, Bangor. Meetings begin at 8pm sharp. Membership enquiries to branch secretary. New members always welcomed

FIRST PORTAFERRY Branch Secretary Dr David Peacock, 34 Shore Road, Portaferry, Northern Ireland BT22 1JZ **Tel 012477 28420 Fax 012477 29834** Chair Tony Cleary Treasurer Hugh Conlon Meetings held on first Tuesday of the month @ 9.00 p.m. Cleary's Bar

FOYLE Branch Secretary Martin Harkin, 2 Harvest Meadows, Dunlade Road, Greysteel, Co Derry, Northern Ireland BT47 3BG Meeting point Ulsterbus Club, Bishop Street, Derry City Travel Arrangements Meet Ulsterbus at midnight, boat at 02.50 on matchday. Hotel Comfort Friendly, Hyde Road. Return boat 14.30, arrive Ulsterbus Club 20.30

GALWAY Branch Secretary Patsy Devlin, 37 Gortgreine, Rahoon, Galway, Ireland **Tel 00 353 091 582634 Fax 00 353 91 582634** (1) Meetings held monthly in Currans Hotel, Eyre Square. (2) All live TV games at Brennans Bar, New Docks; (3) Membership open all year round

GLENOWEN Branch Secretary Jim Turner, 4 Dermot Hill Drive, Belfast, Northern Ireland BT12 7GG **Tel 01232 242682 Mobile 0498 681250** Email jimmy.turner@tesco.net

IVEAGH YOUTH Branch Secretary Russell Allen, 2 Iveagh Crescent, Belfast, Northern Ireland BT12 6AW **Tel 01232 542651** (office) **01232 329621** (home) Assistant Branch Secretary Brendan McBride, 3 Gransha Park, Belfast BT11 8AT **Tel 01232 522400** (work), **01232 203171** (home)

IRELAND (DUBLIN) Branch Secretary Eddie Gibbons, 19 Cherry Orchard Crescent, Ballyfermont, Dublin 10 **Tel 01 626 9759** Membership Secretary Michael O'Toole, 49 Briarwood Lawn, Mulmuddart, Dublin 15 **Tel 01 821 5702**

KILDARE Branch Secretary Maureen McKenna, 'Old Trafford', 19 Curragh Downs, Brownstown, Curragh, Co Kildare, Republic of Ireland

KILKENNY Branch Secretary John Joe Ryan **Tel 056 6565827** (day) **056 65136** (after 6.00pm) **Fax 056 64043** Branch Chairman Pat Murray **Tel 056 71772**

KILLALOE Branch Secretary Michael Flynn, 611 Cross Road, Killaloe, Co Clare, Ireland **Tel 061 376031**

KILLARNEY Branch Secretary Frank Roberts, St Margaret's Road, Killarney, Co Kerry, Republic of Ireland Chairman Bill Keefe; Treasurer Denis Spillane Meetings held on the first Wednesday of every month at which future trips are organised

LAGAN Branch Secretary Sean Finnegan,19 Powerscourt Place, Belfast, BT7 1FX **Tel 01232 209616**

LAOIS Branch Secretary Denis Moran, Newpark, Portlaoise, Co Laois, Ireland **Tel 0502 22681**

LARNE Branch Secretary Brian Haveron, 69 Croft Manor, Ballygally, Larne, Co Antrim BT40 2RU **Tel 01574 583027/01574 261197, 0374 183485** Branch Chairman John Hylands, 43 Olderfleet Road, Larne, Co Antrim BT40 1AS **Tel 01574 277888** Meetings Every second and third Monday of the month at Larne Town Hall Building, 8.00pm sharp

LIMERICK Secretary Dennis O'Sullivan, 14 Rossa Avenue, Mulgrave Street, Limerick, Republic of Ireland **Tel 061 311502 Mobile 086 8435828**

LISBURN Branch Secretary Colin Scott, 7 Barban Hill, Dromore, Co Down, Northern Ireland, BT25 1PR **Tel 01846 699608** Branch meets each Tuesday night at 8.30pm at the Clubrooms in Sackville Street. Families and kids are more than welcome to join. The branch travel to all home games, away games may vary. Anyone wishing to join, please contact the branch secretary

SUPPORTERS' CLUBS
IRISH AND OVERSEAS BRANCHES 1999–2000

LISTOWEL Branch Secretary Aiden O'Connor, 52 Brundetts Road, Chorlton-cum-Hardy, Manchester M21 9DE **Tel 0161 718 1204**

LURGAN Branch Secretary John Furphy, 123 Drumbeg North, Craigavon, Co Armagh, N Ireland BT65 5AE **Tel 01762 341842**

MAYO Branch Secretary Seamus Moran, Belclare, Westport, Co Mayo, Ireland **Tel 00 353 982 7533** (home) **00 353 985 5202** (work) **Mobile 00 353 872 417966 Fax 00 353 982 8874** Chairperson Liam Connell, 70 Knockaphunta, Castlebar, Co Mayo, Ireland Treasurer T J Gannon, 4 The Paddock, Castlebar Road, Westport, Co Mayo, Ireland PRO Kieran Mongey, Blackfort, Castlebar, Co Mayo, Ireland

MEATH Branch Secretary Colm McManus, 46 Beechlawn, Kells, Co Meath, Republic of Ireland **Tel 046 49831** Pick-up points for travel to Old Trafford Jack's Railway Bar, Kells; Fairgreen, Naven

NEWRY Branch Secretary Brendan McConville, 14 Willow Grove, Newry, Co Down, Northern Ireland BT34 1JH **Tel 01693 66996**

NEWTOWNARDS Branch Secretary Leo Cafolla, 11 Strangford Gate Drive, Newtownards, Co Down, Northern Ireland BT23 8ZW **Tel 0410 820300 Fax 01247 811822** Meeting every other Monday 7.30pm at Ards Football Club, Newtownards **Tel 01247 811822**

NORTH BELFAST Branch Secretary Robert Savage, 59 Hollybrook Manor, Glenganely, Belfast, Northern Ireland BT36 7XR **Tel 01232 832270** Meetings are held every second Sunday of the month in the Shamrock Social Club

OMAGH Branch Secretary Brendan McLaughlin, 4 Pinefield Court, Killyclougher, Omagh, Co Tyrone, Northern Ireland BT79 7YT **Tel 01662 250025 Mobile 0410 366 486**

PORTADOWN Branch Secretary Harold Beck, 23 Kernan Grove, Portadown, Co Armagh BT63 5RX

PORTAVOGIE Branch Secretary Robert McMaster, 6 New Road, Portavogie, Co Down BT22 1EN

PORTSTEWART Branch Secretary Ryan McLaughlin, 45 Drumavalley, Bellarena, Limavady, Co. Londonderry, Northern Ireland BT49 0LT **Tel (015047) 50281** after 6.00pm Club meetings held every second Wednesday of the month at 7.30pm, Windsor Hotel, Portstewart

ROSTREVOR Branch Chairman John Parr, 16 Drumreagh Park, Rostrevor BT34 3DU **Tel 016937 39449** Branch Secretary Roger Morgan, 11 St Judes, Rostrevor, Co Down BT34 3EE **Tel 016937 38392** Treasurer John Franklin, 14 Rosswood Park, Rostrevor, Co Down BT34 3DZ **Tel 016937 38906** Meetings Glenside Bar, Bridge Street, Rostrevor, Co Down

SION MILLS Branch Secretary Jim Hunter, 122 Melmount, Sion Mills, Co Tyrone, Northern Ireland BT82 9EW **Tel 01662 658226** (home) **01662 252491** (work) **Fax 01662 252491**

SLIGO Branch Secretary Martin Feeney, 40 Carton Bay, Sligo, Republic of Ireland **Tel 071 71057**

SOUTH BELFAST Branch Secretary James Copeland, 17 Oakhurst Avenue, Blacks Road, Belfast BT10 0PD **Tel 01232 615184** or **01232 871231 Mobile 0467 271648** *Departure point* Balmoral Hotel, Blacks Road, Belfast

STEWARTSTOWN Branch Secretary Robert O'Neill, 6 Castle Farm Road, Stewartstown, Co Tyrone, Northern Ireland

STRABANE Branch Secretary Gerry Donnelly, 27 Dublin Road, Strabane, Co Tyrone, Northern Ireland, BT82 9EA **Tel 01504 883376** Meetings held in Blue Parrot every month

TALLAGHT (CO DUBLIN) Branch Secretary Jimmy Pluck, 32 Kilcarrig Cresent, Fettercairn, Tallaght, Co Dublin 24, Republic of Ireland **Tel/Fax 4597045**

TIPPERARY Branch Secretary John Ryan, 19 Marian Terrace, Tipperary Town, Co Tipperary, Republic of Ireland **Tel 086 811 2974** (24 hours) **Fax 086 911 2974** (24 hours)

TOWER ARDS Branch Secretary Stephen Rowley, 26 Trasnagh Drive, Newtownards, Co Down BT23 4PD **Tel 01247 810457**

TRALEE Branch Secretary Johnny Switzer, 'Toirne Lin', Dromtacker, Tralee, Co Kerry, Republic of Ireland **Tel 066 7124787**

WARRENPOINT Branch Secretary Pat Treanor, 31 Oakland Grove, Warrenpoint **Tel 016937 73921 Mobile 07775 968595** Chairman John Bird, 23 Greendale Crescent, Rostrevor, Co Down **Tel 016937 38376 Mobile 0411 836074** Treasurer Martin McGivern, 2 Lisieux Court, Warrenpoint, Co Down BT34 3TN. Club web site address is http//members.aol.com/mmgmufcwp/manutd.htm Club based at Cearnogs Bar, The Square, Warrenpoint, Co Down, N Ireland **Tel 016937 53429**

WEST BELFAST Branch Secretary John McAllister, 25 Broadway, Belfast BT12 6AS **Tel 01232 329423** Email hoyt@globalnet.co.uk Branch Chairman George McCabe, 21 Beechmount Street, Belfast, BT12 7NG **Tel 01232 294516** Treasurer Mr G Burns Committee Mr G Fox, Mr M Curran, Mr M Mallon, Mr J Walker

OVERSEAS BRANCHES

BELGIUM Chairman Peter Bauwens, Merellaan 52, 9060 Zelzate, Belgium **Tel/Fax 00 32 934 40578** Branch Secretary Björn Tack **Tel/Fax 00 32 934 45860**

CANADA Manchester United Supporters Club, FAO Maureen, 12 St Clair Avenue East, PO Box 69057, Toronto, Ontario, M4T 3AI, Canada **Fax 00 1 416 480 0501** Website www.muscc.com Email toby@muscc.com

CYPRUS Branch President Ronis Soteriades, P.O. Box 51365, 3504 Limassol, Cyprus **Tel 05 337690 Fax 05 388652**

GERMAN FRIENDS Branch President Marco Hornfeck, Silberstein 2A, Geroldsgr,n 95179, Germany **Tel 09267 8111**

GERMAN KREFELD REDS Branch Secretary Andrew Marsh, Innsbrucker Str, 47807 Kreffeld, Germany **Tel/Fax 02151 392908** Chairman Stuart Dykes **Tel 02151 477917 Fax 02151 435168** Email stuart.dykes@ta-online.de

GERMAN REDS Branch Secretary Petra Sengstacke, Konrad-Adenauer Str 70, D-30853 Langenhagen, Germany **Tel 00 49 511 724 3500 Fax 00 49 511 7242886** Email tardis@hannover.sgh-net.de

GIBRALTAR Manchester United Supporters Gibraltar Branch, PO Box 22, Gibraltar **Tel 350 76846 Fax 350 71608 Mobile 587 05000** Branch Chairman Clive A Moberley Branch Secretary Gerald Laguea

HOLLAND Branch Chairman Ron Snellen, P.O. Box 33742, 2503 BA Den Haag, Holland **Tel 00 31 70 329 8602 Fax 00 31 70 367 2247**

HONG KONG Branch Secretary/Treasurer Rick Adkinson, 7D On Hing Building, No 1 On Hing Terrace, Central, Hong Kong **Tel 00 852 2869 1993 Fax 00 852 2869 4312**

ICELAND Branch Secretary Bubbi Avesson, Studningsmannaklubbur, Manchester United, øslandi, PO Box 12170, 132 Reykjavik, Iceland

LUXEMBOURG Branch Secretary Steve Kaiser **Tel 00 352 4301 33073** (work) **00 352 340265** (home)

MALAYSIA Branch Secretary Laurence How, 47A Jalan SS 2/75, 47300 Petaling Jaya, Selangor, D.E.Malaysia **Tel 6 03 7773070 & 6 03 7775339 Fax 6 03 7774511**

OUTPOSTS 1 & 2 These two outlets act as meeting places for branch members and also for any United fan visiting the Far East. Details are as follows
Outpost 1 – Central Market in Kuala Lumpar City Centre
Open daily (except Thursdays) from 11.00am to 7.00pm **Tel 6 03 2010651/652**
Outpost 2 – L1-L12 First Floor, Amcorp Mall, 18 Persiaran Barat, 46050 Petaling Jaya
Open daily from 11.00am to 7.00pm (except Wednesdays) **Tel 6 03 7552698**

MALTA Branch President John Buttigieg, Quarries Square, MSIDA MSD 03, Malta

MAURITIUS Branch Secretary Yacoob Atchia, Flamingo Pool House, Remeno Street, Rose Hill, Mauritius, Indian Ocean **Tel 464 7382/454 7761/454 3570/464 7750 Fax 454 7839** Email abyss.manutd@intnet.mu Chairman Swallay Banhoo **Tel 464 4450** (home) Treasurer Naniel Baichoo **Tel 454 3570** (work) **465 0387** (home)

NEW SOUTH WALES Branch Secretary Graham Shakespeare, P.O. Box 693, Sutherland, New South Wales 1499, Australia **Tel/Fax 00 61 2 9589 2578**

NEW ZEALAND Branch Chairman Brian Wood, 55 Pine Street, Mount Eden, Auckland, New Zealand Secretary Gillian Goodinson, 20 Sandown Road, Rothesay Bay, Auckland, New Zealand

SCANDANAVIA Branch Secretary Per H Larsen, P.O. Box 4003 Dreggen, N-5023 Bergan, Norway **Tel +47 5531 3889** (Mon – Fri 08-21, Sat 08-14) **Fax +47 5596 2033** Email muscsb@united.no.

SOUTH AFRICA Branch Secretary Ethel Sleith, P.O. Box 13990, Witfield 1467, Gauteng, South Africa **Tel/Fax (011) 826 2181** Email ethelred@web.co.za

SOUTH AUSTRALIA P.O. Box 276, Ingle Farm, South Australia 5098 **Fax 08 82816731** Branch Secretary Mick Griffiths **Tel 08 82644499** Branch Chairman Chris Golder **Tel 08 82630602** Vice-Chairman John Harrison **Tel 08 82603413** Treasurer Charlie Kelly **Tel 08 82628245** Meetings are held at the Para Hills Soccer Club, Bridge Road, Para Hills, SA. The Manchester United Supporters Amateur League soccer team train and play at Para Hills Soccer Club

SWISS DEVILS Branch Secretary Marc Tanner, Soodstrasse 64, 8134 Adliswil, Switzerland **Tel (411) 710 5986/ (411) 267 5513 Fax (411) 252 20 02**

TOKYO Branch Secretary Hiroki Miyaji, 2-24-10 Minami-Ayoma, Minato-ku, Tokyo, Japan **Tel +81 3 3470 3441** English Information Stephen Ryan **Tel +81 3 3380 8441** Email best-oz@kk.iij4u.or.jp

U.S.A. Branch Secretary Peter Holland, MUSC USA HQ, 139 West Neck Road, Huntingdon, N.Y. 11743, U.S.A. **Tel 00 1 516 547 5500 Fax 00 1 516 547 6800** (day) **Tel/Fax 00 1 516 261 7314** (evening) Email muscusa@datacapture.com (day) muscusa@muscusa.com (evening); Web Site www.muscusa.com Webmaster john@muscusa.com

VICTORIAN AUSTRALIA President Kieran Dunleavy, P.O. Box 1199, Camberwell, 3124 Victoria **Tel/Fax 9 804 0244** Web Page Http.//www.strug.com.au~sidcol Email muscovic@vicnet.net.au

WESTERN AUSTRALIA Branch Chairman Graham Wyche, 19 Frobisher Avenue, Sorrento 6020, Perth, Western Australia **Tel/Fax (08) 9 447 1144; Mobile 0417 903 101** Email freobook@omen.com.au